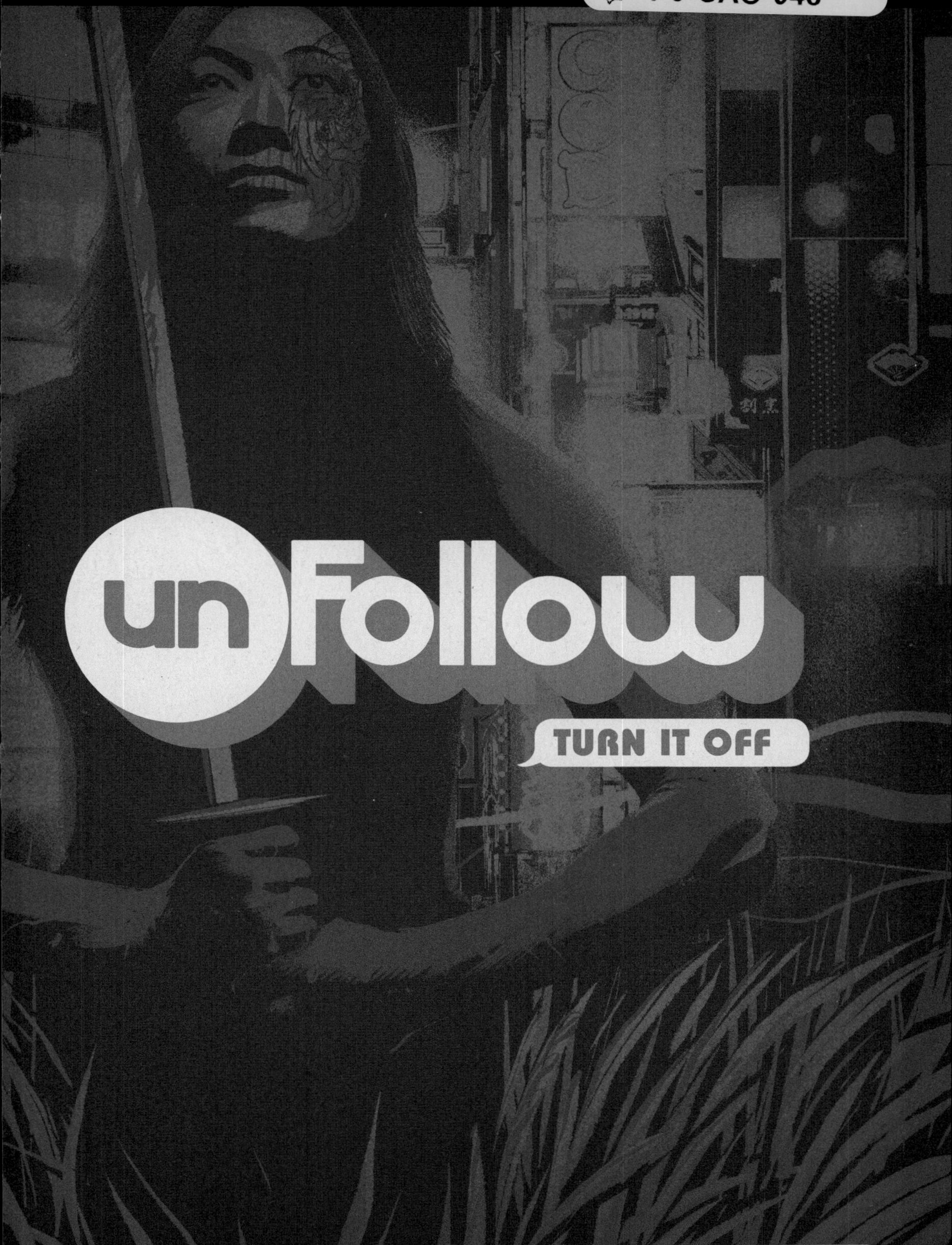
unFollow
TURN IT OFF

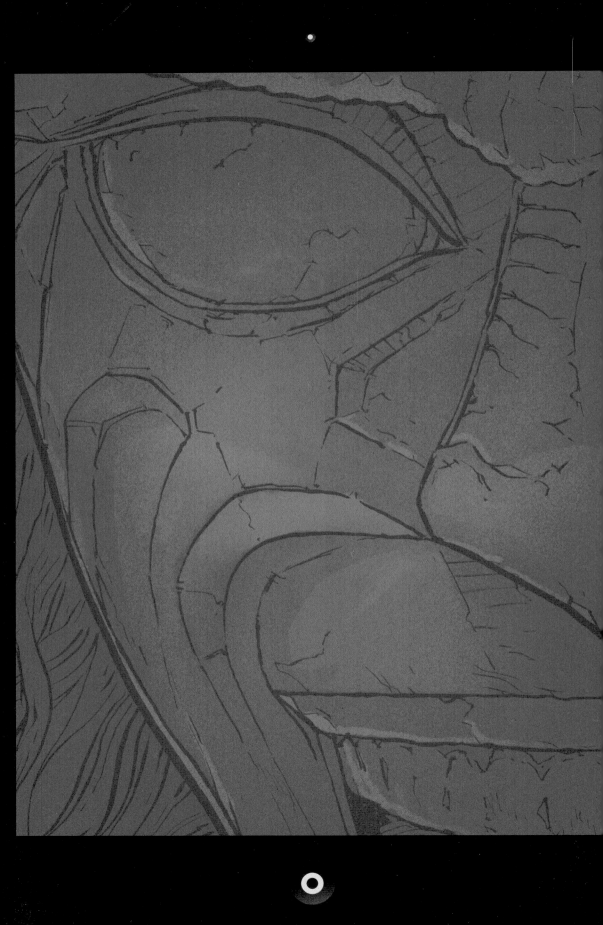

unFollow

TURN IT OFF

ROB WILLIAMS Writer

MIKE DOWLING
SIMON GANE
JAVIER PULIDO
Artists

QUINTON WINTER
JORDIE BELLAIRE
MUNTSA VICENTE
Colorists

CLEM ROBINS
Letterer

MATT TAYLOR
Cover Art and
Original Series Covers

UNFOLLOW created by **ROB WILLIAMS** and **MIKE DOWLING**

Ellie Pyle Editor – Original Series
Maggie Howell Assistant Editor – Original Series
Jamie S. Rich Group Editor – Vertigo Comics
Jeb Woodard Group Editor – Collected Editions
Scott Nybakken Editor – Collected Edition
Steve Cook Design Director – Books
Damian Ryland Publication Design

Diane Nelson President
Dan DiDio Publisher
Jim Lee Publisher
Geoff Johns President & Chief Creative Officer
Amit Desai Executive VP – Business & Marketing Strategy, Direct to Consumer &
Global Franchise Management
Sam Ades Senior VP – Direct to Consumer
Bobbie Chase VP – Talent Development
Mark Chiarello Senior VP – Art, Design & Collected Editions
John Cunningham Senior VP – Sales & Trade Marketing
Anne DePies Senior VP – Business Strategy, Finance & Administration
Don Falletti VP – Manufacturing Operations
Lawrence Ganem VP – Editorial Administration & Talent Relations
Alison Gill Senior VP – Manufacturing & Operations
Hank Kanalz Senior VP – Editorial Strategy & Administration
Jay Kogan VP – Legal Affairs
Thomas Loftus VP – Business Affairs
Jack Mahan VP – Business Affairs
Nick Napolitano VP – Manufacturing Administration
Eddie Scannell VP – Consumer Marketing
Courtney Simmons Senior VP – Publicity & Communications
Jim (Ski) Sokolowski VP – Comic Book Specialty Sales & Trade Marketing
Nancy Spears VP – Mass, Book, Digital Sales & Trade Marketing

Logo design by **Tom Muller**

PEFC Certified

This product is from
sustainably managed
forests, recycled and
controlled sources

PEFC/26-31-02   www.pefc.org

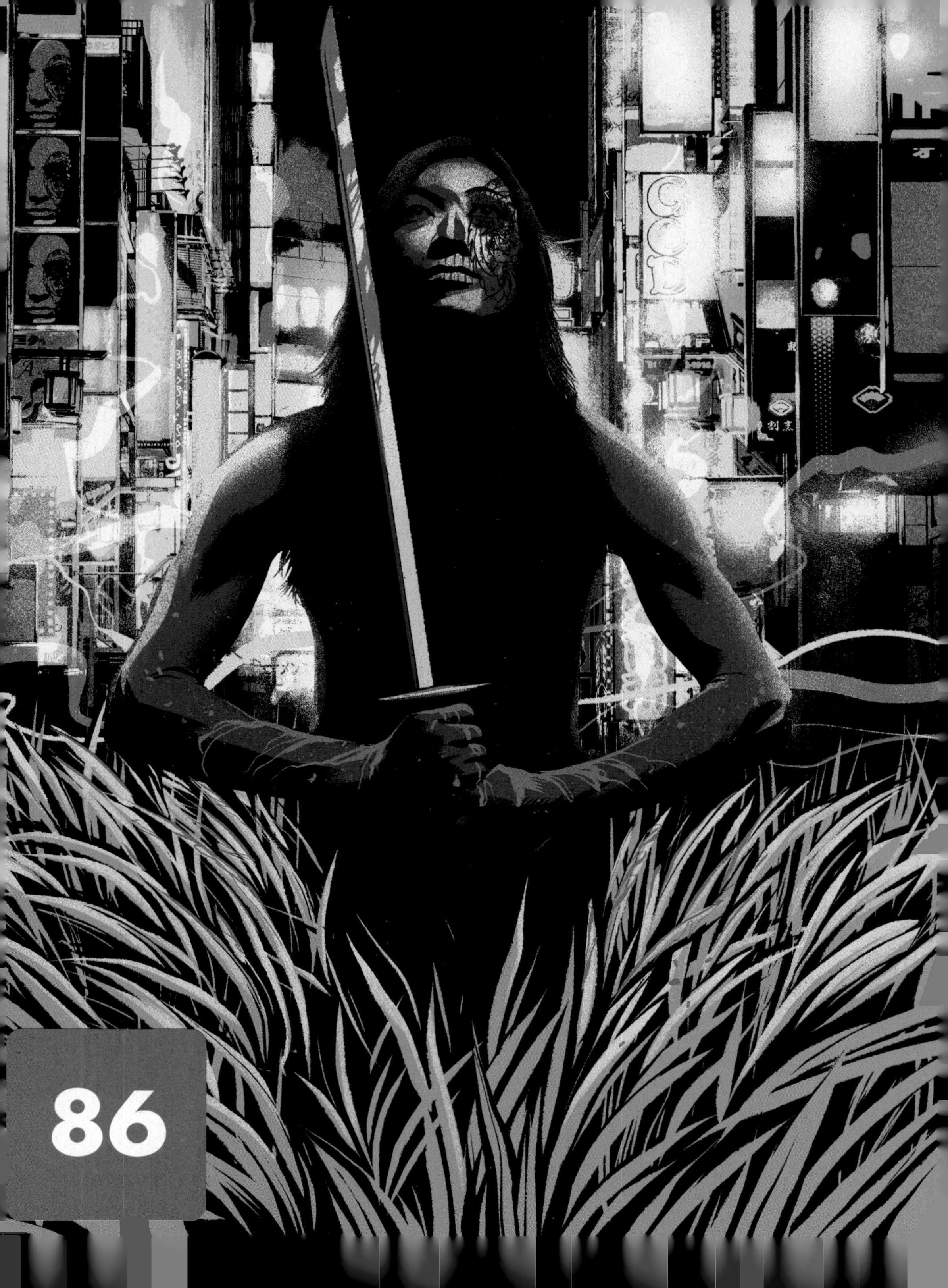
86

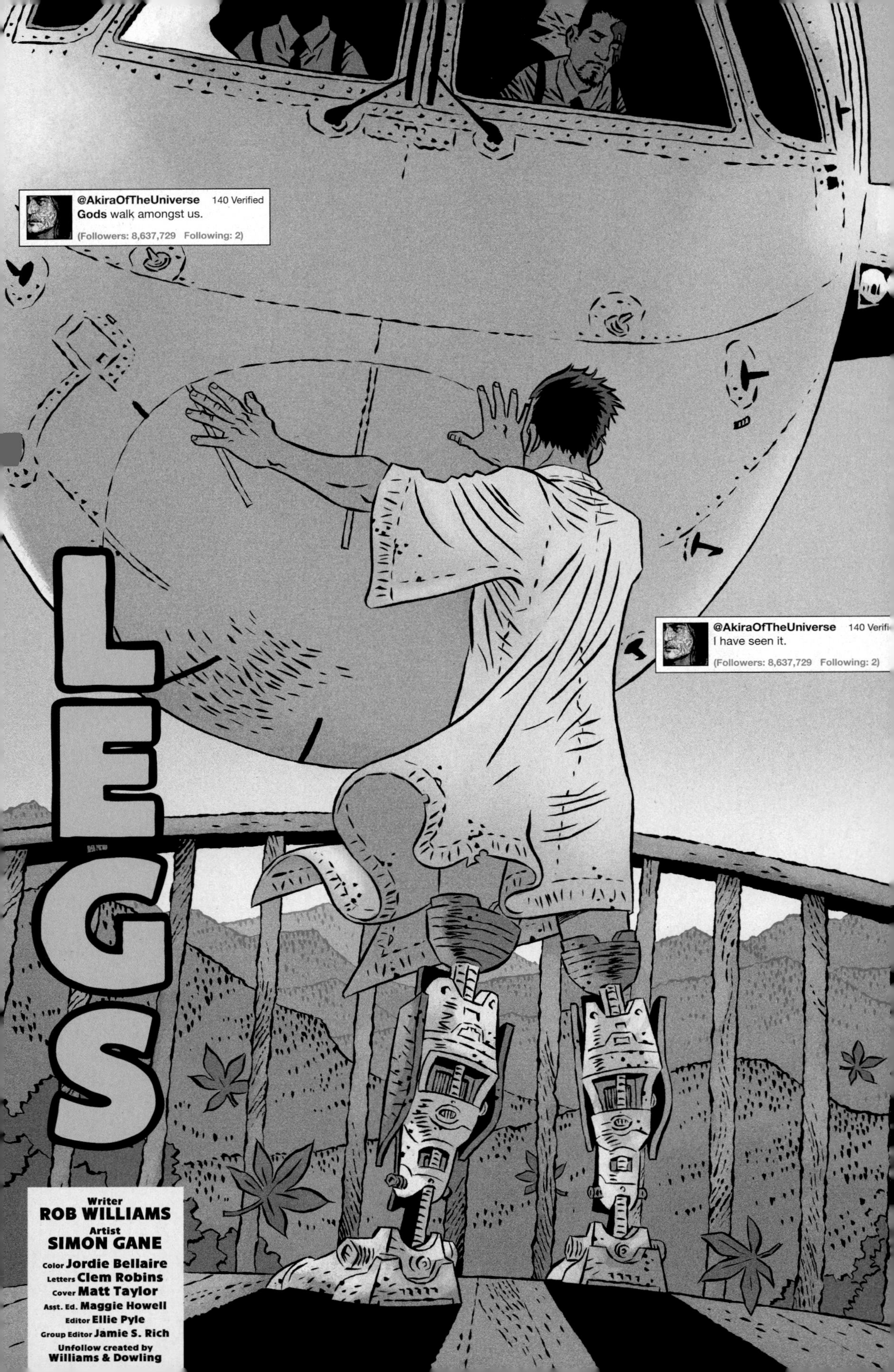
@AkiraOfTheUniverse 140 Verified
Gods walk amongst us.
(Followers: 8,637,729 Following: 2)
@AkiraOfTheUniverse 140 Verifi
I have seen it.
(Followers: 8,637,729 Following: 2)
LEGS
Writer ROB WILLIAMS
Artist SIMON GANE
Color Jordie Bellaire
Letters Clem Robins
Cover Matt Taylor
Asst. Ed. Maggie Howell
Editor Ellie Pyle
Group Editor Jamie S. Rich
Unfollow created by Williams & Dowling

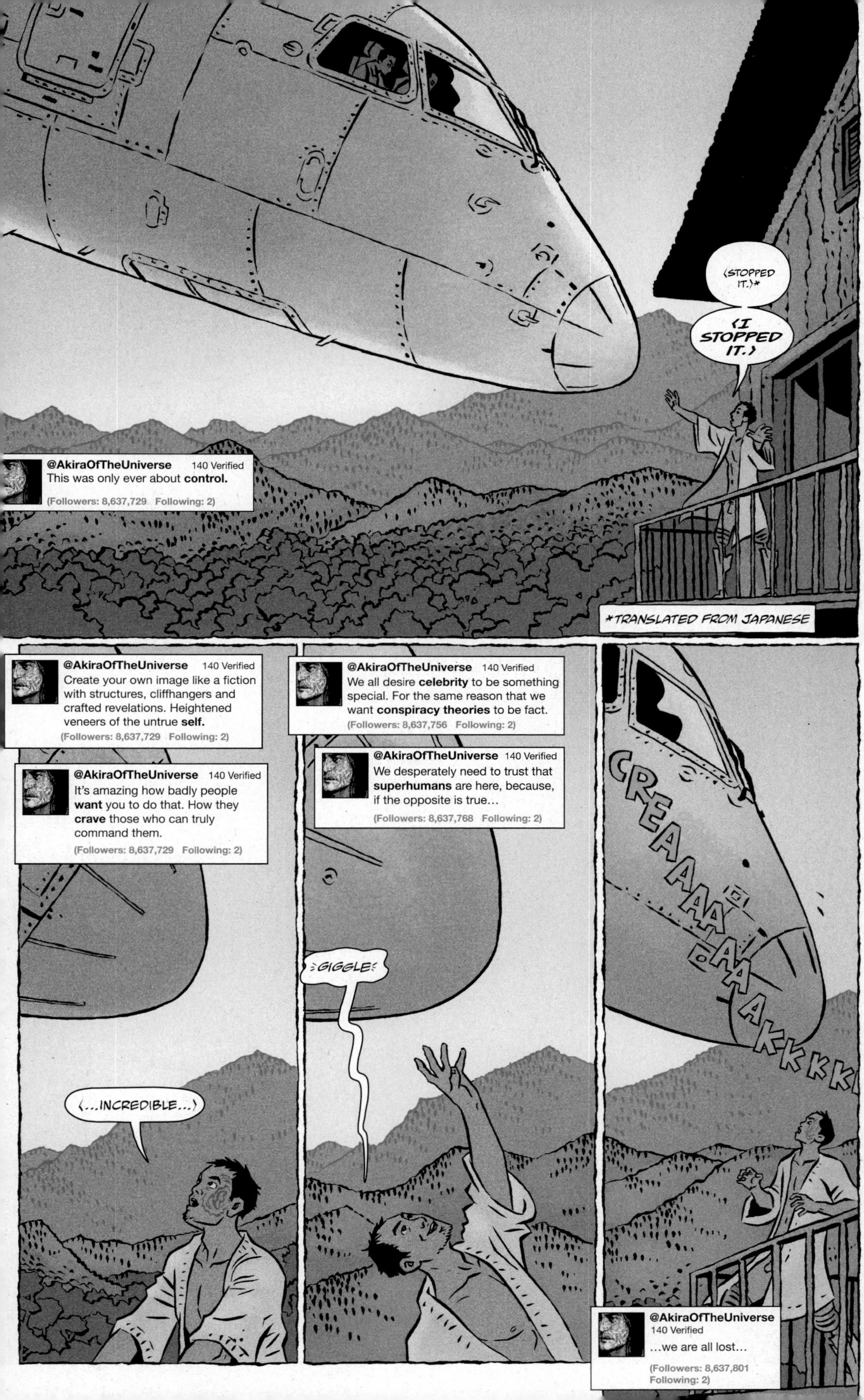

⟨STOPPED IT.⟩*
⟨I STOPPED IT.⟩
@AkiraOfTheUniverse 140 Verified
This was only ever about control.
(Followers: 8,637,729 Following: 2)
*TRANSLATED FROM JAPANESE
@AkiraOfTheUniverse 140 Verified
Create your own image like a fiction with structures, cliffhangers and crafted revelations. Heightened veneers of the untrue self.
(Followers: 8,637,729 Following: 2)
@AkiraOfTheUniverse 140 Verified
It's amazing how badly people want you to do that. How they crave those who can truly command them.
(Followers: 8,637,729 Following: 2)
⟨...INCREDIBLE...⟩
@AkiraOfTheUniverse 140 Verified
We all desire celebrity to be something special. For the same reason that we want conspiracy theories to be fact.
(Followers: 8,637,756 Following: 2)
@AkiraOfTheUniverse 140 Verified
We desperately need to trust that superhumans are here, because, if the opposite is true...
(Followers: 8,637,768 Following: 2)
GIGGLE
CREAAAAAAAKKKKK
@AkiraOfTheUniverse
140 Verified
...we are all lost...
(Followers: 8,637,801
Following: 2)

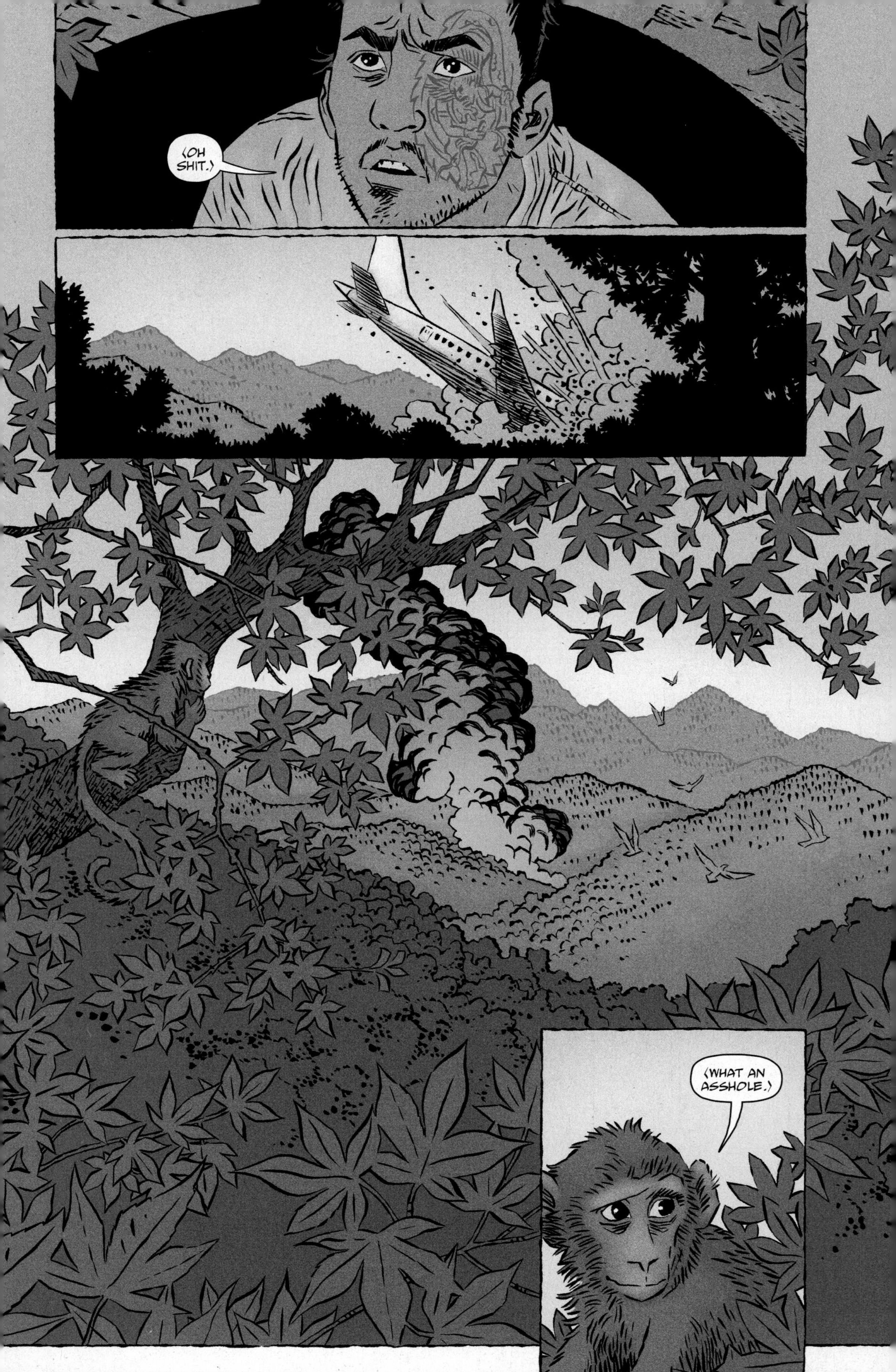
‹OH SHIT.›
‹WHAT AN ASSHOLE.›

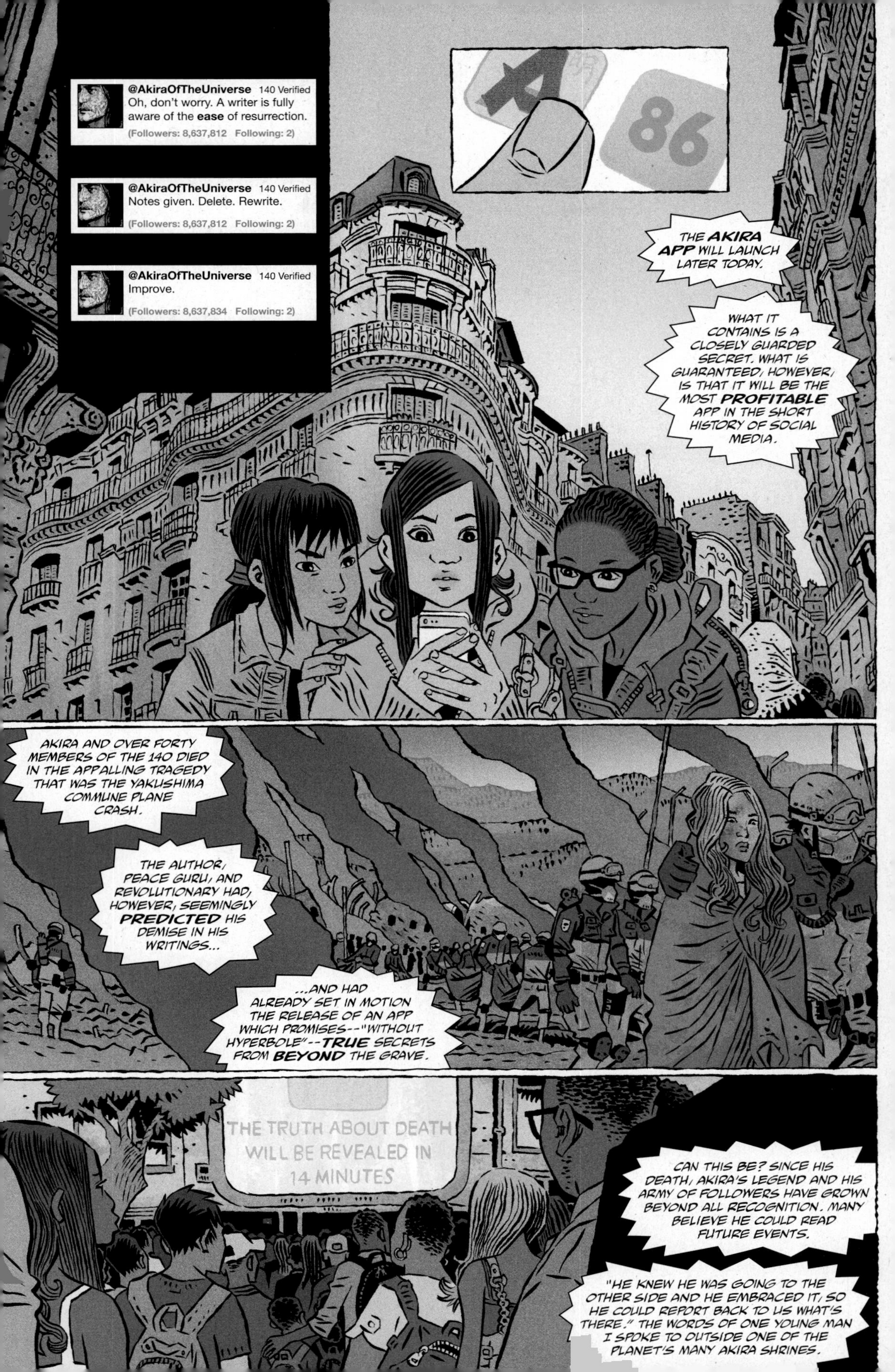
@AkiraOfTheUniverse 140 Verified
Oh, don't worry. A writer is fully aware of the ease of resurrection.
(Followers: 8,637,812 Following: 2)
@AkiraOfTheUniverse 140 Verified
Notes given. Delete. Rewrite.
(Followers: 8,637,812 Following: 2)
@AkiraOfTheUniverse 140 Verified
Improve.
(Followers: 8,637,834 Following: 2)
86
THE AKIRA APP WILL LAUNCH LATER TODAY.
WHAT IT CONTAINS IS A CLOSELY GUARDED SECRET. WHAT IS GUARANTEED, HOWEVER, IS THAT IT WILL BE THE MOST PROFITABLE APP IN THE SHORT HISTORY OF SOCIAL MEDIA.
AKIRA AND OVER FORTY MEMBERS OF THE 140 DIED IN THE APPALLING TRAGEDY THAT WAS THE YAKUSHIMA COMMUNE PLANE CRASH.
THE AUTHOR, PEACE GURU, AND REVOLUTIONARY HAD, HOWEVER, SEEMINGLY PREDICTED HIS DEMISE IN HIS WRITINGS...
...AND HAD ALREADY SET IN MOTION THE RELEASE OF AN APP WHICH PROMISES--"WITHOUT HYPERBOLE"--TRUE SECRETS FROM BEYOND THE GRAVE.
THE TRUTH ABOUT DEATH WILL BE REVEALED IN 14 MINUTES
CAN THIS BE? SINCE HIS DEATH, AKIRA'S LEGEND AND HIS ARMY OF FOLLOWERS HAVE GROWN BEYOND ALL RECOGNITION. MANY BELIEVE HE COULD READ FUTURE EVENTS.
"HE KNEW HE WAS GOING TO THE OTHER SIDE AND HE EMBRACED IT, SO HE COULD REPORT BACK TO US WHAT'S THERE." THE WORDS OF ONE YOUNG MAN I SPOKE TO OUTSIDE ONE OF THE PLANET'S MANY AKIRA SHRINES.

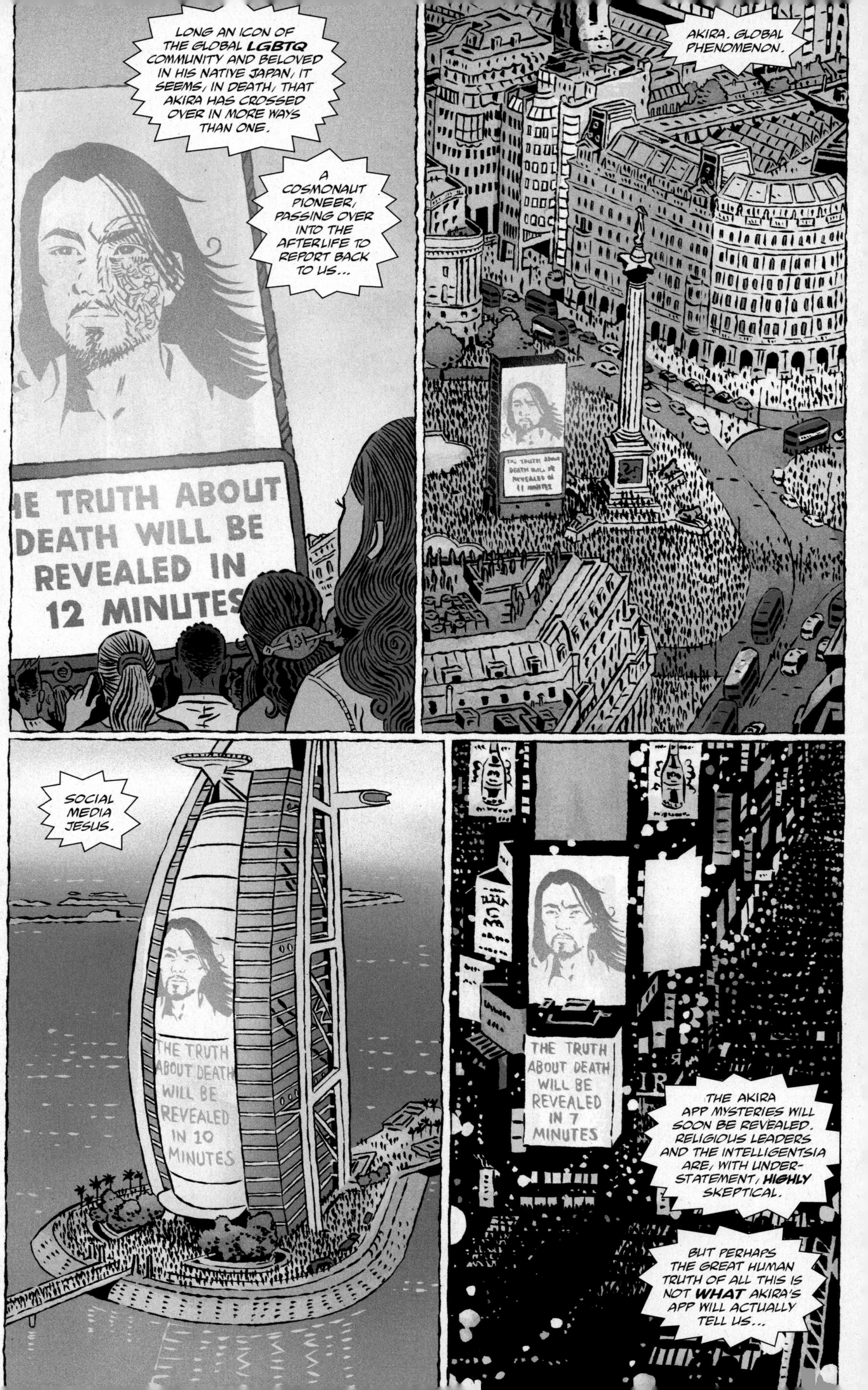
LONG AN ICON OF THE GLOBAL LGBTQ COMMUNITY AND BELOVED IN HIS NATIVE JAPAN, IT SEEMS, IN DEATH, THAT AKIRA HAS CROSSED OVER IN MORE WAYS THAN ONE.
A COSMONAUT PIONEER, PASSING OVER INTO THE AFTERLIFE TO REPORT BACK TO US...
HE TRUTH ABOUT DEATH WILL BE REVEALED IN 12 MINUTES
AKIRA. GLOBAL PHENOMENON.
SOCIAL MEDIA JESUS.
THE TRUTH ABOUT DEATH WILL BE REVEALED IN 10 MINUTES
THE TRUTH ABOUT DEATH WILL BE REVEALED IN 7 MINUTES
THE AKIRA APP MYSTERIES WILL SOON BE REVEALED. RELIGIOUS LEADERS AND THE INTELLIGENTSIA ARE, WITH UNDER-STATEMENT, HIGHLY SKEPTICAL.
BUT PERHAPS THE GREAT HUMAN TRUTH OF ALL THIS IS NOT WHAT AKIRA'S APP WILL ACTUALLY TELL US...

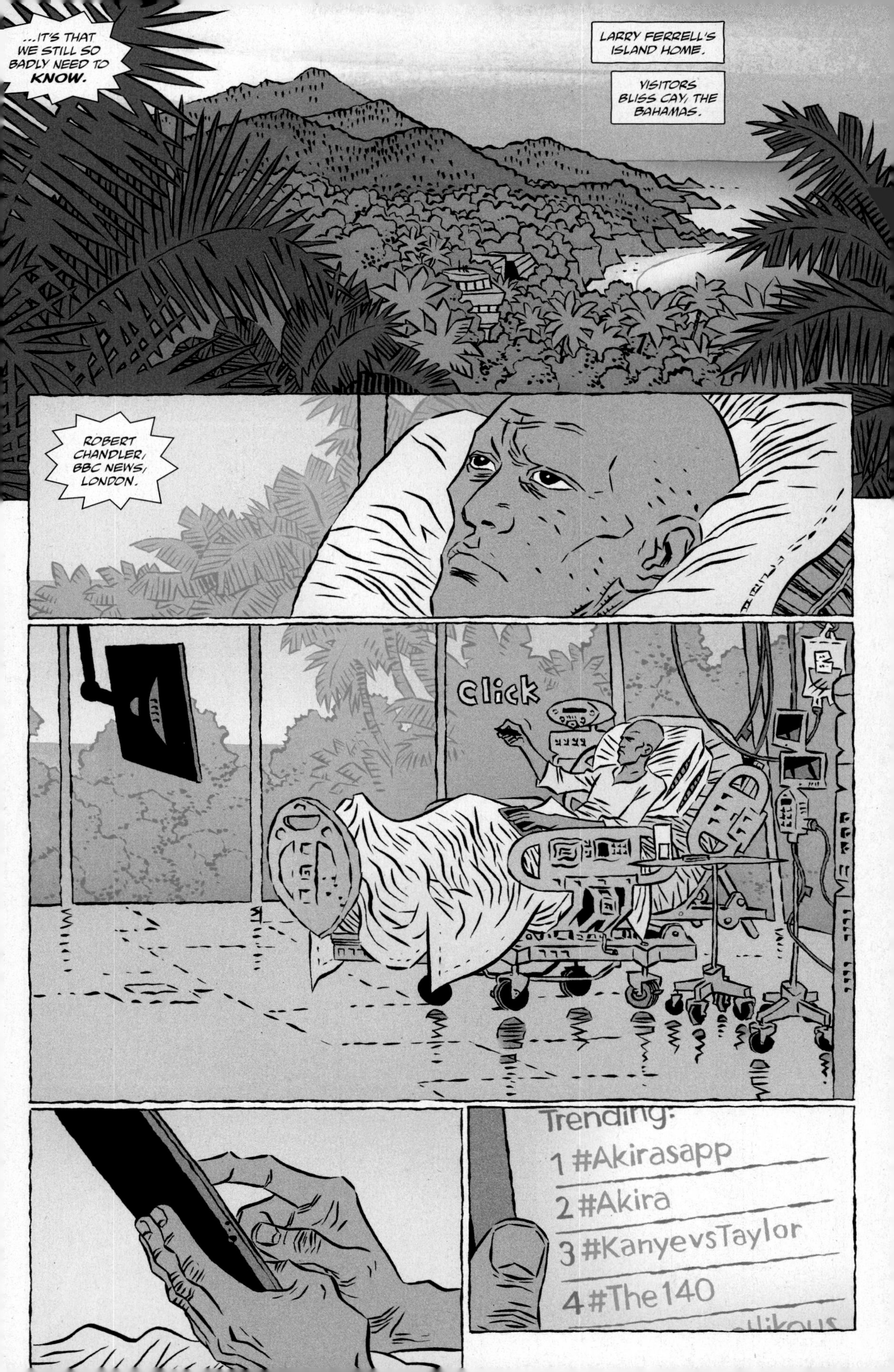
...IT'S THAT WE STILL SO BADLY NEED TO KNOW.
LARRY FERRELL'S ISLAND HOME.
VISITORS BLISS CAY, THE BAHAMAS.
ROBERT CHANDLER, BBC NEWS, LONDON.
Click
Trending:
1 #Akirasapp
2 #Akira
3 #KanyevsTaylor
4 #The140

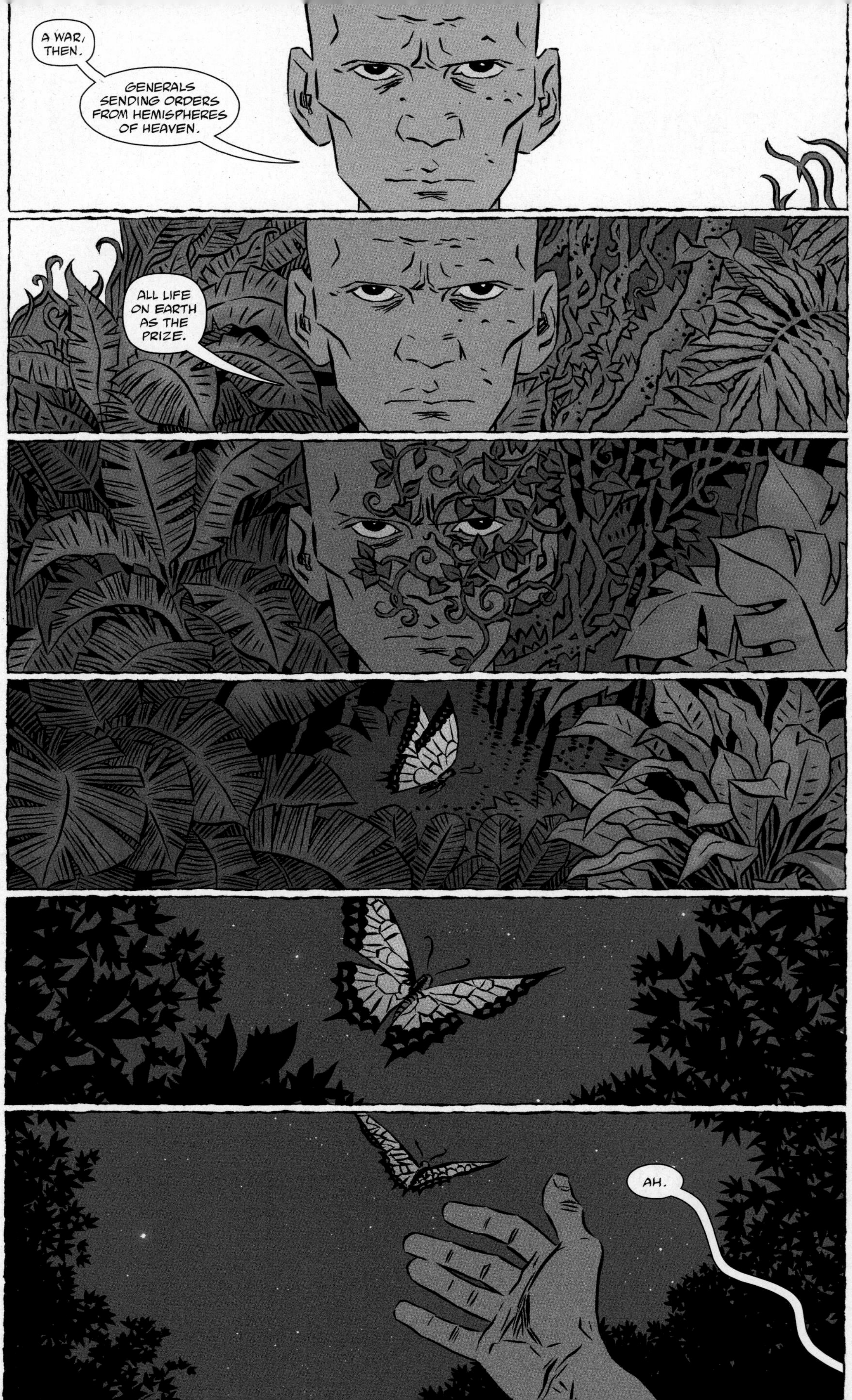
A WAR, THEN.
GENERALS SENDING ORDERS FROM HEMISPHERES OF HEAVEN.
ALL LIFE ON EARTH AS THE PRIZE.
AH.

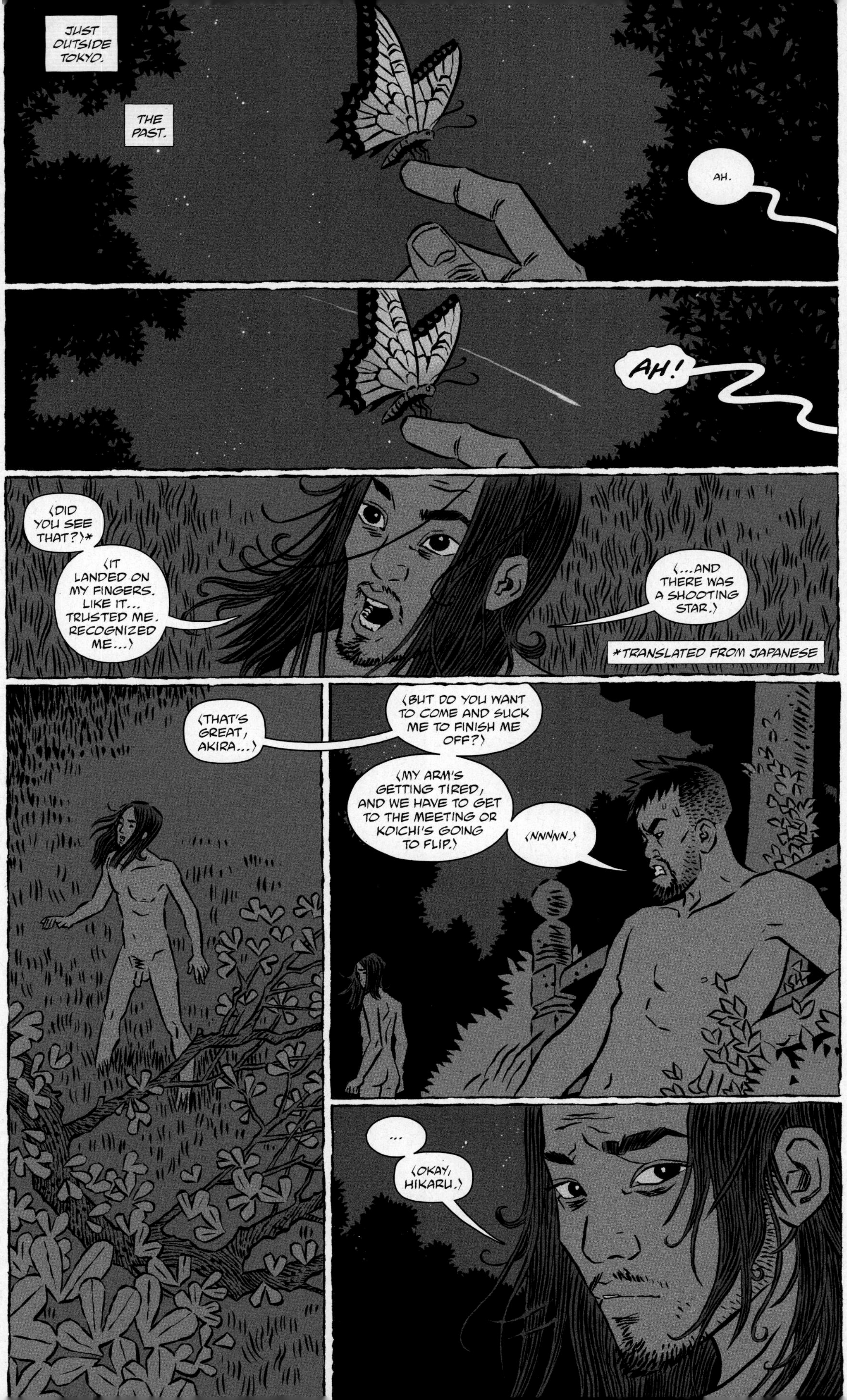
JUST OUTSIDE TOKYO.
THE PAST.
AH.
AH!
⟨DID YOU SEE THAT?⟩*
⟨IT LANDED ON MY FINGERS. LIKE IT... TRUSTED ME. RECOGNIZED ME...⟩
⟨...AND THERE WAS A SHOOTING STAR.⟩
*TRANSLATED FROM JAPANESE
⟨THAT'S GREAT, AKIRA...⟩
⟨BUT DO YOU WANT TO COME AND SUCK ME TO FINISH ME OFF?⟩
⟨MY ARM'S GETTING TIRED, AND WE HAVE TO GET TO THE MEETING OR KOICHI'S GOING TO FLIP.⟩
⟨NNNNN.⟩
...
⟨OKAY, HIKARU.⟩

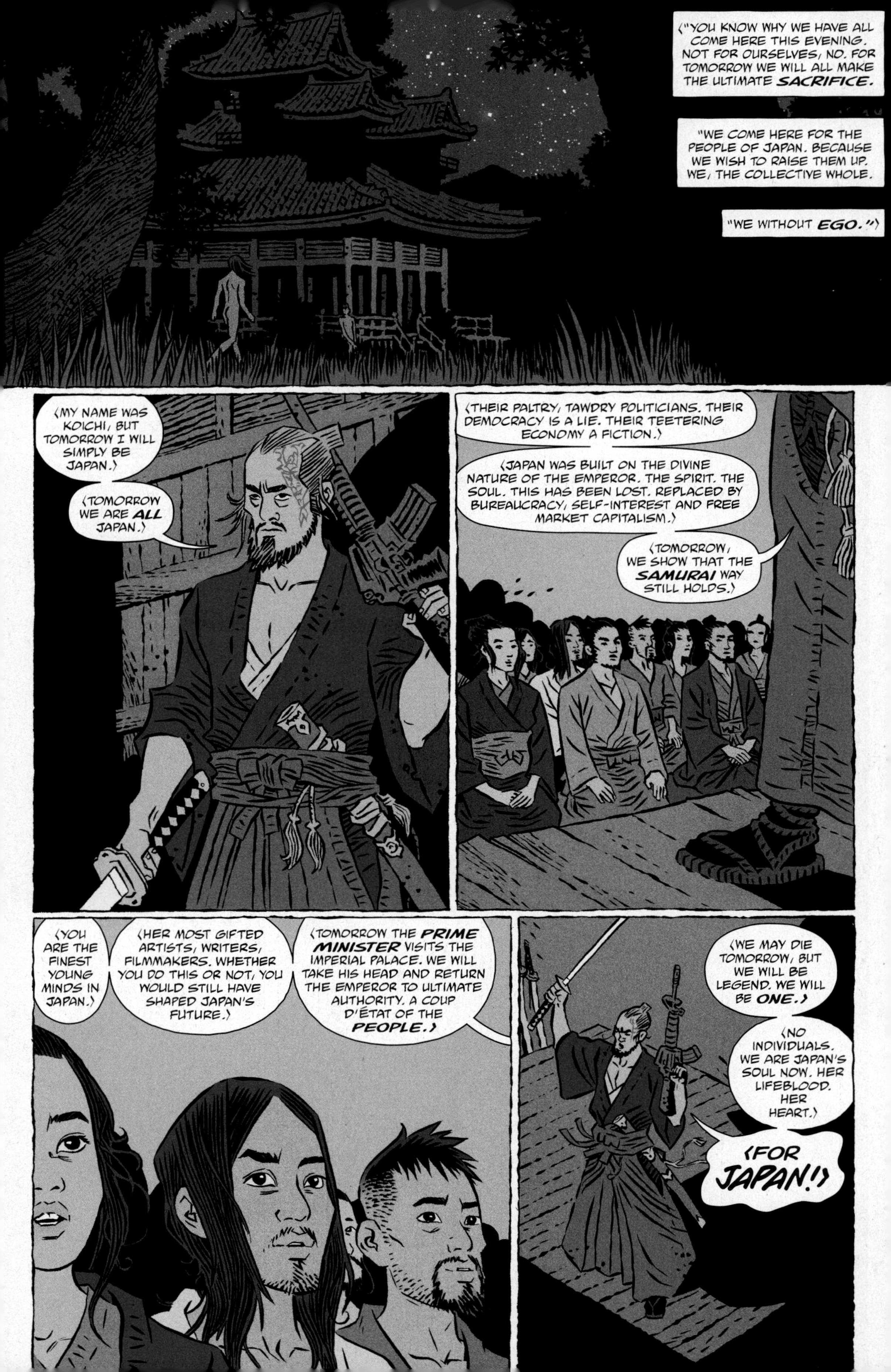
("YOU KNOW WHY WE HAVE ALL COME HERE THIS EVENING. NOT FOR OURSELVES, NO. FOR TOMORROW WE WILL ALL MAKE THE ULTIMATE SACRIFICE.
"WE COME HERE FOR THE PEOPLE OF JAPAN. BECAUSE WE WISH TO RAISE THEM UP. WE, THE COLLECTIVE WHOLE.
"WE WITHOUT EGO.")
(MY NAME WAS KOICHI, BUT TOMORROW I WILL SIMPLY BE JAPAN.)
(TOMORROW WE ARE ALL JAPAN.)
(THEIR PALTRY, TAWDRY POLITICIANS. THEIR DEMOCRACY IS A LIE. THEIR TEETERING ECONOMY A FICTION.)
(JAPAN WAS BUILT ON THE DIVINE NATURE OF THE EMPEROR. THE SPIRIT. THE SOUL. THIS HAS BEEN LOST. REPLACED BY BUREAUCRACY, SELF-INTEREST AND FREE MARKET CAPITALISM.)
(TOMORROW, WE SHOW THAT THE SAMURAI WAY STILL HOLDS.)
(YOU ARE THE FINEST YOUNG MINDS IN JAPAN.)
(HER MOST GIFTED ARTISTS, WRITERS, FILMMAKERS. WHETHER YOU DO THIS OR NOT, YOU WOULD STILL HAVE SHAPED JAPAN'S FUTURE.)
(TOMORROW THE PRIME MINISTER VISITS THE IMPERIAL PALACE. WE WILL TAKE HIS HEAD AND RETURN THE EMPEROR TO ULTIMATE AUTHORITY. A COUP D'ÉTAT OF THE PEOPLE.)
(WE MAY DIE TOMORROW, BUT WE WILL BE LEGEND. WE WILL BE ONE.)
(NO INDIVIDUALS. WE ARE JAPAN'S SOUL NOW. HER LIFEBLOOD. HER HEART.)
(FOR JAPAN!)

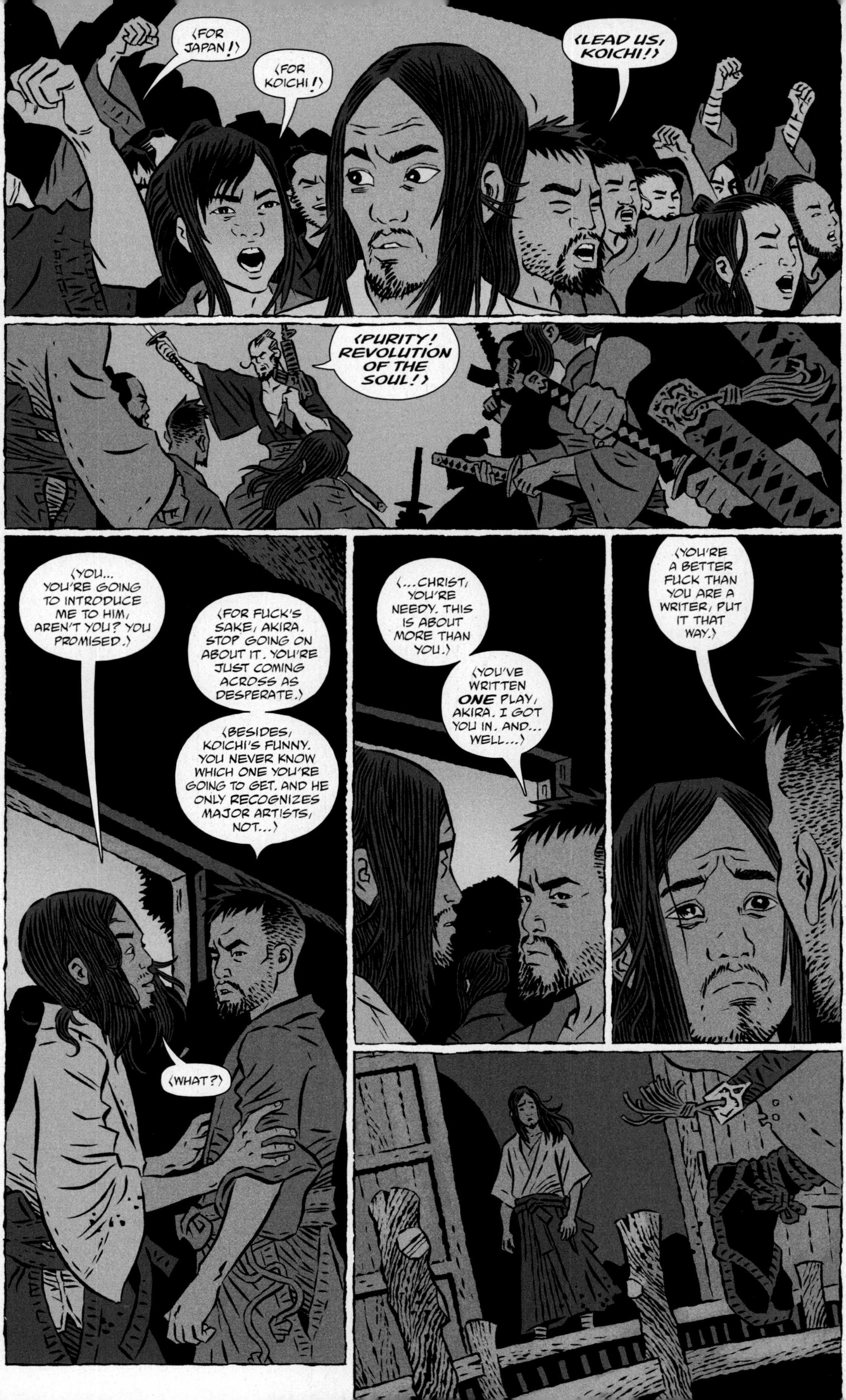

‹FOR JAPAN!›
‹FOR KOICHI!›
‹LEAD US, KOICHI!›
‹PURITY! REVOLUTION OF THE SOUL!›
‹YOU... YOU'RE GOING TO INTRODUCE ME TO HIM, AREN'T YOU? YOU PROMISED.›
‹FOR FUCK'S SAKE, AKIRA. STOP GOING ON ABOUT IT. YOU'RE JUST COMING ACROSS AS DESPERATE.›
‹BESIDES, KOICHI'S FUNNY. YOU NEVER KNOW WHICH ONE YOU'RE GOING TO GET. AND HE ONLY RECOGNIZES MAJOR ARTISTS, NOT...›
‹WHAT?›
‹...CHRIST, YOU'RE NEEDY. THIS IS ABOUT MORE THAN YOU.›
‹YOU'VE WRITTEN ONE PLAY, AKIRA. I GOT YOU IN. AND... WELL...›
‹YOU'RE A BETTER FUCK THAN YOU ARE A WRITER, PUT IT THAT WAY.›

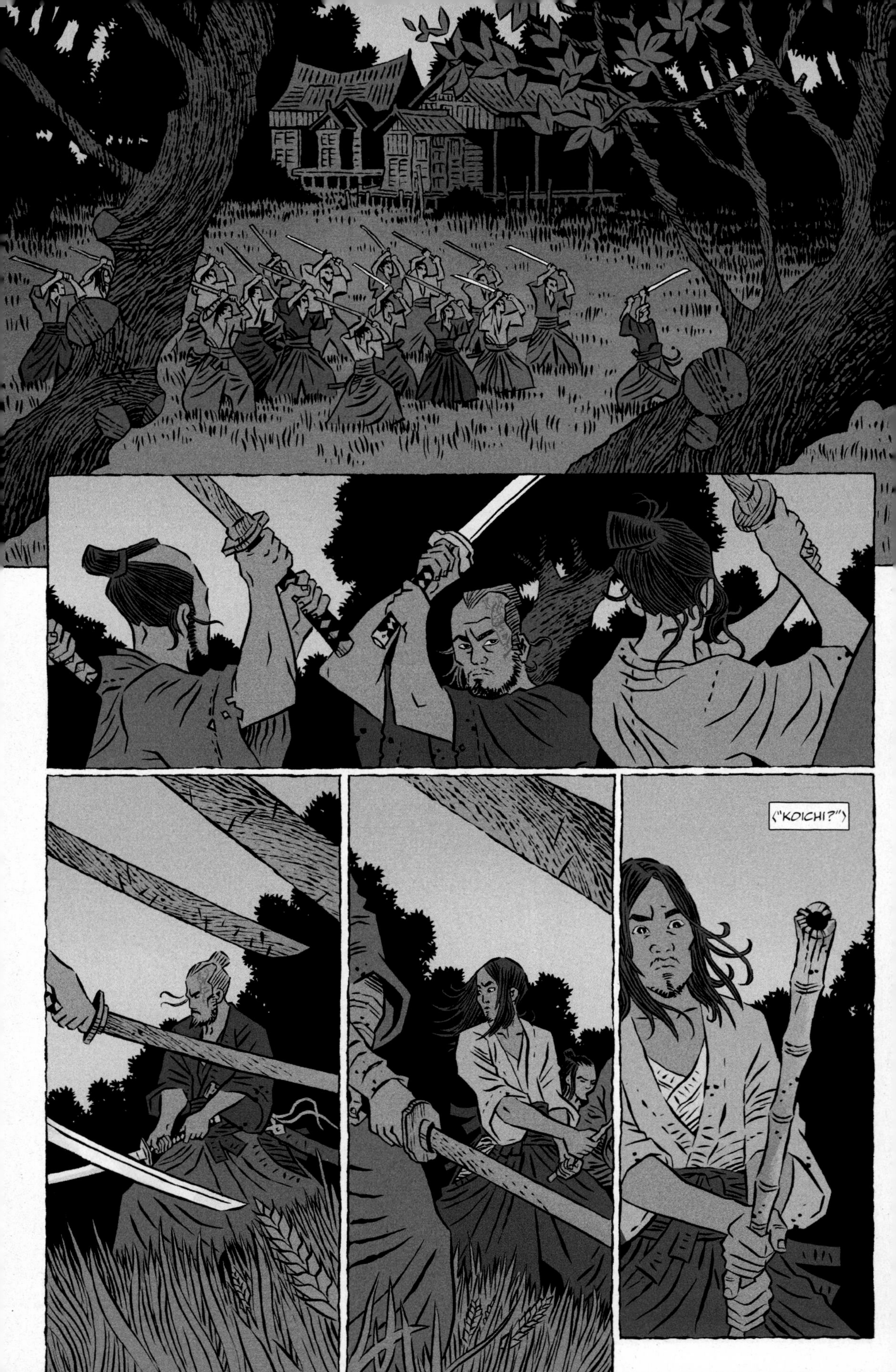
<"KOICHI?">

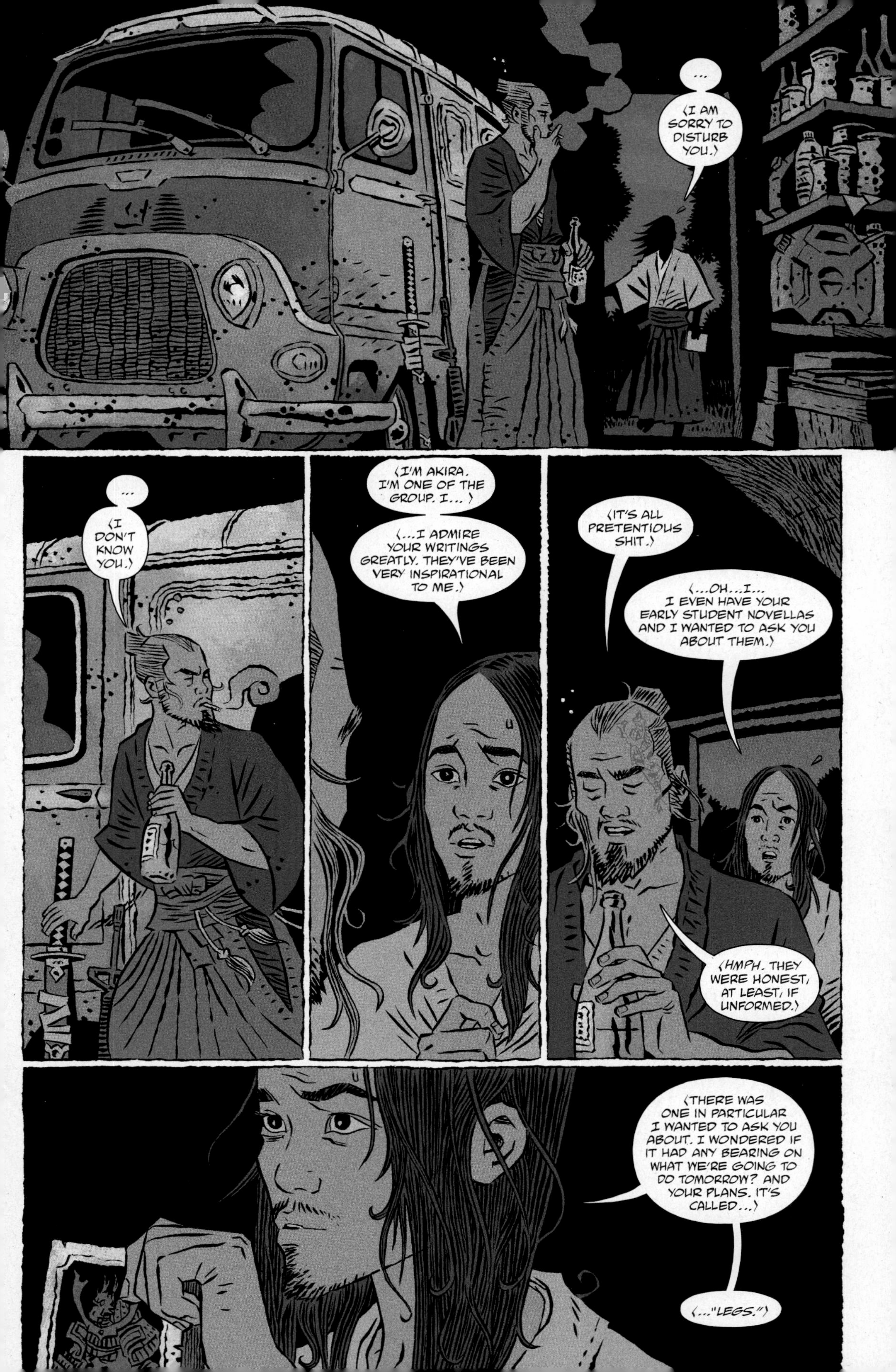
...
⟨I AM SORRY TO DISTURB YOU.⟩
...
⟨I DON'T KNOW YOU.⟩
⟨I'M AKIRA. I'M ONE OF THE GROUP. I...⟩
⟨...I ADMIRE YOUR WRITINGS GREATLY. THEY'VE BEEN VERY INSPIRATIONAL TO ME.⟩
⟨IT'S ALL PRETENTIOUS SHIT.⟩
⟨...OH...I... I EVEN HAVE YOUR EARLY STUDENT NOVELLAS AND I WANTED TO ASK YOU ABOUT THEM.⟩
⟨HMPH. THEY WERE HONEST, AT LEAST, IF UNFORMED.⟩
⟨THERE WAS ONE IN PARTICULAR I WANTED TO ASK YOU ABOUT. I WONDERED IF IT HAD ANY BEARING ON WHAT WE'RE GOING TO DO TOMORROW? AND YOUR PLANS. IT'S CALLED...⟩
⟨..."LEGS."⟩

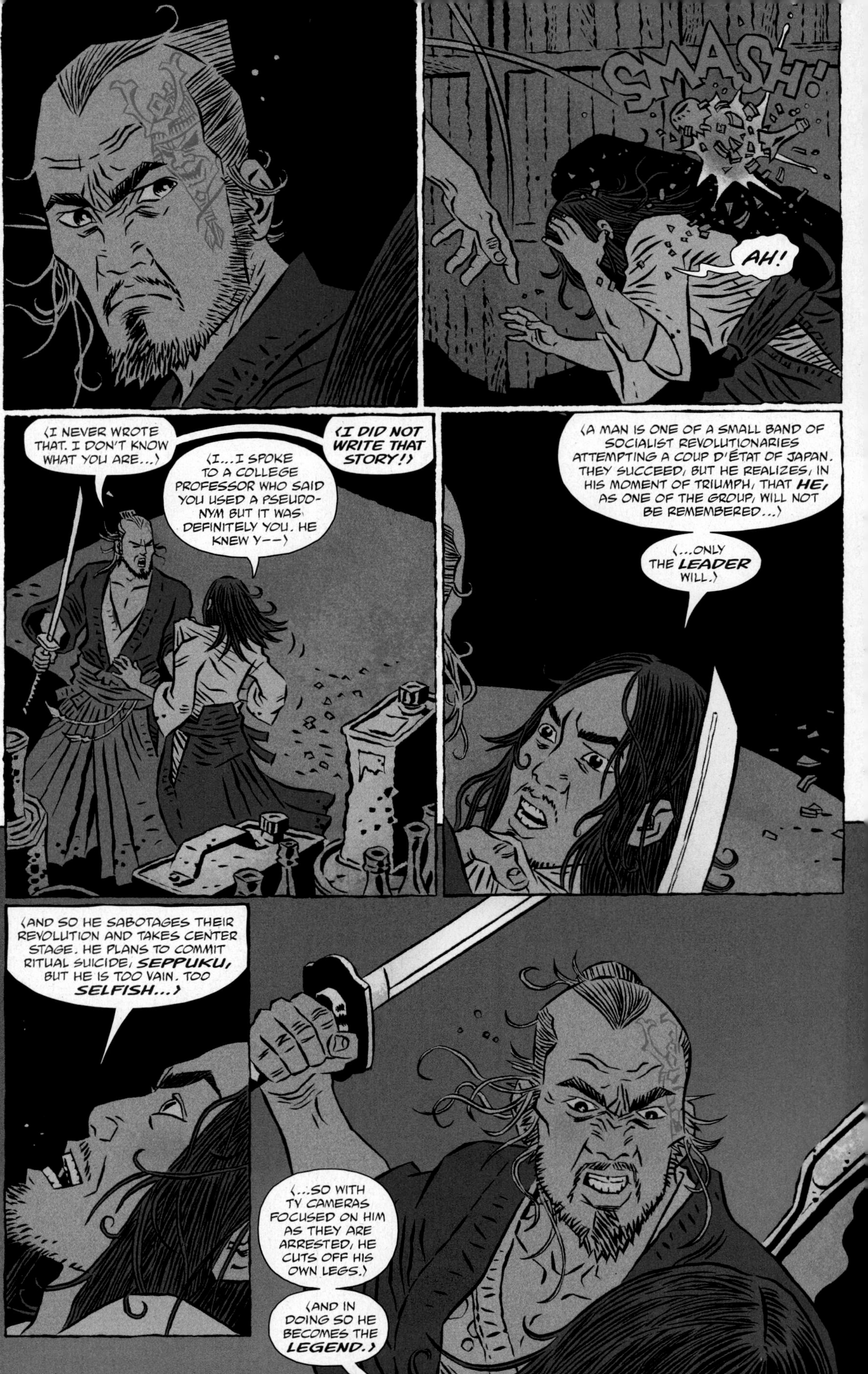
SMASH!
AH!
⟨I NEVER WROTE THAT. I DON'T KNOW WHAT YOU ARE...⟩
⟨I DID NOT WRITE THAT STORY!⟩
⟨I...I SPOKE TO A COLLEGE PROFESSOR WHO SAID YOU USED A PSEUDONYM BUT IT WAS DEFINITELY YOU. HE KNEW Y--⟩
⟨A MAN IS ONE OF A SMALL BAND OF SOCIALIST REVOLUTIONARIES ATTEMPTING A COUP D'ÉTAT OF JAPAN. THEY SUCCEED, BUT HE REALIZES, IN HIS MOMENT OF TRIUMPH, THAT HE, AS ONE OF THE GROUP, WILL NOT BE REMEMBERED...⟩
⟨...ONLY THE LEADER WILL.⟩
⟨AND SO HE SABOTAGES THEIR REVOLUTION AND TAKES CENTER STAGE. HE PLANS TO COMMIT RITUAL SUICIDE, SEPPUKU, BUT HE IS TOO VAIN. TOO SELFISH...⟩
⟨...SO WITH TV CAMERAS FOCUSED ON HIM AS THEY ARE ARRESTED, HE CUTS OFF HIS OWN LEGS.⟩
⟨AND IN DOING SO HE BECOMES THE LEGEND.⟩

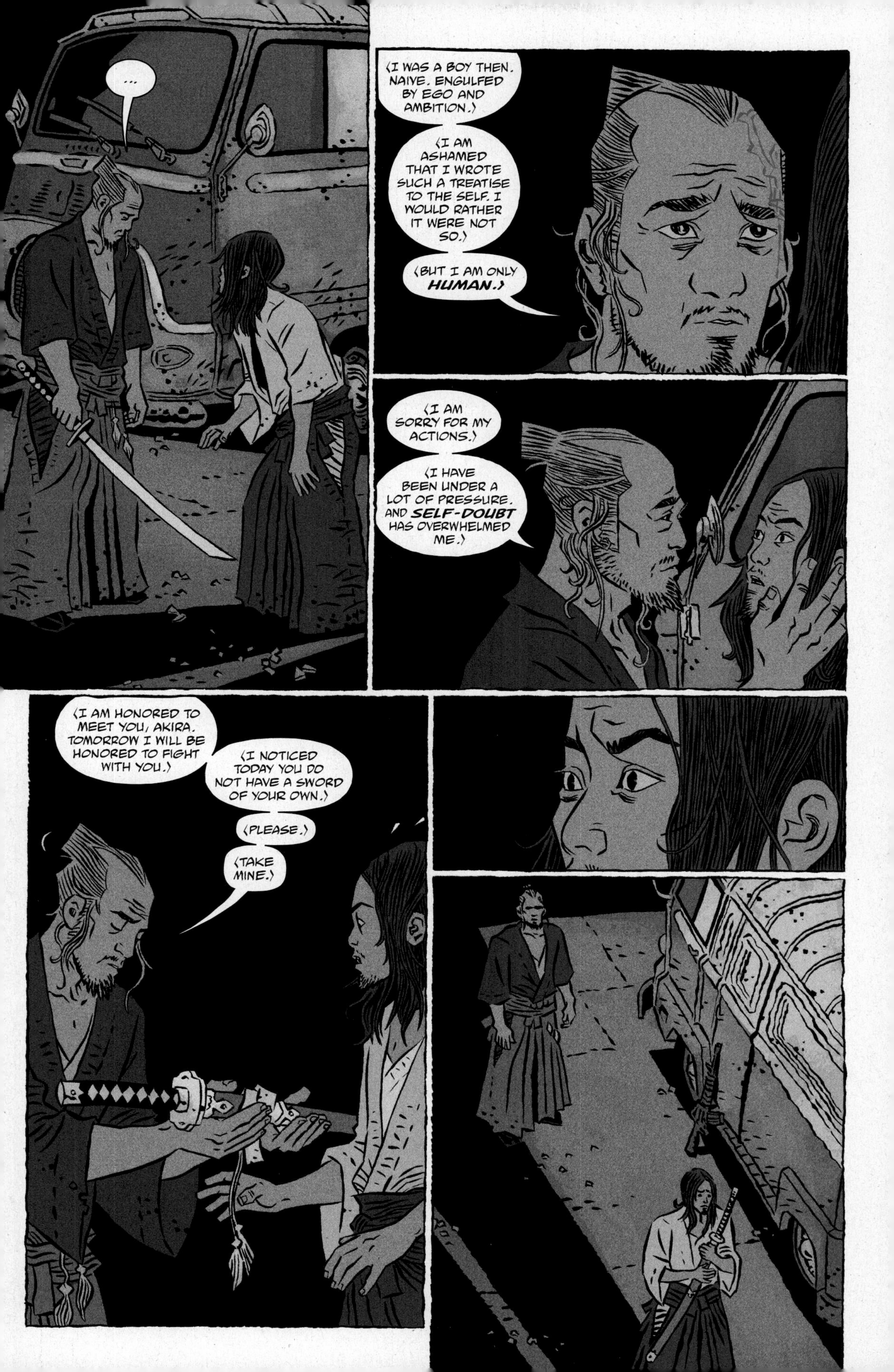
...
⟨I WAS A BOY THEN. NAIVE. ENGULFED BY EGO AND AMBITION.⟩
⟨I AM ASHAMED THAT I WROTE SUCH A TREATISE TO THE SELF. I WOULD RATHER IT WERE NOT SO.⟩
⟨BUT I AM ONLY HUMAN.⟩
⟨I AM SORRY FOR MY ACTIONS.⟩
⟨I HAVE BEEN UNDER A LOT OF PRESSURE. AND SELF-DOUBT HAS OVERWHELMED ME.⟩
⟨I AM HONORED TO MEET YOU, AKIRA. TOMORROW I WILL BE HONORED TO FIGHT WITH YOU.⟩
⟨I NOTICED TODAY YOU DO NOT HAVE A SWORD OF YOUR OWN.⟩
⟨PLEASE.⟩
⟨TAKE MINE.⟩

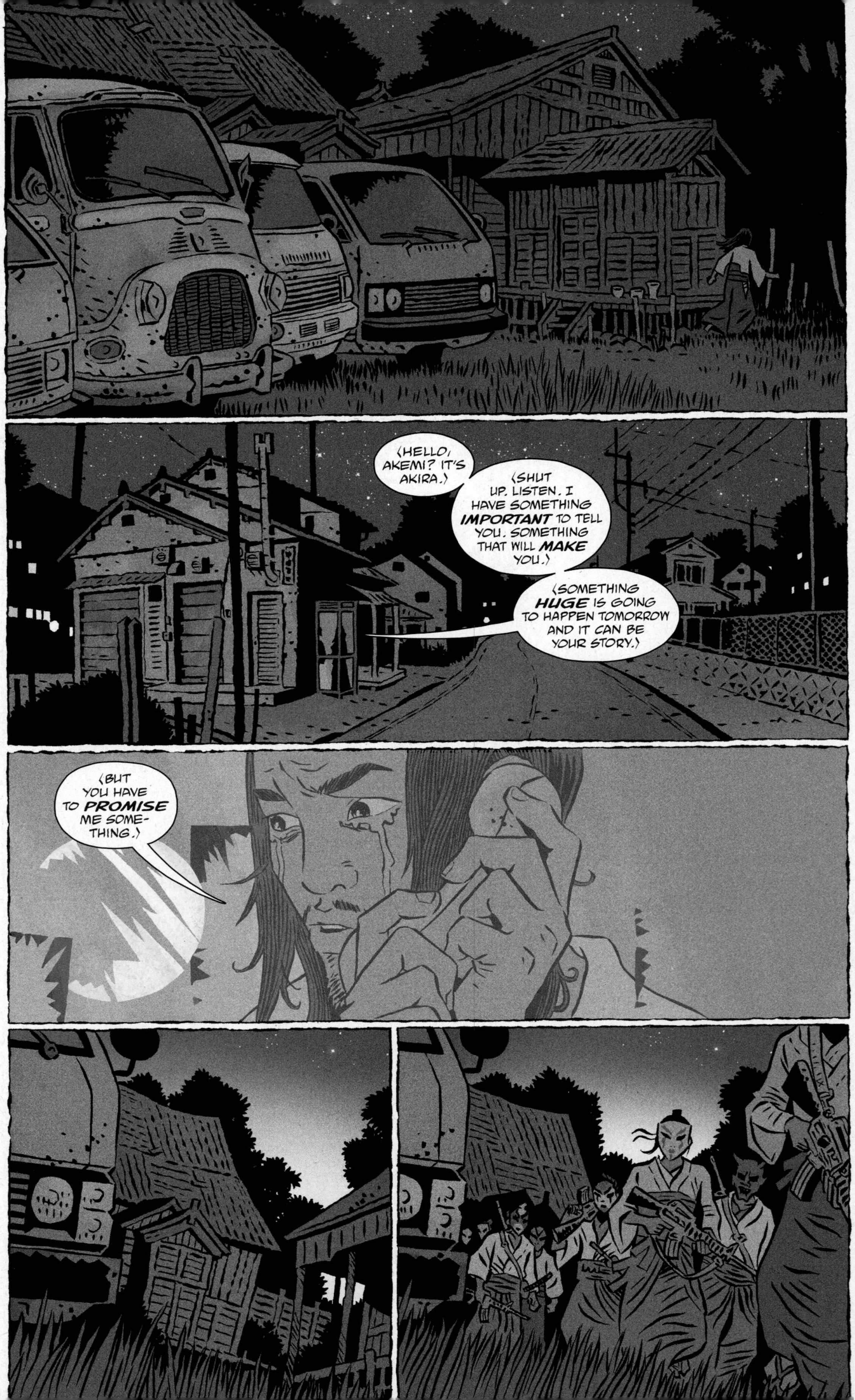
⟨HELLO, AKEMI? IT'S AKIRA.⟩
⟨SHUT UP. LISTEN. I HAVE SOMETHING **IMPORTANT** TO TELL YOU. SOMETHING THAT WILL **MAKE** YOU.⟩
⟨SOMETHING **HUGE** IS GOING TO HAPPEN TOMORROW AND IT CAN BE YOUR STORY.⟩
⟨BUT YOU HAVE TO **PROMISE** ME SOME-THING.⟩

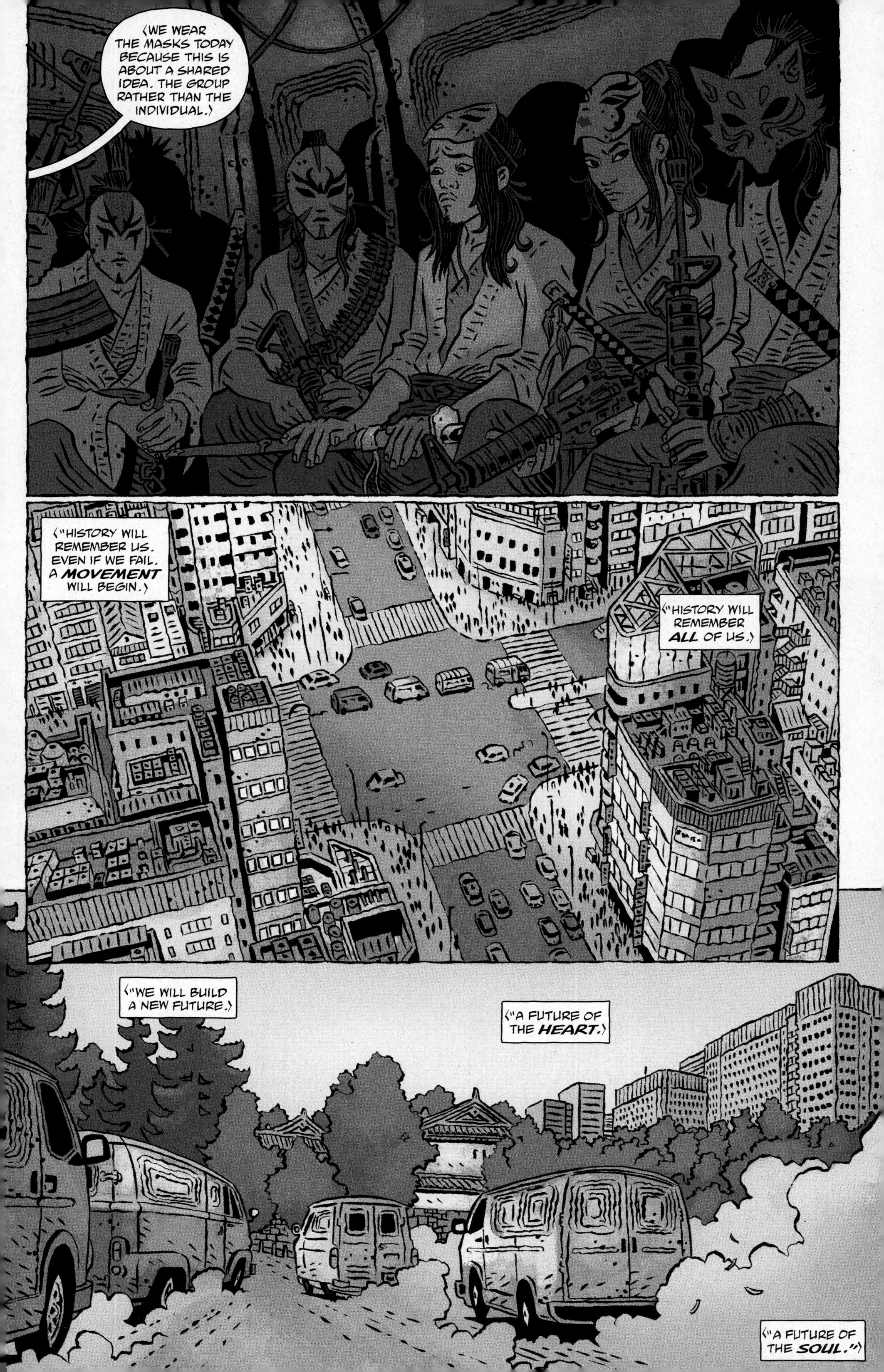
⟨WE WEAR THE MASKS TODAY BECAUSE THIS IS ABOUT A SHARED IDEA. THE GROUP RATHER THAN THE INDIVIDUAL.⟩
⟨"HISTORY WILL REMEMBER US. EVEN IF WE FAIL. A MOVEMENT WILL BEGIN.⟩
⟨"HISTORY WILL REMEMBER ALL OF US.⟩
⟨"WE WILL BUILD A NEW FUTURE.⟩
⟨"A FUTURE OF THE HEART.⟩
⟨"A FUTURE OF THE SOUL."⟩

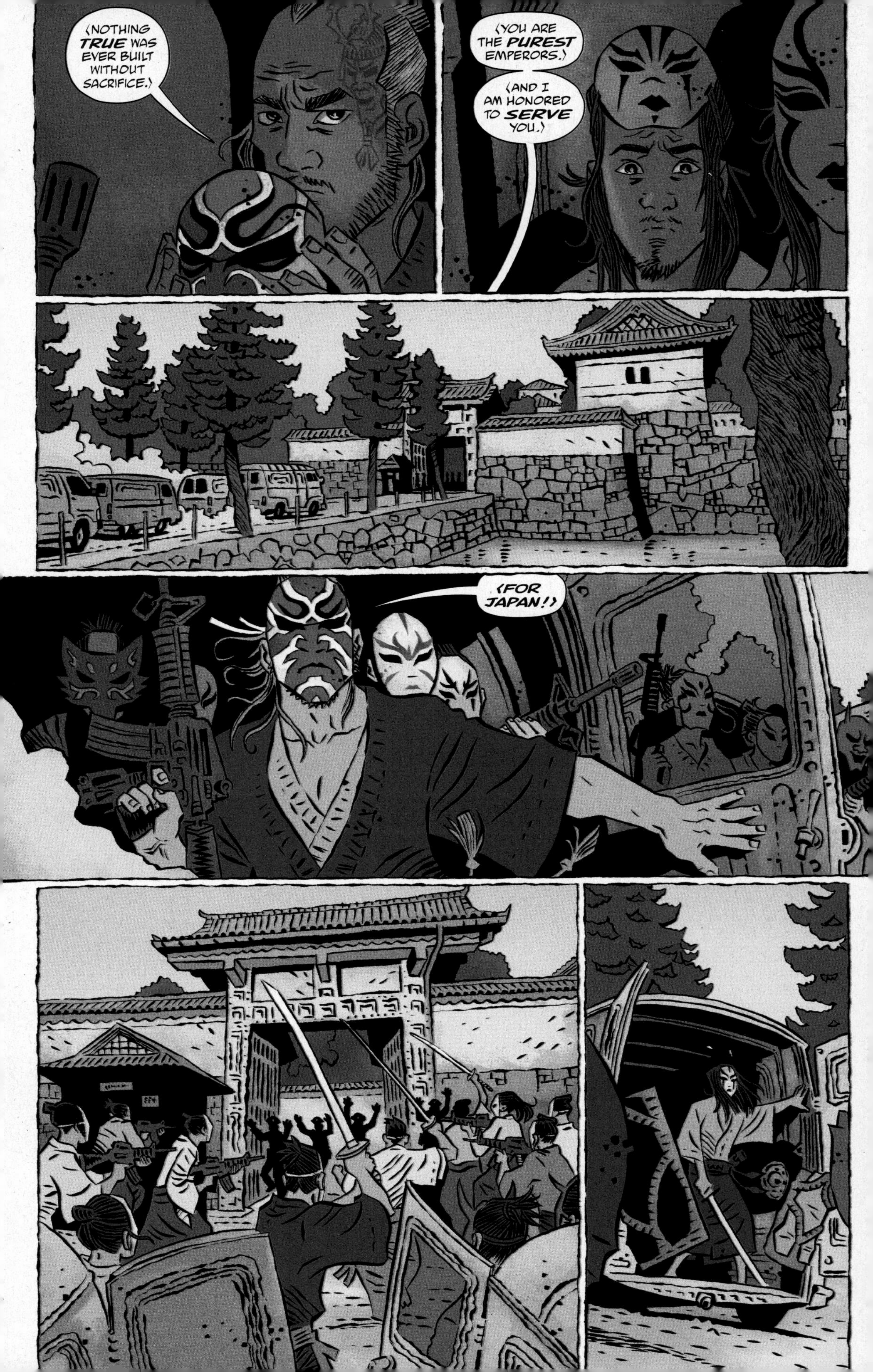

‹NOTHING TRUE WAS EVER BUILT WITHOUT SACRIFICE.›
‹YOU ARE THE PUREST EMPERORS.›
‹AND I AM HONORED TO SERVE YOU.›
‹FOR JAPAN!›

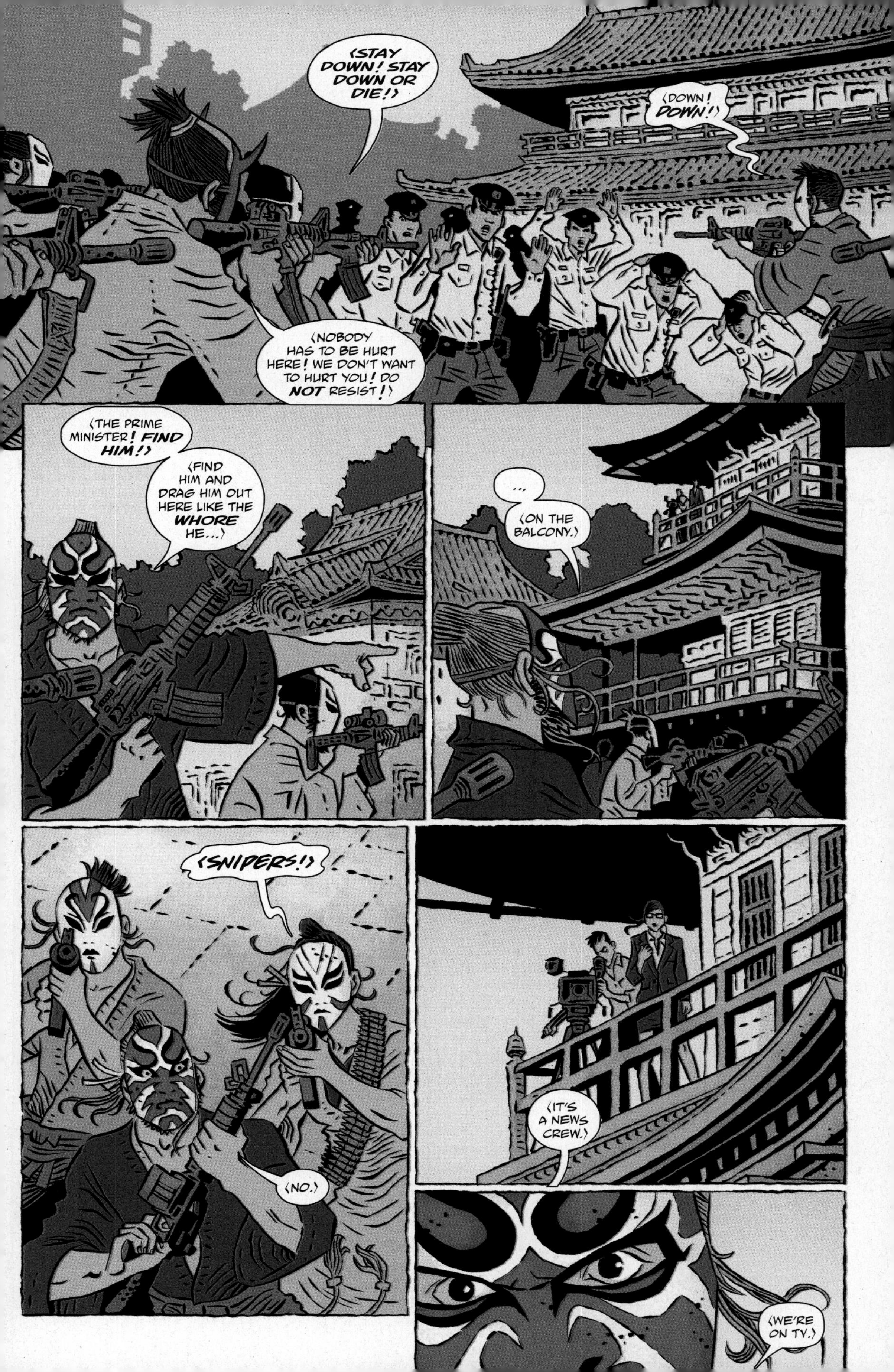
‹STAY DOWN! STAY DOWN OR DIE!›
‹DOWN! DOWN!›
‹NOBODY HAS TO BE HURT HERE! WE DON'T WANT TO HURT YOU! DO NOT RESIST!›
‹THE PRIME MINISTER! FIND HIM!›
‹FIND HIM AND DRAG HIM OUT HERE LIKE THE WHORE HE...›
...
‹ON THE BALCONY.›
‹SNIPERS!›
‹NO.›
‹IT'S A NEWS CREW.›
‹WE'RE ON TV.›

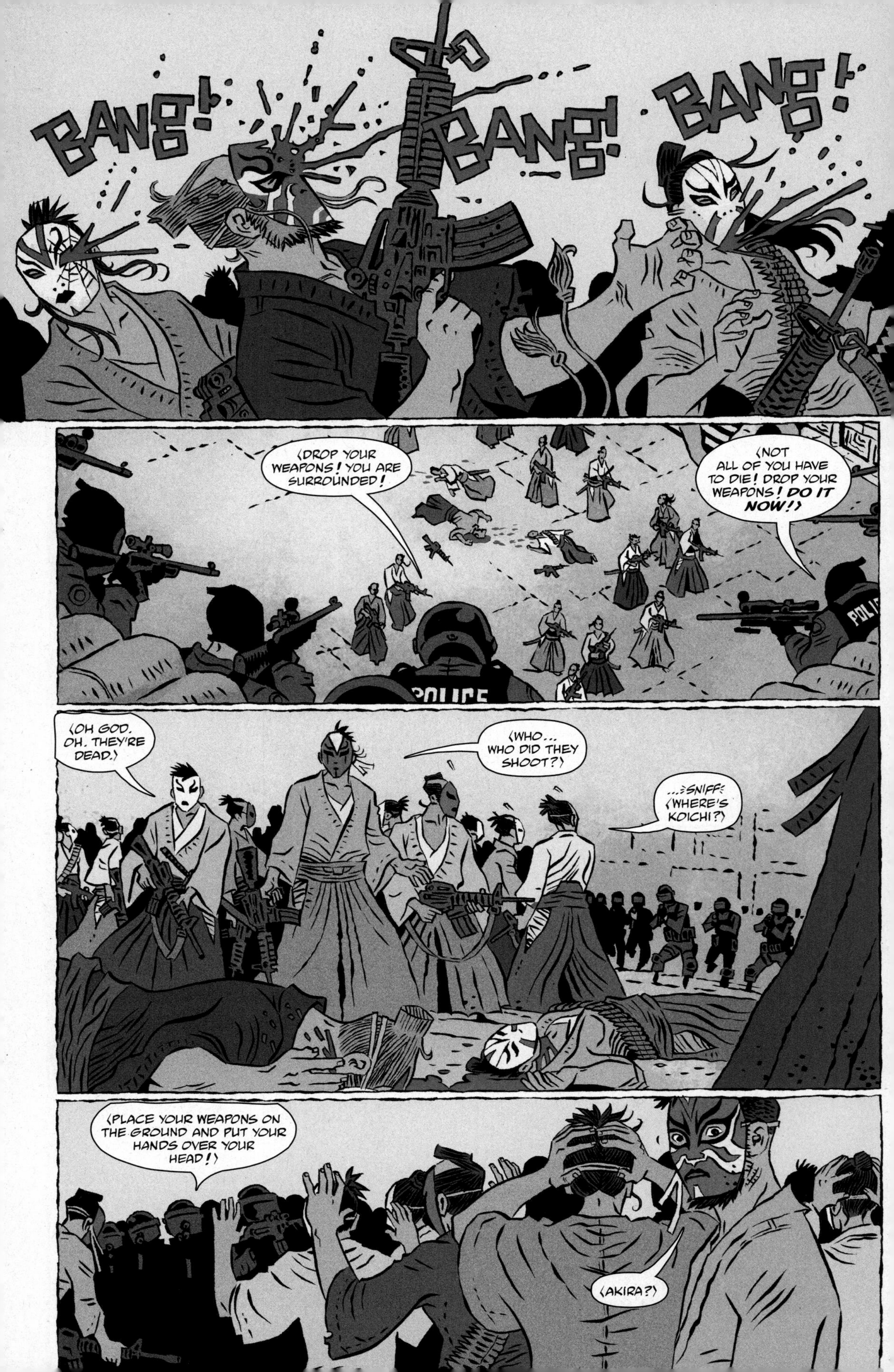
BANG! BANG! BANG!
‹DROP YOUR WEAPONS! YOU ARE SURROUNDED!›
‹NOT ALL OF YOU HAVE TO DIE! DROP YOUR WEAPONS! DO IT NOW!›
POLICE
POLI
‹OH GOD. OH. THEY'RE DEAD.›
‹WHO... WHO DID THEY SHOOT?›
...SNIFF ‹WHERE'S KOICHI?›
‹PLACE YOUR WEAPONS ON THE GROUND AND PUT YOUR HANDS OVER YOUR HEAD!›
‹AKIRA?›

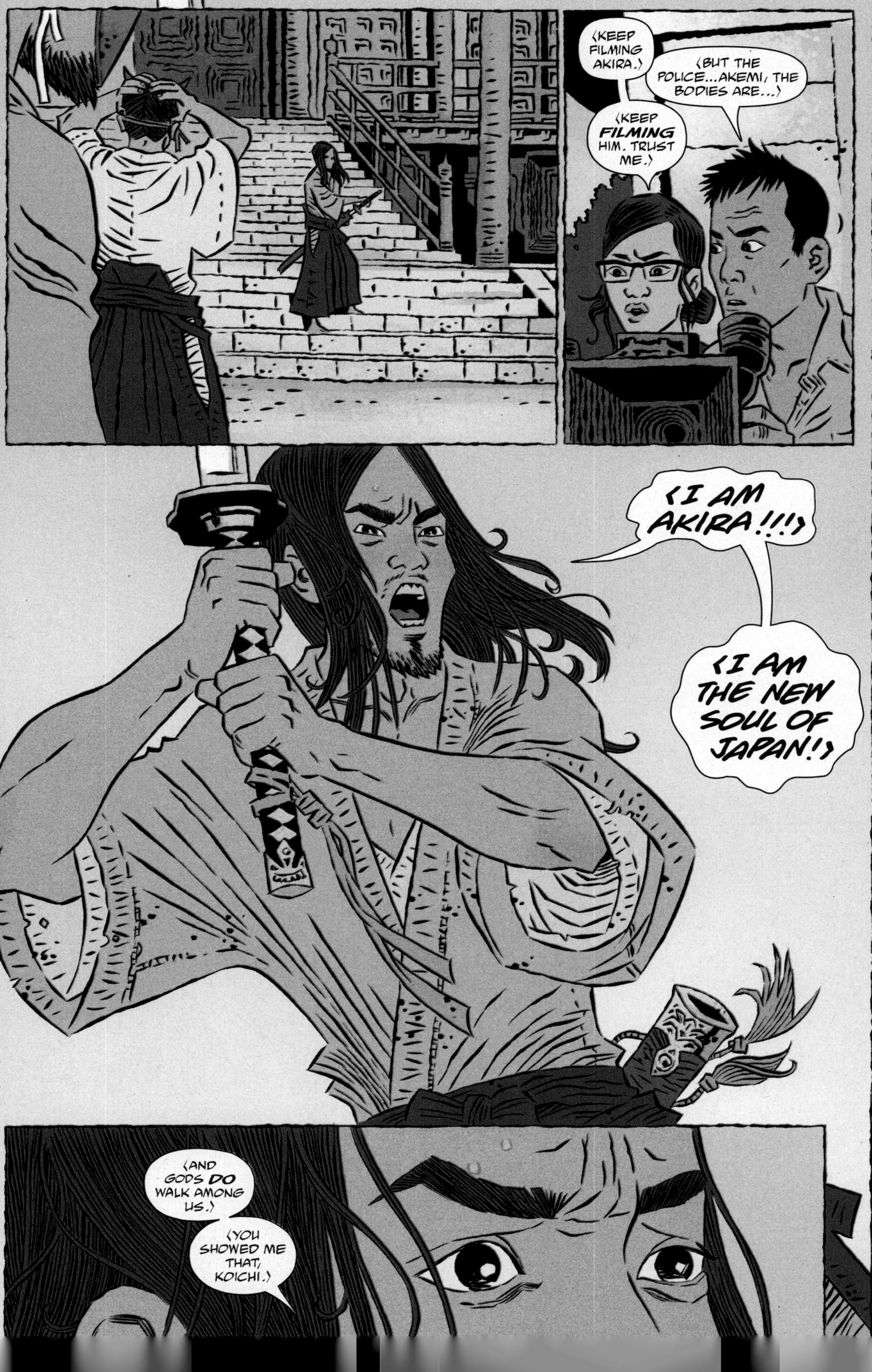

‹KEEP FILMING AKIRA.›
‹BUT THE POLICE...AKEMI, THE BODIES ARE...›
‹KEEP **FILMING** HIM. TRUST ME.›
‹I AM AKIRA!!!›
‹I AM THE NEW SOUL OF JAPAN!›
‹AND GODS **DO** WALK AMONG US.›
‹YOU SHOWED ME THAT, KOICHI.›

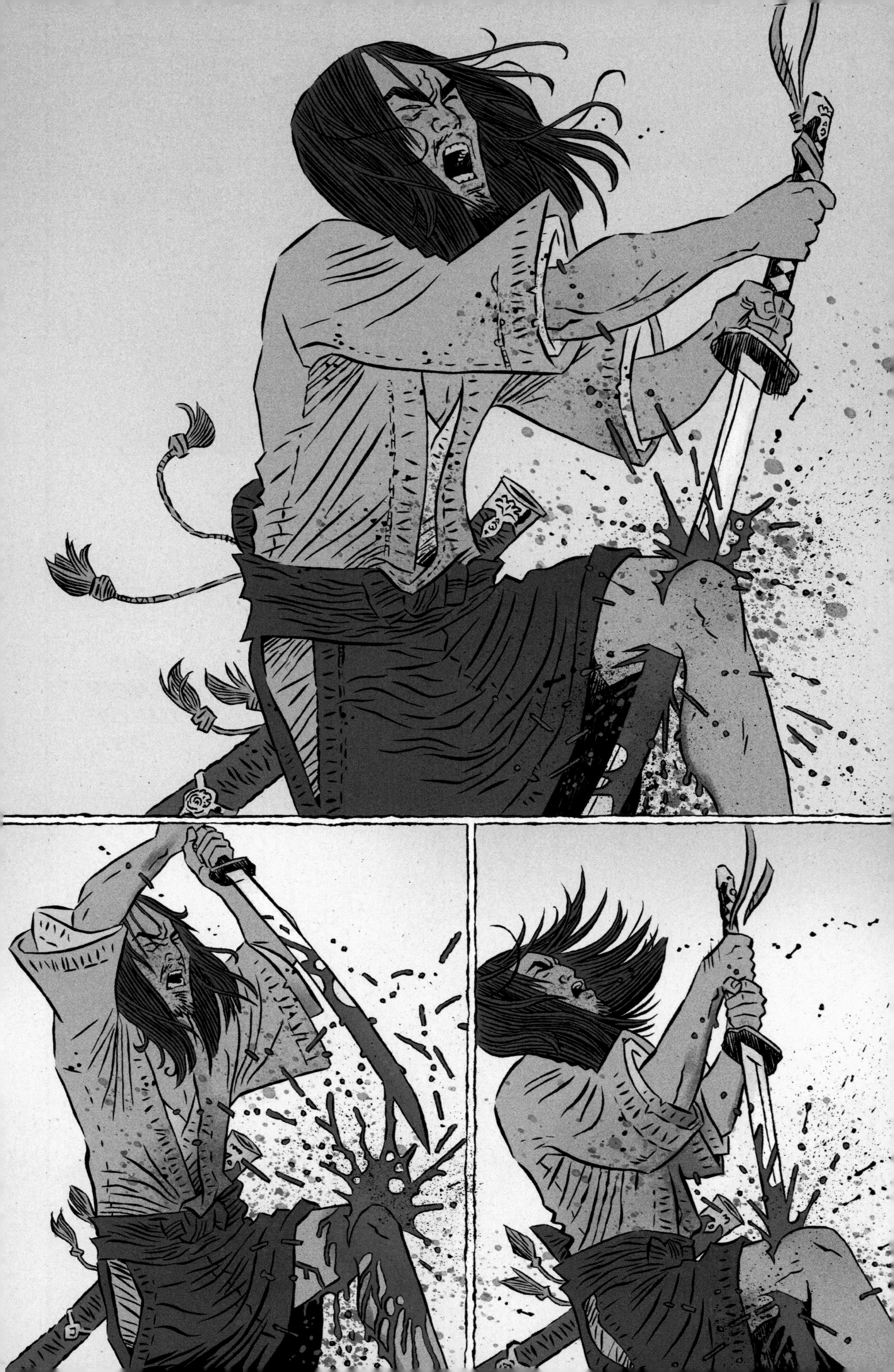

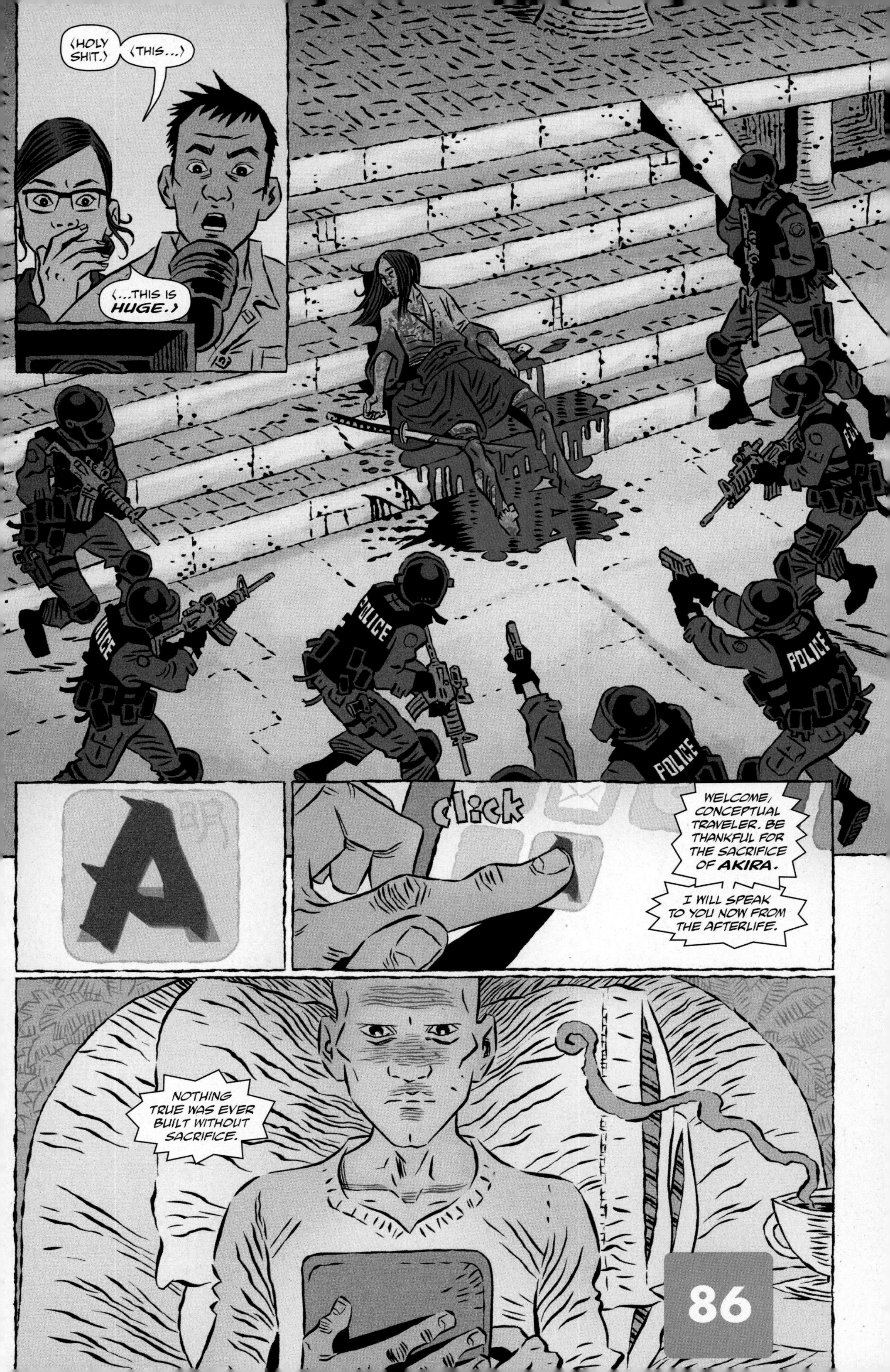
⟨HOLY SHIT.⟩
⟨THIS...⟩
⟨...THIS IS **HUGE**.⟩
POLICE
POLICE
POLICE
POLICE
click
WELCOME, CONCEPTUAL TRAVELER. BE THANKFUL FOR THE SACRIFICE OF **AKIRA**.
I WILL SPEAK TO YOU NOW FROM THE AFTERLIFE.
NOTHING TRUE WAS EVER BUILT WITHOUT SACRIFICE.

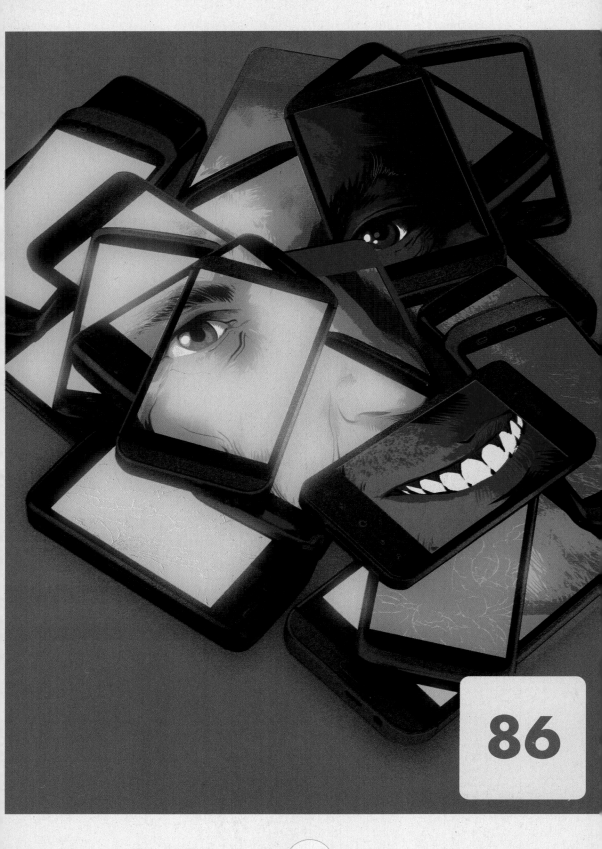

86

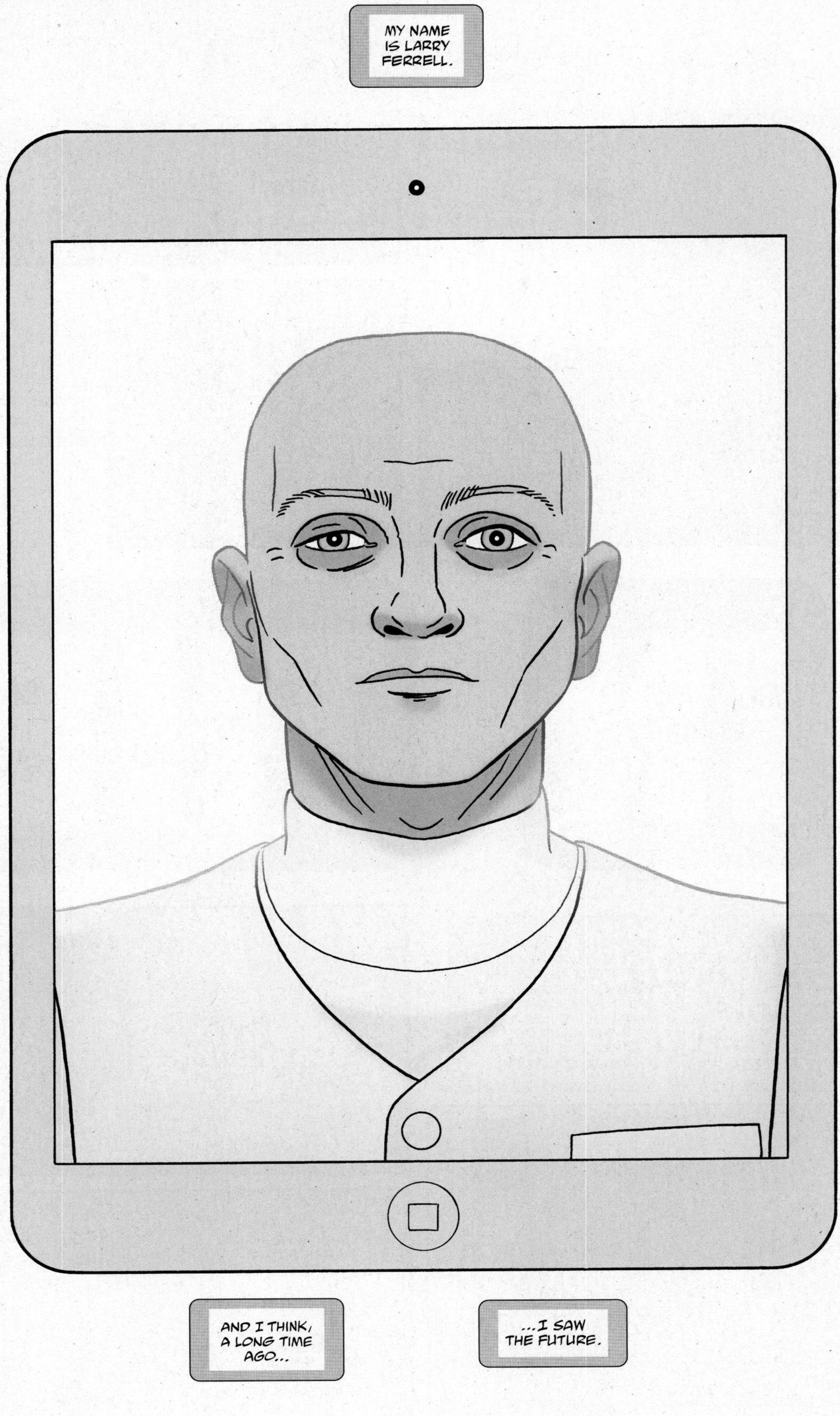
MY NAME IS LARRY FERRELL.
AND I THINK, A LONG TIME AGO...
...I SAW THE FUTURE.

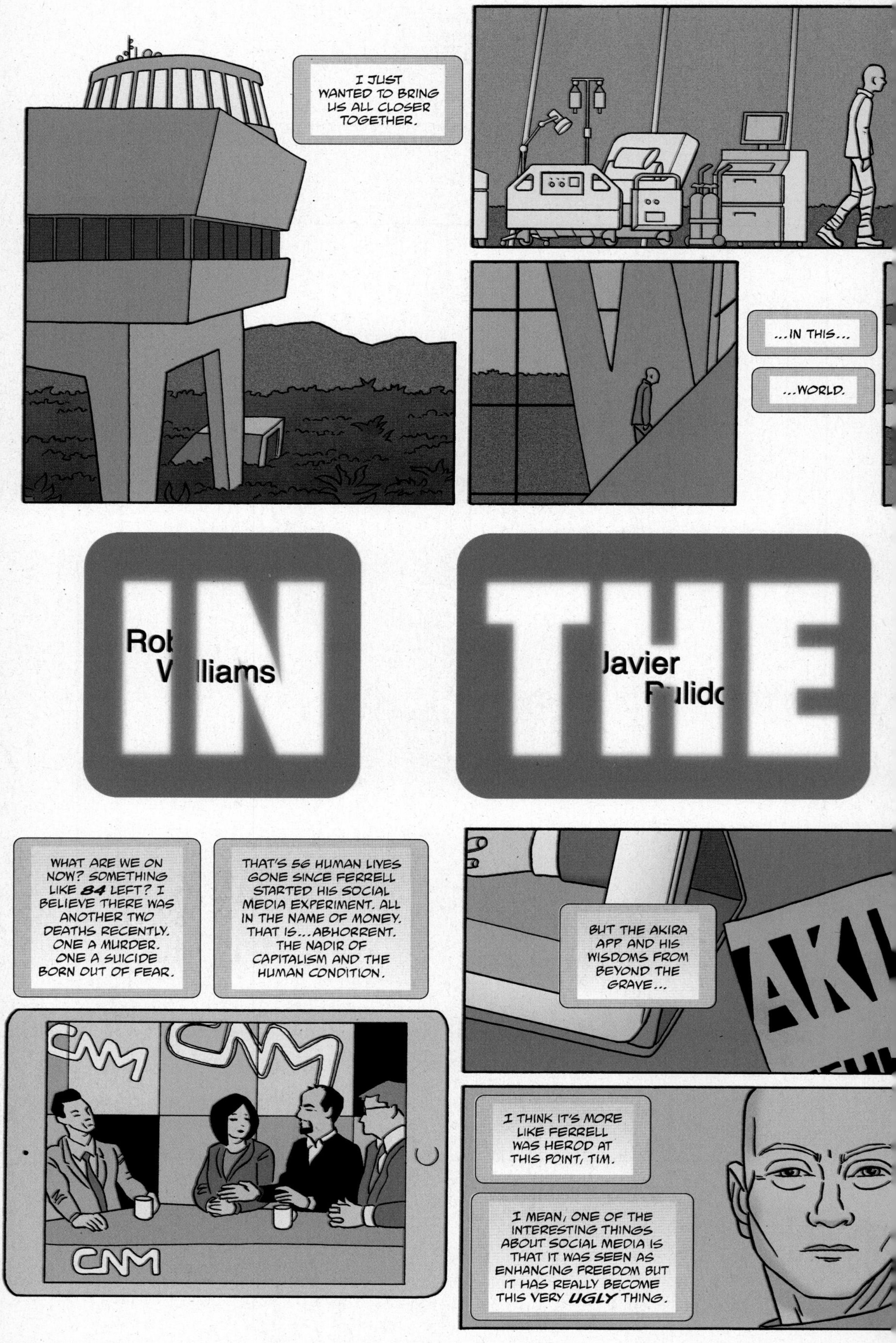
I JUST WANTED TO BRING US ALL CLOSER TOGETHER.
...IN THIS...
...WORLD.
IN THE
Rob Williams
Javier Pulido
WHAT ARE WE ON NOW? SOMETHING LIKE 84 LEFT? I BELIEVE THERE WAS ANOTHER TWO DEATHS RECENTLY. ONE A MURDER. ONE A SUICIDE BORN OUT OF FEAR.
THAT'S 56 HUMAN LIVES GONE SINCE FERRELL STARTED HIS SOCIAL MEDIA EXPERIMENT. ALL IN THE NAME OF MONEY. THAT IS...ABHORRENT. THE NADIR OF CAPITALISM AND THE HUMAN CONDITION.
CNM
CNM
CNM
BUT THE AKIRA APP AND HIS WISDOMS FROM BEYOND THE GRAVE...
I THINK IT'S MORE LIKE FERRELL WAS HEROD AT THIS POINT, TIM.
I MEAN, ONE OF THE INTERESTING THINGS ABOUT SOCIAL MEDIA IS THAT IT WAS SEEN AS ENHANCING FREEDOM BUT IT HAS REALLY BECOME THIS VERY UGLY THING.

EVERYONE.

IT'S AN INTERESTING CONTRADICTION. LARRY FERRELL'S 140 LIST SEEMS TO HAVE BROUGHT OUT THE BEST OF US AND THE WORST OF US.

FUTURE

Cle m Robins
Letter

M ggie Howe
ssista Editor

Muntsa Vicen
Colori

Ell Pyle
Editor

C ted by
Willia & Dowling

...THIS...THIS HAS BECOME A GENUINE WORLDWIDE PHENOMENON. AN AWFUL LOT OF PEOPLE ARE LISTENING TO THIS APP, WITH ITS PROCLAMATIONS OF PURE LOVE.

IT'S BECOME A SOCIAL MEDIA *CHURCH.* AKIRA AS A 140-CHARACTER *JESUS.*

SO, NOW, WE HAVE TO WONDER...WAS LARRY FERRELL HIS JOHN THE BAPTIST?

AND LARRY FERRELL *INVENTED* IT.

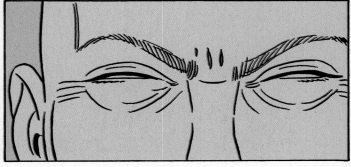

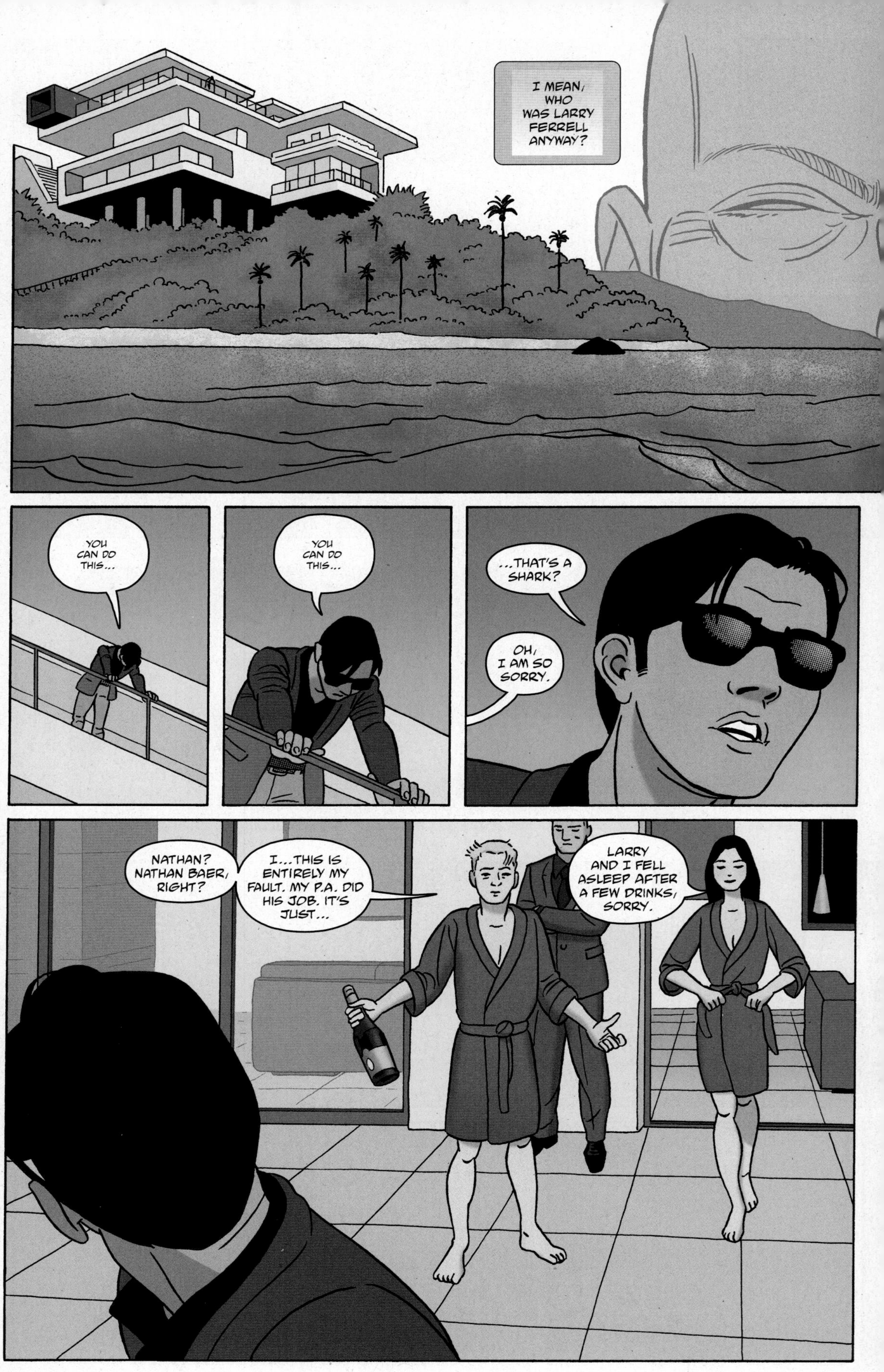
I MEAN, WHO WAS LARRY FERRELL ANYWAY?
YOU CAN DO THIS...
YOU CAN DO THIS...
...THAT'S A SHARK?
OH, I AM SO SORRY.
NATHAN? NATHAN BAER, RIGHT?
I...THIS IS ENTIRELY MY FAULT. MY P.A. DID HIS JOB. IT'S JUST...
LARRY AND I FELL ASLEEP AFTER A FEW DRINKS, SORRY.

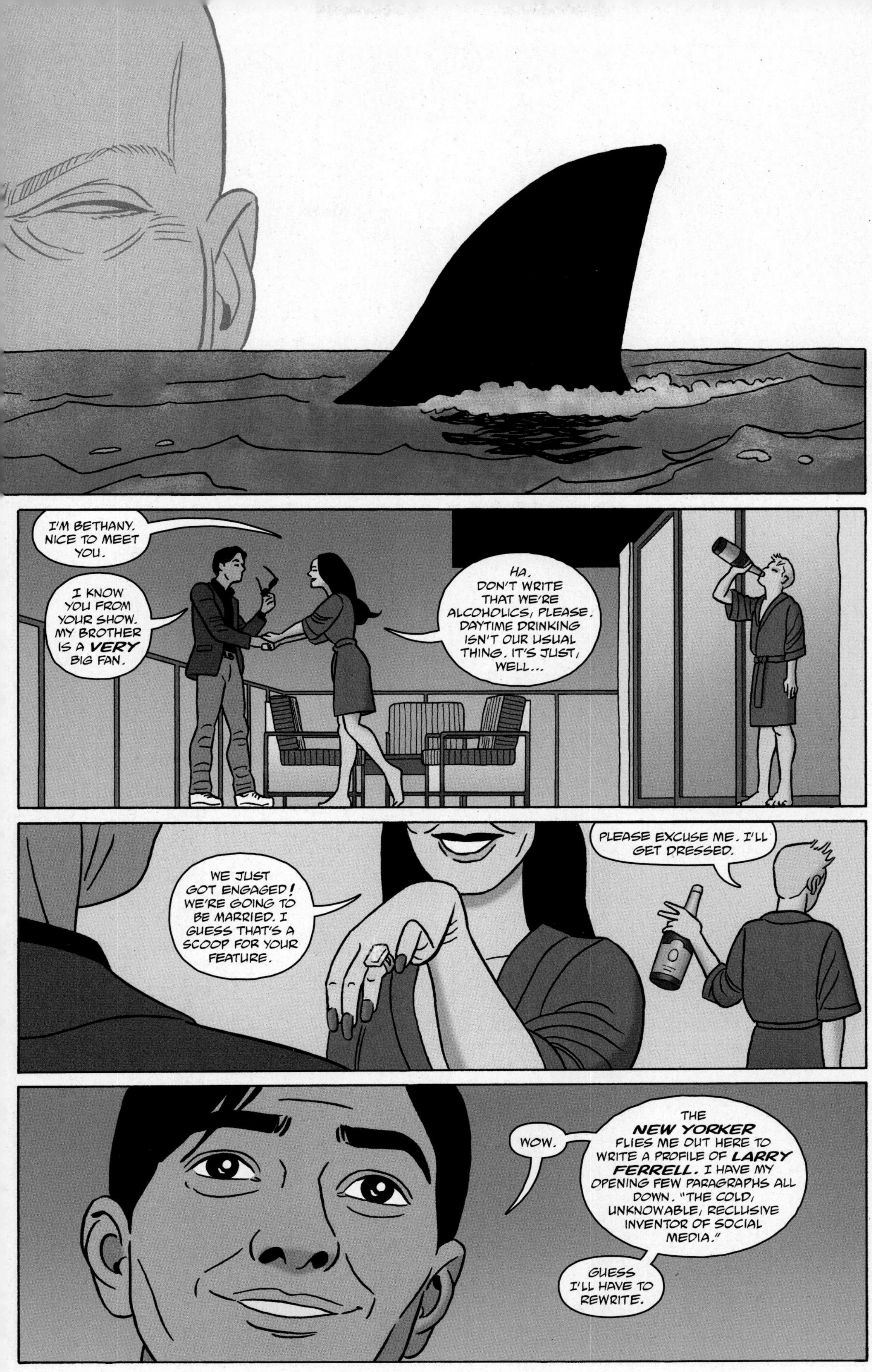
I'M BETHANY. NICE TO MEET YOU.
I KNOW YOU FROM YOUR SHOW. MY BROTHER IS A VERY BIG FAN.
HA. DON'T WRITE THAT WE'RE ALCOHOLICS, PLEASE. DAYTIME DRINKING ISN'T OUR USUAL THING. IT'S JUST, WELL...
WE JUST GOT ENGAGED! WE'RE GOING TO BE MARRIED. I GUESS THAT'S A SCOOP FOR YOUR FEATURE.
PLEASE EXCUSE ME. I'LL GET DRESSED.
WOW.
THE NEW YORKER FLIES ME OUT HERE TO WRITE A PROFILE OF LARRY FERRELL. I HAVE MY OPENING FEW PARAGRAPHS ALL DOWN. "THE COLD, UNKNOWABLE, RECLUSIVE INVENTOR OF SOCIAL MEDIA."
GUESS I'LL HAVE TO REWRITE.

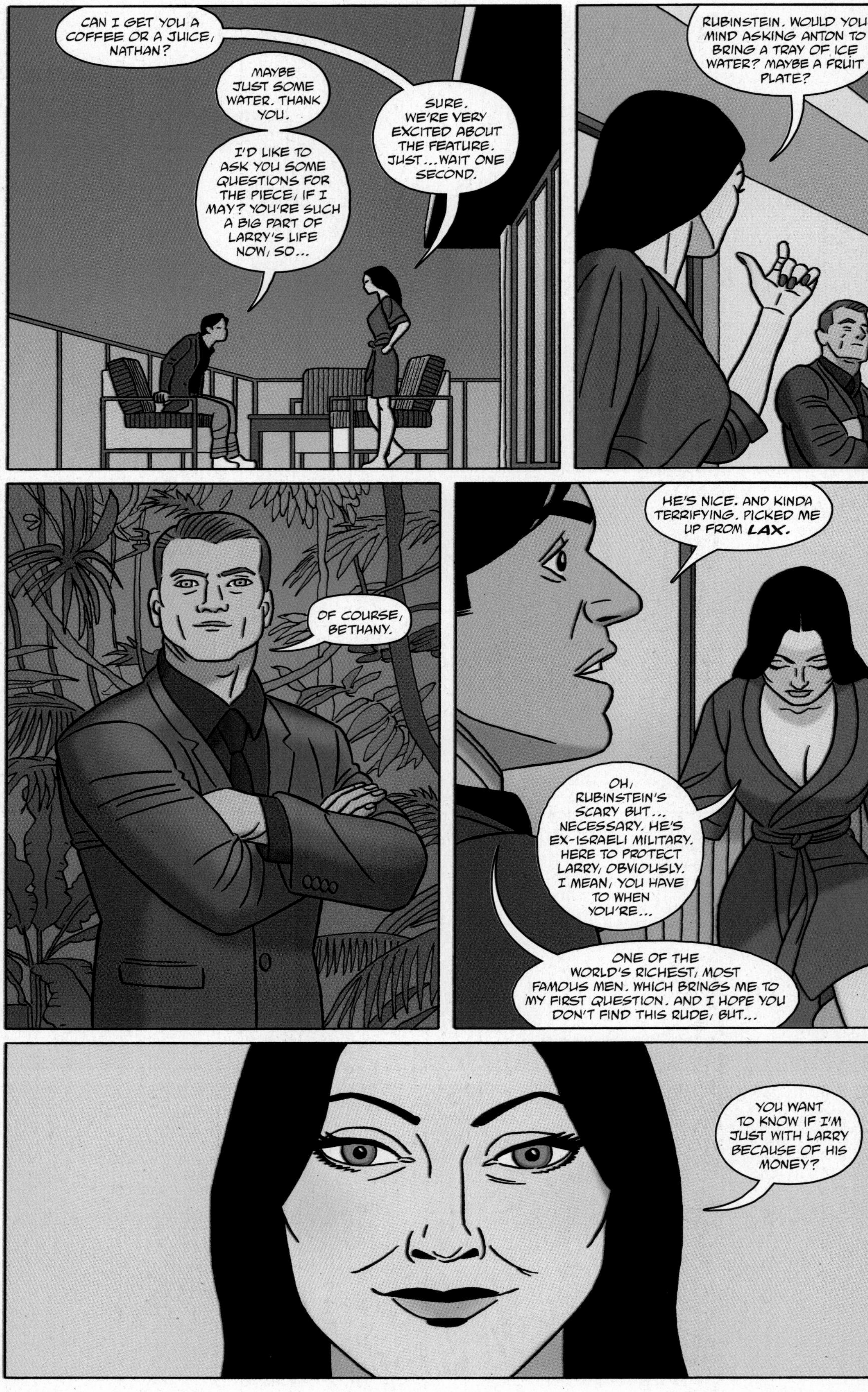
CAN I GET YOU A COFFEE OR A JUICE, NATHAN?
MAYBE JUST SOME WATER. THANK YOU.
I'D LIKE TO ASK YOU SOME QUESTIONS FOR THE PIECE, IF I MAY? YOU'RE SUCH A BIG PART OF LARRY'S LIFE NOW, SO...
SURE. WE'RE VERY EXCITED ABOUT THE FEATURE. JUST...WAIT ONE SECOND.
RUBINSTEIN. WOULD YOU MIND ASKING ANTON TO BRING A TRAY OF ICE WATER? MAYBE A FRUIT PLATE?
OF COURSE, BETHANY.
HE'S NICE. AND KINDA TERRIFYING. PICKED ME UP FROM LAX.
OH, RUBINSTEIN'S SCARY BUT... NECESSARY. HE'S EX-ISRAELI MILITARY. HERE TO PROTECT LARRY, OBVIOUSLY. I MEAN, YOU HAVE TO WHEN YOU'RE...
ONE OF THE WORLD'S RICHEST, MOST FAMOUS MEN. WHICH BRINGS ME TO MY FIRST QUESTION. AND I HOPE YOU DON'T FIND THIS RUDE, BUT...
YOU WANT TO KNOW IF I'M JUST WITH LARRY BECAUSE OF HIS MONEY?

YES.

I...

WHAT'S THE RIGHT THING TO SAY? LARRY AND I TALK A LOT ABOUT THE IMPORTANCE OF HONESTY.

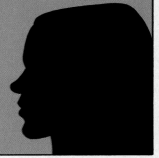

WERE IT NOT FOR HIS MONEY, LARRY AND I WOULD NEVER HAVE MET. THAT MUCH IS TRUE. LARRY IS ALL ABOUT LINES OF COMMUNICATION.

MY SHOW'S A HIT. MY LIFE'S HOLLYWOOD. BEFORE LARRY I DATED A LOT OF VERY FAMOUS ACTORS.

AND I MET LARRY AT A HOLLYWOOD PARTY, WHICH HE WOULD NEVER HAVE GOT INTO WERE HE NOT WHO HE IS. HE SENT ME THE MOST GORGEOUS FLOWERS EVERY DAY FOR TWO WEEKS BEFORE I AGREED TO ONE DATE.

MONEY OFFERS OPPORTUNITY. AND THAT'S SOMETHING LARRY WOULD LIKE TO OFFER EVERY-ONE.

I FELL IN LOVE WITH LARRY FERRELL FOR ONE REASON.

THE PURITY OF HIS HEART.

THAT'S WHY WE SPECIFICALLY ASKED FOR YOU, NATHAN. WE BOTH LOVED YOUR BOOK SO MUCH. IT REALLY SPOKE TO ME. AND WE WANTED TO TALK TO YOU ABOUT OUR PLANS...

I'D REALLY LIKE IT IF WE COULD BE FRIENDS.

WOW. WELL, I DID WONDER WHY YOU REQUESTED ME. I'M VERY MUCH LOOKING FORWARD TO SPEAKING TO LARR...

SKRREEEE

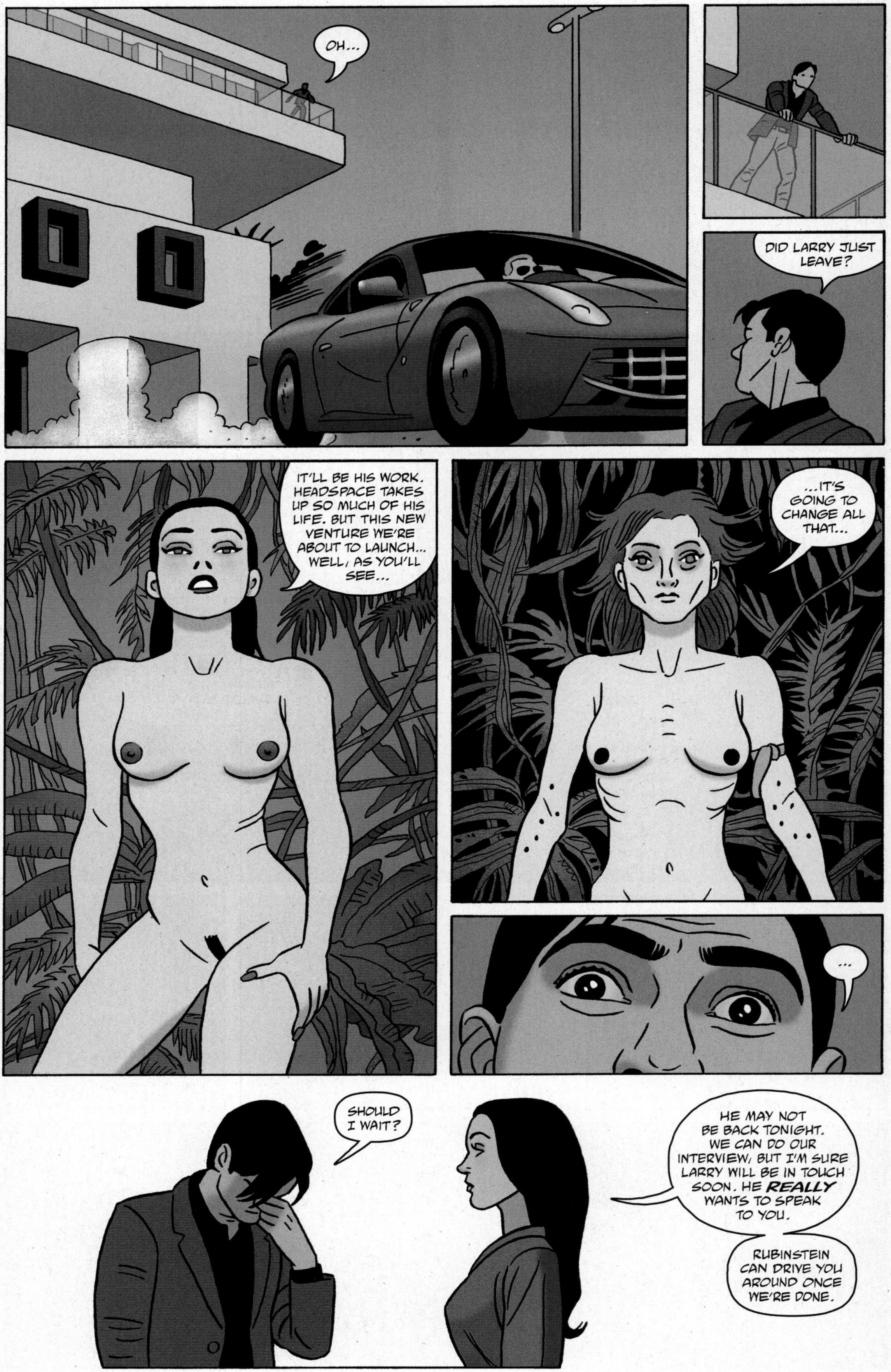
OH...
DID LARRY JUST LEAVE?
IT'LL BE HIS WORK. HEADSPACE TAKES UP SO MUCH OF HIS LIFE. BUT THIS NEW VENTURE WE'RE ABOUT TO LAUNCH... WELL, AS YOU'LL SEE...
...IT'S GOING TO CHANGE ALL THAT...
...
SHOULD I WAIT?
HE MAY NOT BE BACK TONIGHT. WE CAN DO OUR INTERVIEW, BUT I'M SURE LARRY WILL BE IN TOUCH SOON. HE **REALLY** WANTS TO SPEAK TO YOU.
RUBINSTEIN CAN DRIVE YOU AROUND ONCE WE'RE DONE.

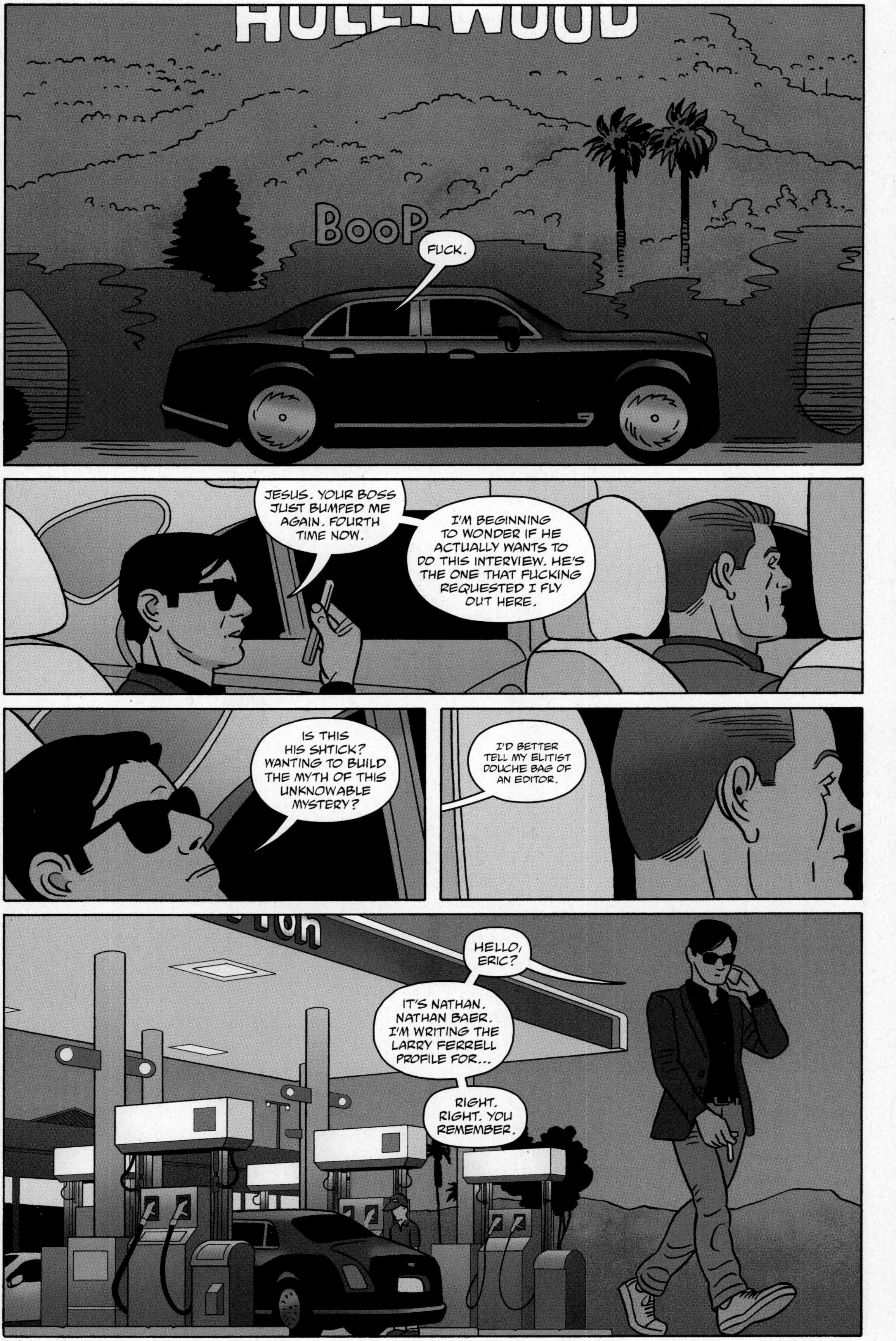
HOLLYWOOD
BOOP
FUCK.
JESUS. YOUR BOSS JUST BUMPED ME AGAIN. FOURTH TIME NOW.
I'M BEGINNING TO WONDER IF HE ACTUALLY WANTS TO DO THIS INTERVIEW. HE'S THE ONE THAT FUCKING REQUESTED I FLY OUT HERE.
IS THIS HIS SHTICK? WANTING TO BUILD THE MYTH OF THIS UNKNOWABLE MYSTERY?
I'D BETTER TELL MY ELITIST DOUCHE BAG OF AN EDITOR.
HELLO, ERIC?
IT'S NATHAN. NATHAN BAER. I'M WRITING THE LARRY FERRELL PROFILE FOR...
RIGHT. RIGHT. YOU REMEMBER.

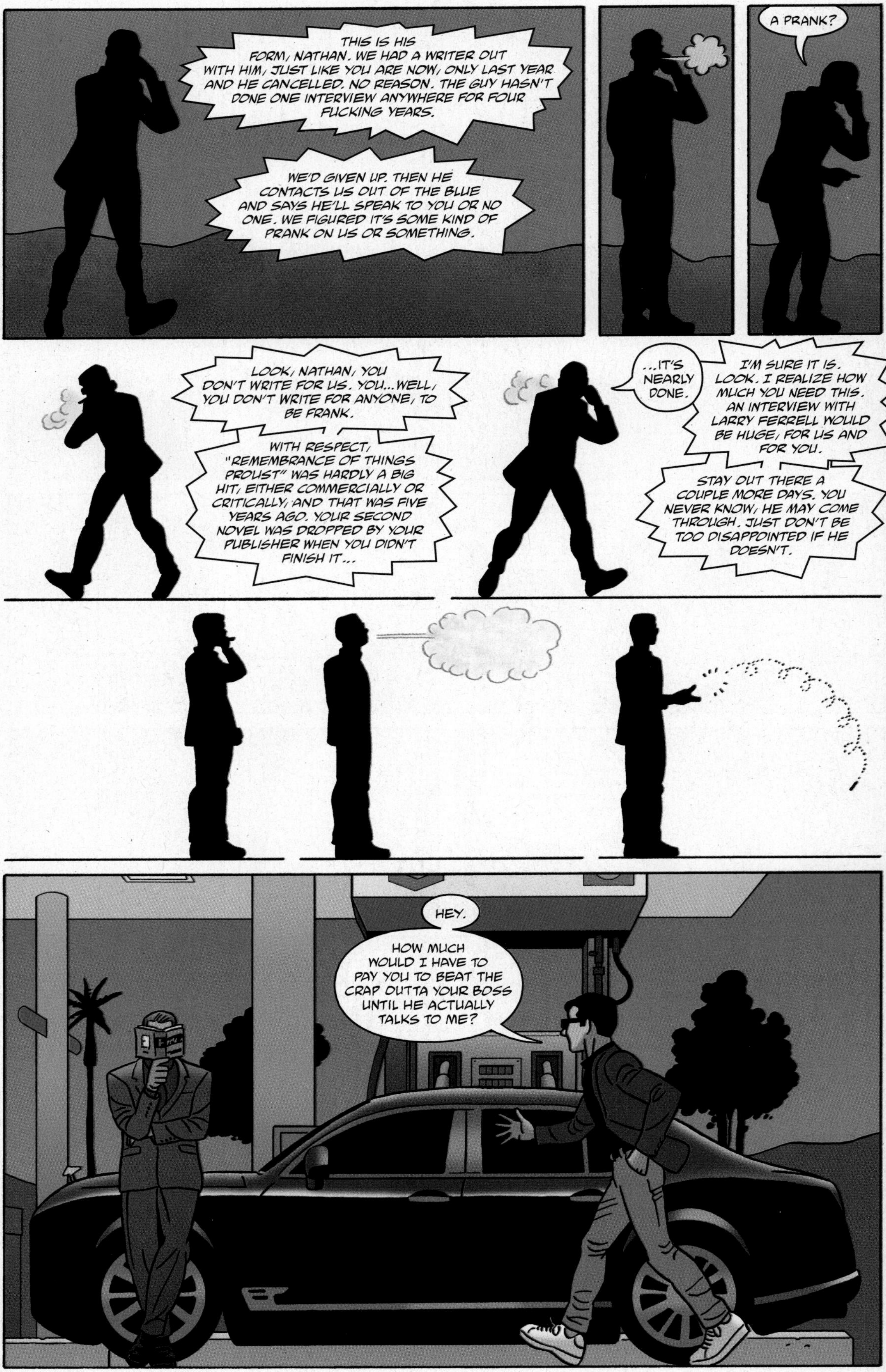
THIS IS HIS FORM, NATHAN. WE HAD A WRITER OUT WITH HIM, JUST LIKE YOU ARE NOW, ONLY LAST YEAR AND HE CANCELLED. NO REASON. THE GUY HASN'T DONE ONE INTERVIEW ANYWHERE FOR FOUR FUCKING YEARS.
WE'D GIVEN UP. THEN HE CONTACTS US OUT OF THE BLUE AND SAYS HE'LL SPEAK TO YOU OR NO ONE. WE FIGURED IT'S SOME KIND OF PRANK ON US OR SOMETHING.
A PRANK?
LOOK, NATHAN, YOU DON'T WRITE FOR US. YOU...WELL, YOU DON'T WRITE FOR ANYONE, TO BE FRANK.
WITH RESPECT, "REMEMBRANCE OF THINGS PROUST" WAS HARDLY A BIG HIT, EITHER COMMERCIALLY OR CRITICALLY, AND THAT WAS FIVE YEARS AGO. YOUR SECOND NOVEL WAS DROPPED BY YOUR PUBLISHER WHEN YOU DIDN'T FINISH IT...
...IT'S NEARLY DONE.
I'M SURE IT IS. LOOK. I REALIZE HOW MUCH YOU NEED THIS. AN INTERVIEW WITH LARRY FERRELL WOULD BE HUGE, FOR US AND FOR YOU.
STAY OUT THERE A COUPLE MORE DAYS. YOU NEVER KNOW, HE MAY COME THROUGH. JUST DON'T BE TOO DISAPPOINTED IF HE DOESN'T.
HEY.
HOW MUCH WOULD I HAVE TO PAY YOU TO BEAT THE CRAP OUTTA YOUR BOSS UNTIL HE ACTUALLY TALKS TO ME?

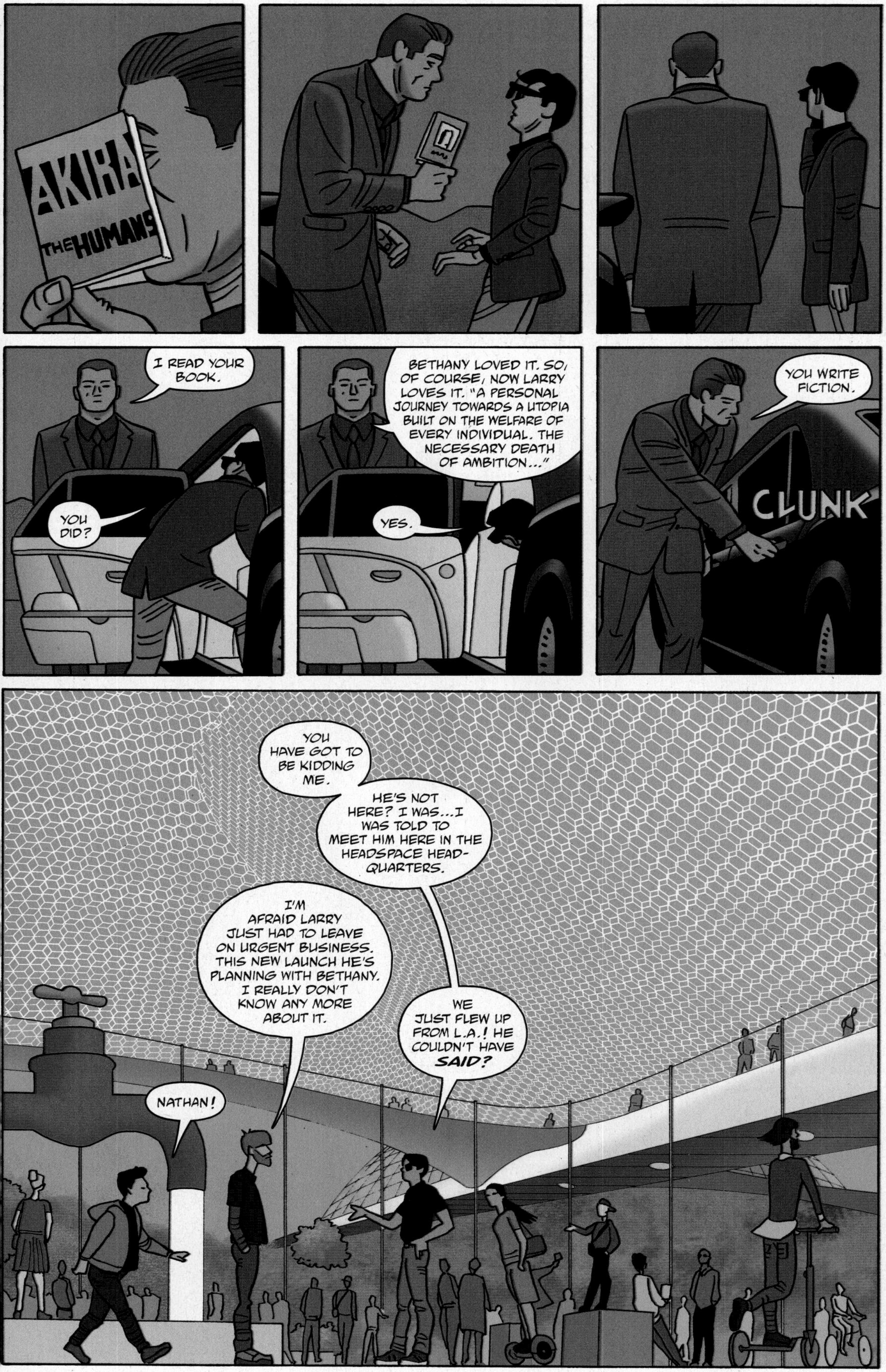
AKIRA
THE HUMANS
I READ YOUR BOOK.
YOU DID?
BETHANY LOVED IT. SO, OF COURSE, NOW LARRY LOVES IT. "A PERSONAL JOURNEY TOWARDS A UTOPIA BUILT ON THE WELFARE OF EVERY INDIVIDUAL. THE NECESSARY DEATH OF AMBITION..."
YES.
YOU WRITE FICTION.
CLUNK
YOU HAVE GOT TO BE KIDDING ME.
HE'S NOT HERE? I WAS...I WAS TOLD TO MEET HIM HERE IN THE HEADSPACE HEAD-QUARTERS.
I'M AFRAID LARRY JUST HAD TO LEAVE ON URGENT BUSINESS. THIS NEW LAUNCH HE'S PLANNING WITH BETHANY. I REALLY DON'T KNOW ANY MORE ABOUT IT.
WE JUST FLEW UP FROM L.A.! HE COULDN'T HAVE SAID?
NATHAN!

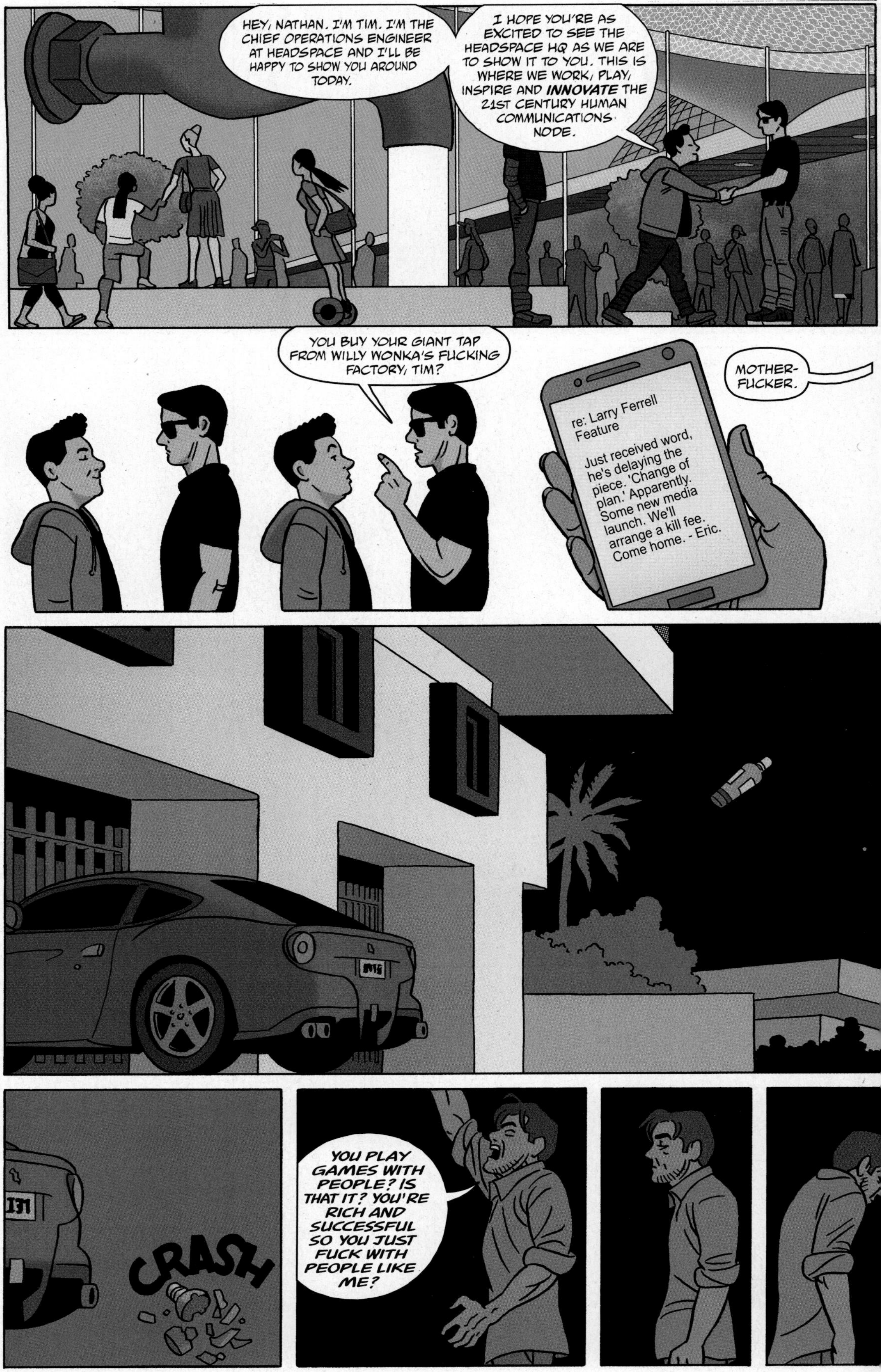
HEY, NATHAN. I'M TIM. I'M THE CHIEF OPERATIONS ENGINEER AT HEADSPACE AND I'LL BE HAPPY TO SHOW YOU AROUND TODAY.
I HOPE YOU'RE AS EXCITED TO SEE THE HEADSPACE HQ AS WE ARE TO SHOW IT TO YOU. THIS IS WHERE WE WORK, PLAY, INSPIRE AND ***INNOVATE*** THE 21ST CENTURY HUMAN COMMUNICATIONS NODE.
YOU BUY YOUR GIANT TAP FROM WILLY WONKA'S FUCKING FACTORY, TIM?
re: Larry Ferrell Feature
Just received word, he's delaying the piece. 'Change of plan.' Apparently. Some new media launch. We'll arrange a kill fee. Come home. - Eric.
MOTHER-FUCKER.
CRASH
YOU PLAY GAMES WITH PEOPLE? IS THAT IT? YOU'RE RICH AND SUCCESSFUL SO YOU JUST FUCK WITH PEOPLE LIKE ME?

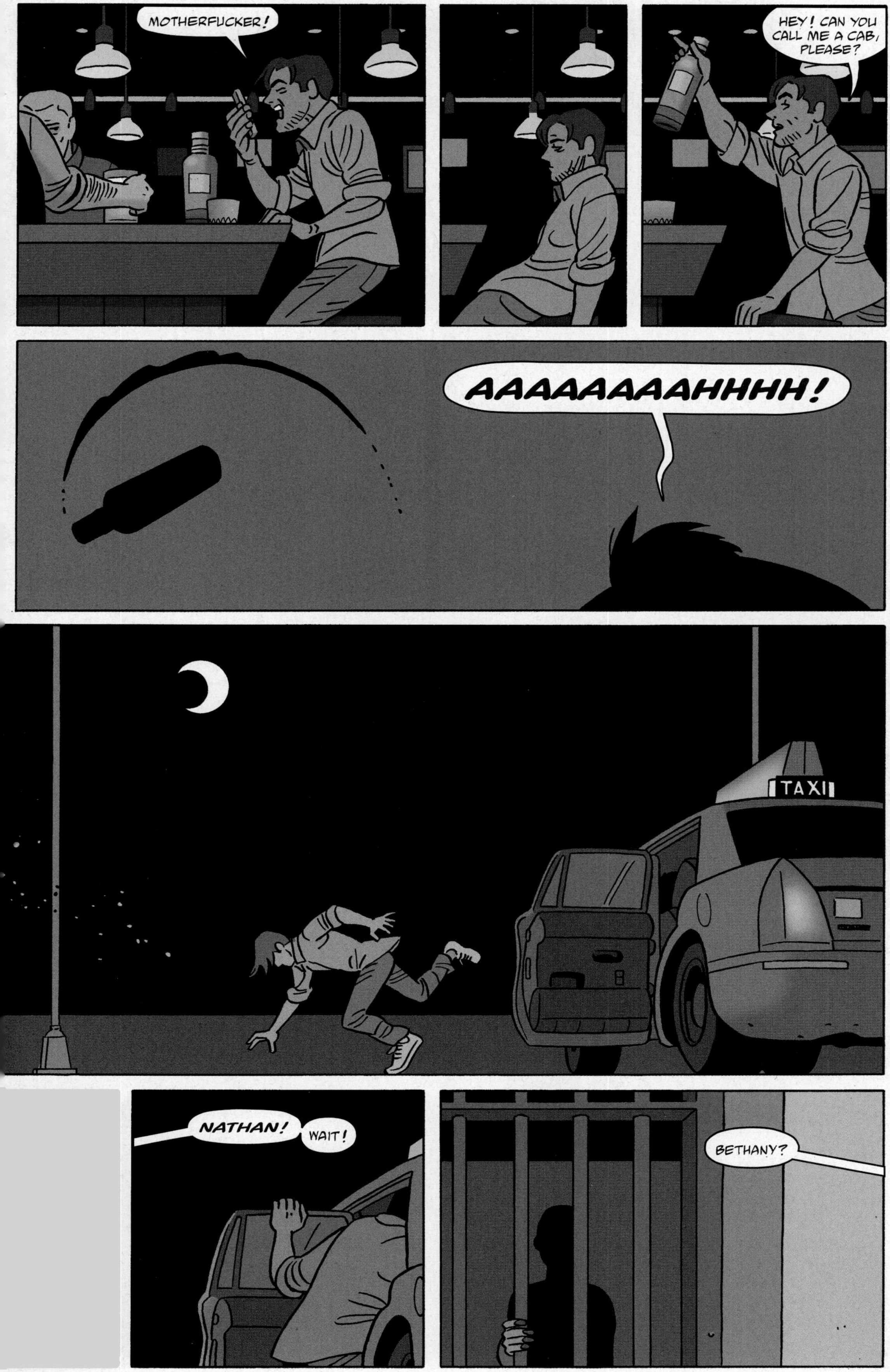
MOTHERFUCKER!
HEY! CAN YOU CALL ME A CAB, PLEASE?
AAAAAAAAHHHH!
TAXI
NATHAN!
WAIT!
BETHANY?

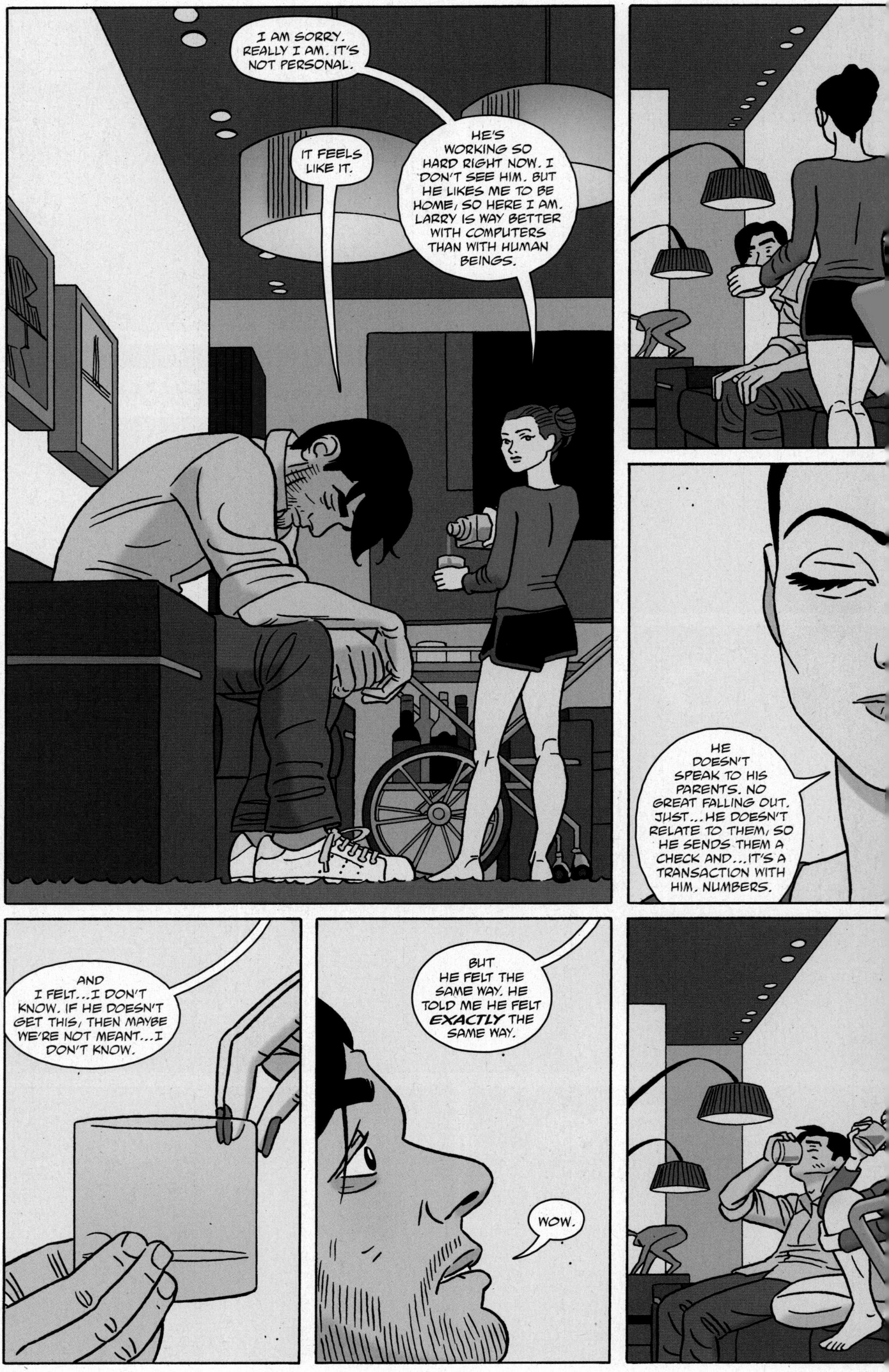
I AM SORRY. REALLY I AM. IT'S NOT PERSONAL.
IT FEELS LIKE IT.
HE'S WORKING SO HARD RIGHT NOW. I DON'T SEE HIM. BUT HE LIKES ME TO BE HOME, SO HERE I AM. LARRY IS WAY BETTER WITH COMPUTERS THAN WITH HUMAN BEINGS.
. . .
HE DOESN'T SPEAK TO HIS PARENTS. NO GREAT FALLING OUT. JUST... HE DOESN'T RELATE TO THEM, SO HE SENDS THEM A CHECK AND... IT'S A TRANSACTION WITH HIM. NUMBERS.
AND I FELT... I DON'T KNOW. IF HE DOESN'T GET THIS, THEN MAYBE WE'RE NOT MEANT... I DON'T KNOW.
BUT HE FELT THE SAME WAY. HE TOLD ME HE FELT *EXACTLY* THE SAME WAY.
WOW.

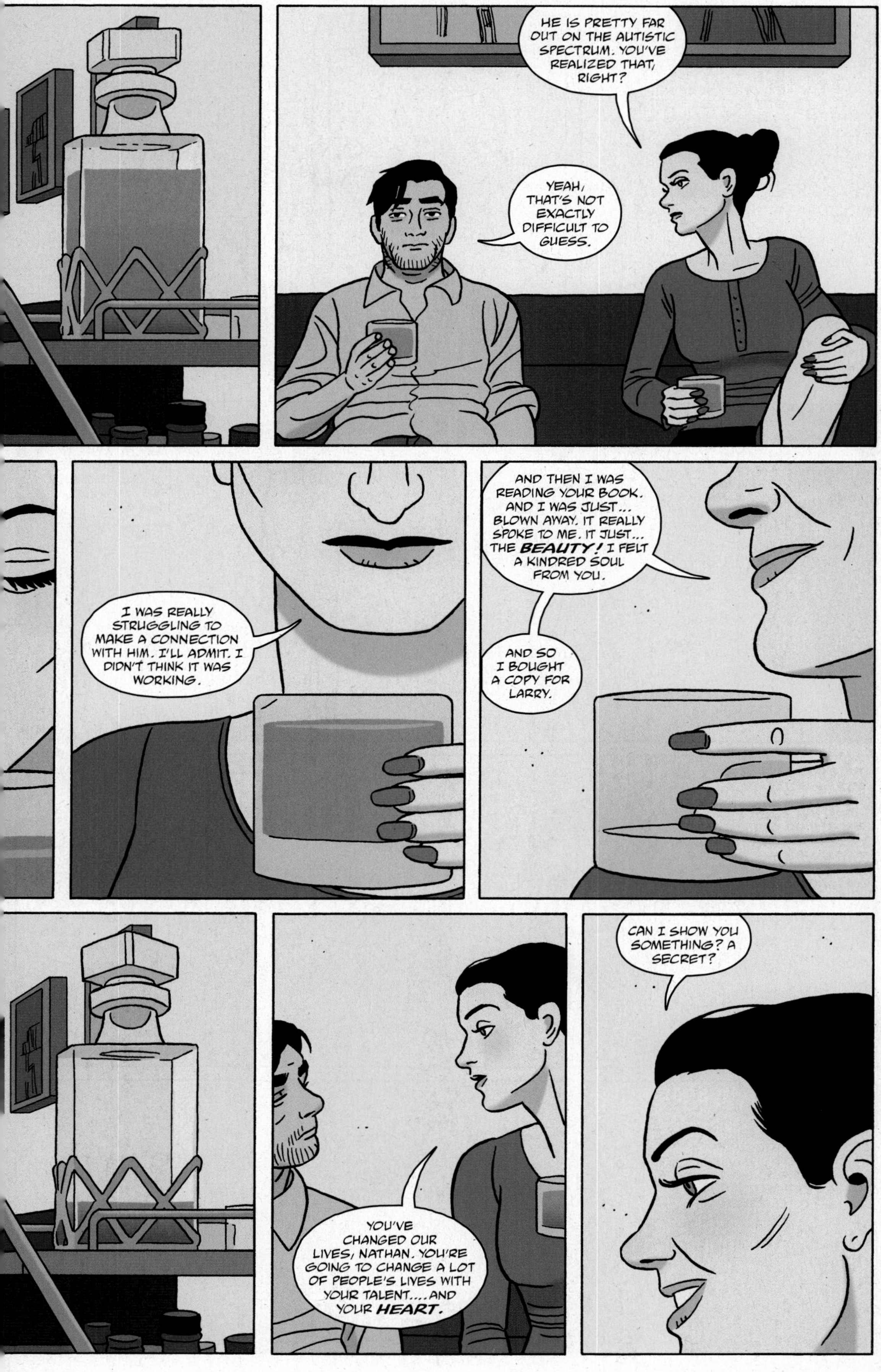
HE IS PRETTY FAR OUT ON THE AUTISTIC SPECTRUM. YOU'VE REALIZED THAT, RIGHT?
YEAH, THAT'S NOT EXACTLY DIFFICULT TO GUESS.
I WAS REALLY STRUGGLING TO MAKE A CONNECTION WITH HIM. I'LL ADMIT. I DIDN'T THINK IT WAS WORKING.
AND THEN I WAS READING YOUR BOOK. AND I WAS JUST... BLOWN AWAY. IT REALLY SPOKE TO ME. IT JUST... THE BEAUTY! I FELT A KINDRED SOUL FROM YOU.
AND SO I BOUGHT A COPY FOR LARRY.
YOU'VE CHANGED OUR LIVES, NATHAN. YOU'RE GOING TO CHANGE A LOT OF PEOPLE'S LIVES WITH YOUR TALENT.... AND YOUR HEART.
CAN I SHOW YOU SOMETHING? A SECRET?

HELLO, MY NAME IS LARRY FERRELL. AND I CREATED SOCIAL MEDIA TO BRING EVERY HUMAN BEING ON THIS PLANET CLOSER TOGETHER.

TO END CONFLICT. TO INCREASE EMPATHY. TO SEE THE COMMONALITY IN ALL OF US. I HOPE I'VE ACHIEVED THAT, TO SOME EXTENT.

BUT NOW I REALIZE I HAVE TO DO MORE.

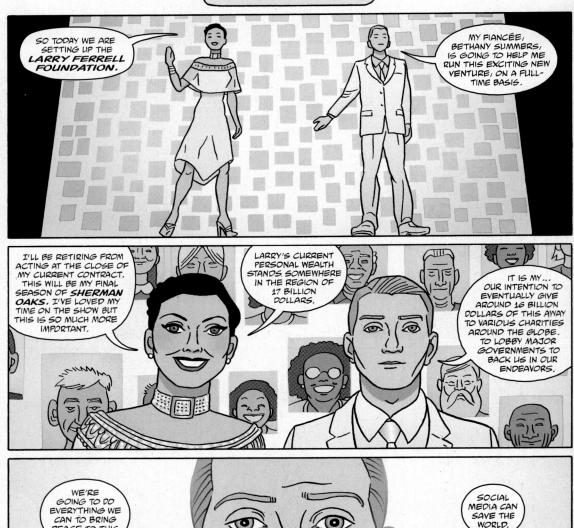

SO TODAY WE ARE SETTING UP THE *LARRY FERRELL FOUNDATION.*

MY FIANCÉE, BETHANY SUMMERS, IS GOING TO HELP ME RUN THIS EXCITING NEW VENTURE, ON A FULL-TIME BASIS.

I'LL BE RETIRING FROM ACTING AT THE CLOSE OF MY CURRENT CONTRACT. THIS WILL BE MY FINAL SEASON OF *SHERMAN OAKS.* I'VE LOVED MY TIME ON THE SHOW BUT THIS IS SO MUCH MORE IMPORTANT.

LARRY'S CURRENT PERSONAL WEALTH STANDS SOMEWHERE IN THE REGION OF 17 BILLION DOLLARS.

IT IS MY... OUR INTENTION TO EVENTUALLY GIVE AROUND 16 BILLION DOLLARS OF THIS AWAY TO VARIOUS CHARITIES AROUND THE GLOBE. TO LOBBY MAJOR GOVERNMENTS TO BACK US IN OUR ENDEAVORS.

WE'RE GOING TO DO EVERYTHING WE CAN TO BRING PEACE TO THIS PLANET.

SOCIAL MEDIA CAN SAVE THE WORLD.

AND IT WILL.

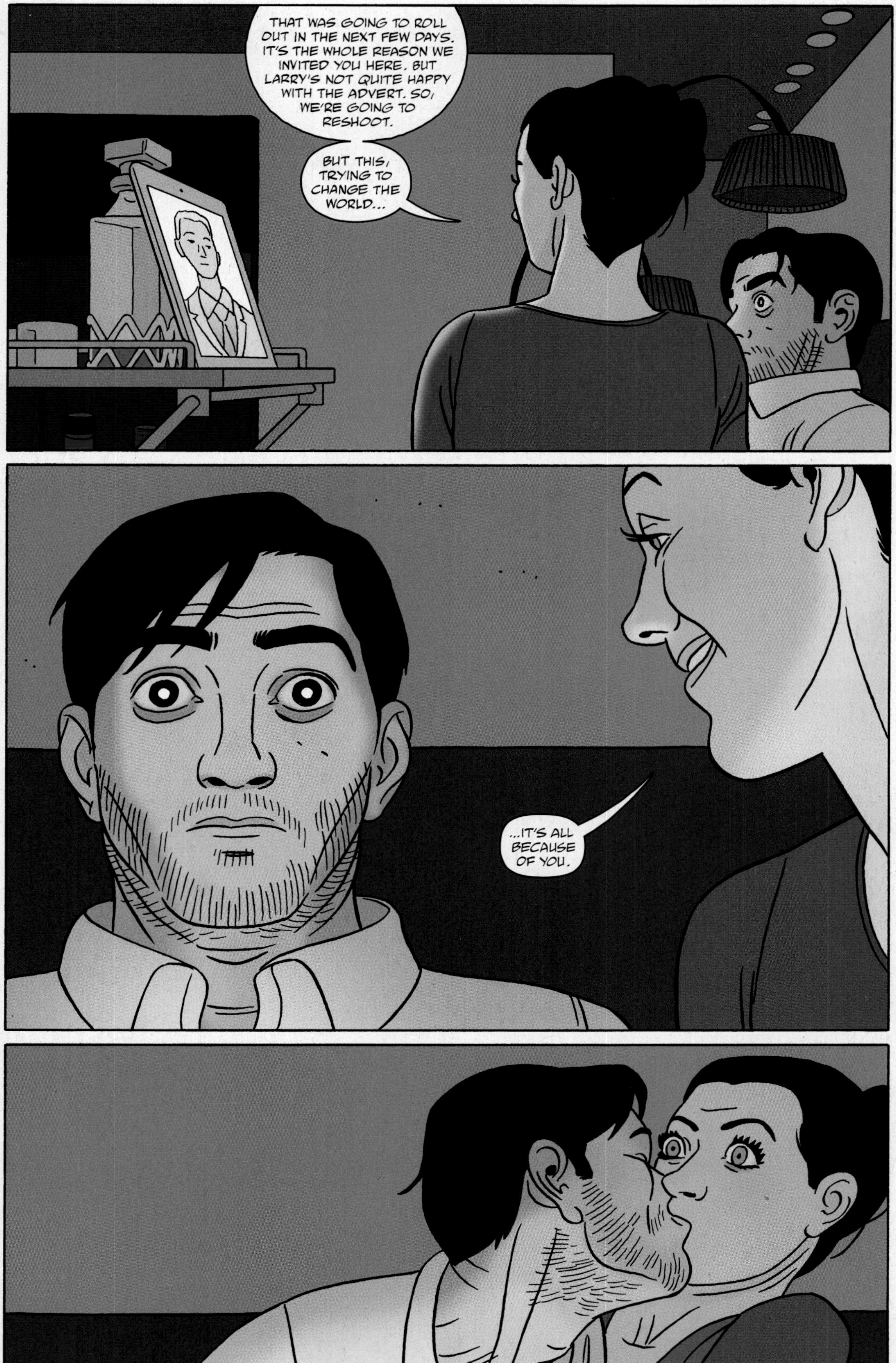
THAT WAS GOING TO ROLL OUT IN THE NEXT FEW DAYS. IT'S THE WHOLE REASON WE INVITED YOU HERE. BUT LARRY'S NOT QUITE HAPPY WITH THE ADVERT. SO, WE'RE GOING TO RESHOOT.
BUT THIS, TRYING TO CHANGE THE WORLD...
...IT'S ALL BECAUSE OF YOU.

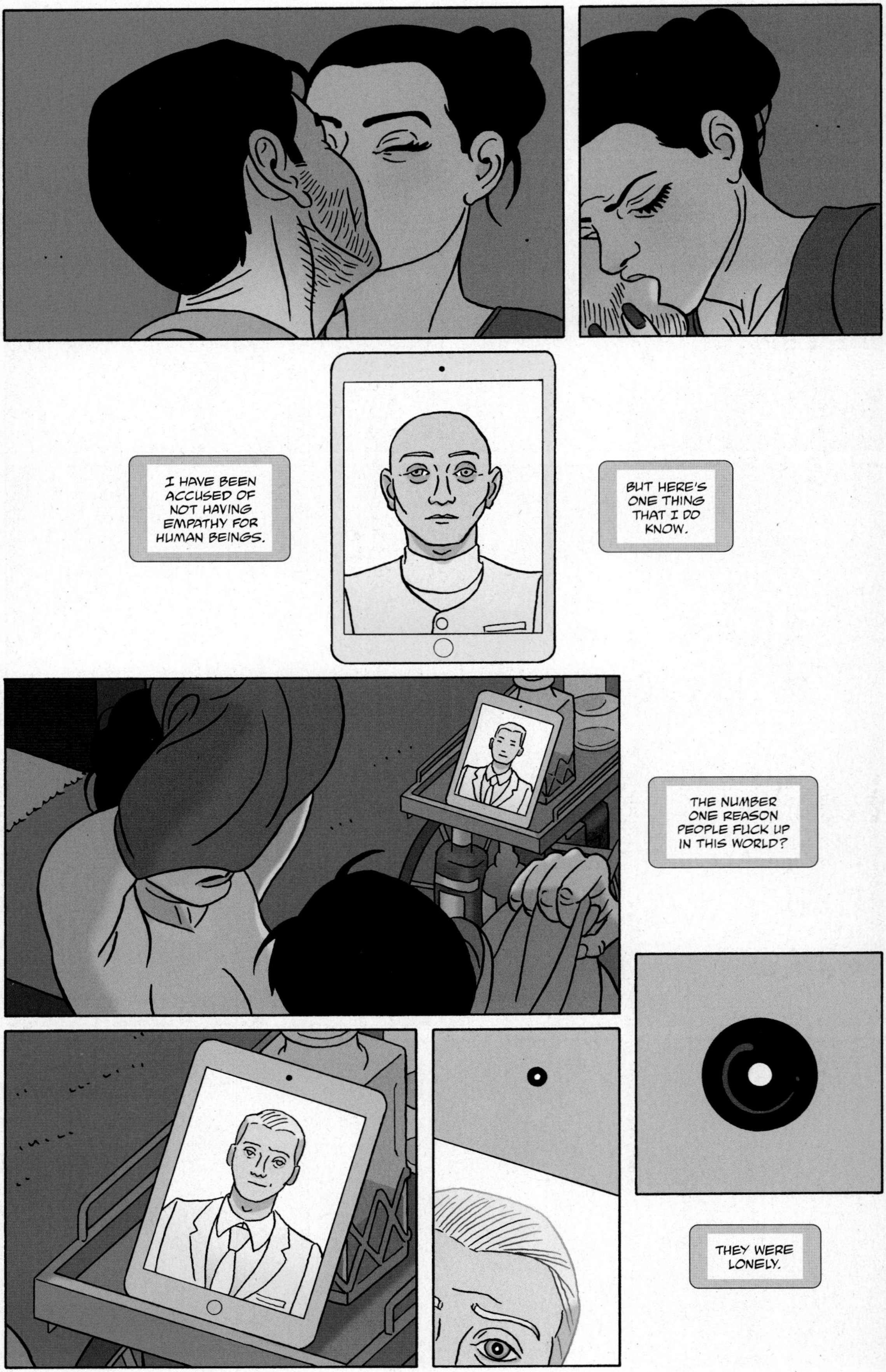
I HAVE BEEN ACCUSED OF NOT HAVING EMPATHY FOR HUMAN BEINGS.
BUT HERE'S ONE THING THAT I DO KNOW.
THE NUMBER ONE REASON PEOPLE FUCK UP IN THIS WORLD?
THEY WERE LONELY.

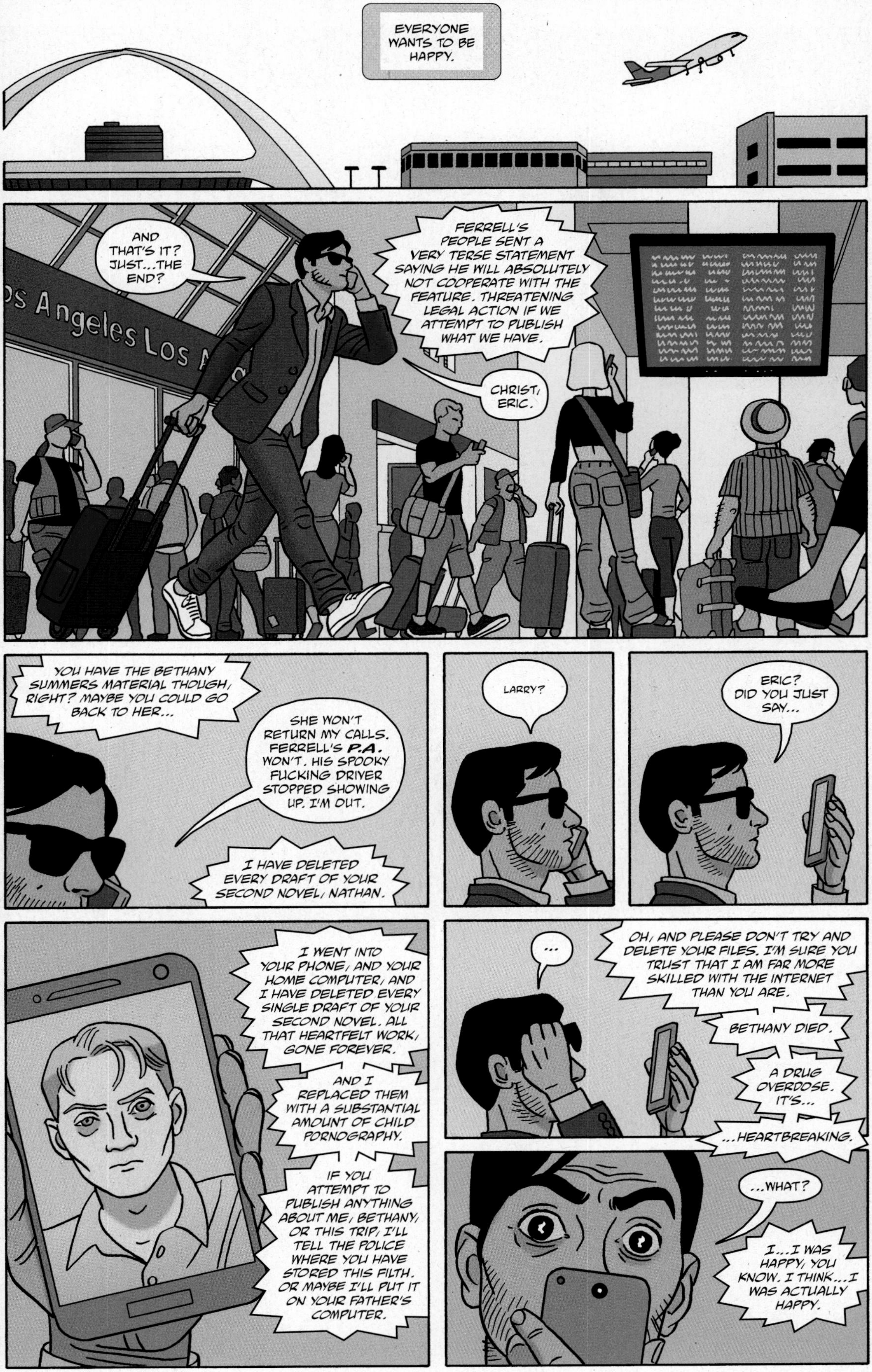
EVERYONE WANTS TO BE HAPPY.
AND THAT'S IT? JUST...THE END?
FERRELL'S PEOPLE SENT A VERY TERSE STATEMENT SAYING HE WILL ABSOLUTELY NOT COOPERATE WITH THE FEATURE. THREATENING LEGAL ACTION IF WE ATTEMPT TO PUBLISH WHAT WE HAVE.
CHRIST, ERIC.
Los Angeles Los A
YOU HAVE THE BETHANY SUMMERS MATERIAL THOUGH, RIGHT? MAYBE YOU COULD GO BACK TO HER...
SHE WON'T RETURN MY CALLS. FERRELL'S P.A. WON'T. HIS SPOOKY FUCKING DRIVER STOPPED SHOWING UP. I'M OUT.
I HAVE DELETED EVERY DRAFT OF YOUR SECOND NOVEL, NATHAN.
LARRY?
ERIC? DID YOU JUST SAY...
I WENT INTO YOUR PHONE, AND YOUR HOME COMPUTER, AND I HAVE DELETED EVERY SINGLE DRAFT OF YOUR SECOND NOVEL. ALL THAT HEARTFELT WORK, GONE FOREVER.
AND I REPLACED THEM WITH A SUBSTANTIAL AMOUNT OF CHILD PORNOGRAPHY.
IF YOU ATTEMPT TO PUBLISH ANYTHING ABOUT ME, BETHANY, OR THIS TRIP, I'LL TELL THE POLICE WHERE YOU HAVE STORED THIS FILTH. OR MAYBE I'LL PUT IT ON YOUR FATHER'S COMPUTER.
...
OH, AND PLEASE DON'T TRY AND DELETE YOUR FILES. I'M SURE YOU TRUST THAT I AM FAR MORE SKILLED WITH THE INTERNET THAN YOU ARE.
BETHANY DIED.
A DRUG OVERDOSE. IT'S...
...HEARTBREAKING.
...WHAT?
I...I WAS HAPPY, YOU KNOW. I THINK...I WAS ACTUALLY HAPPY.

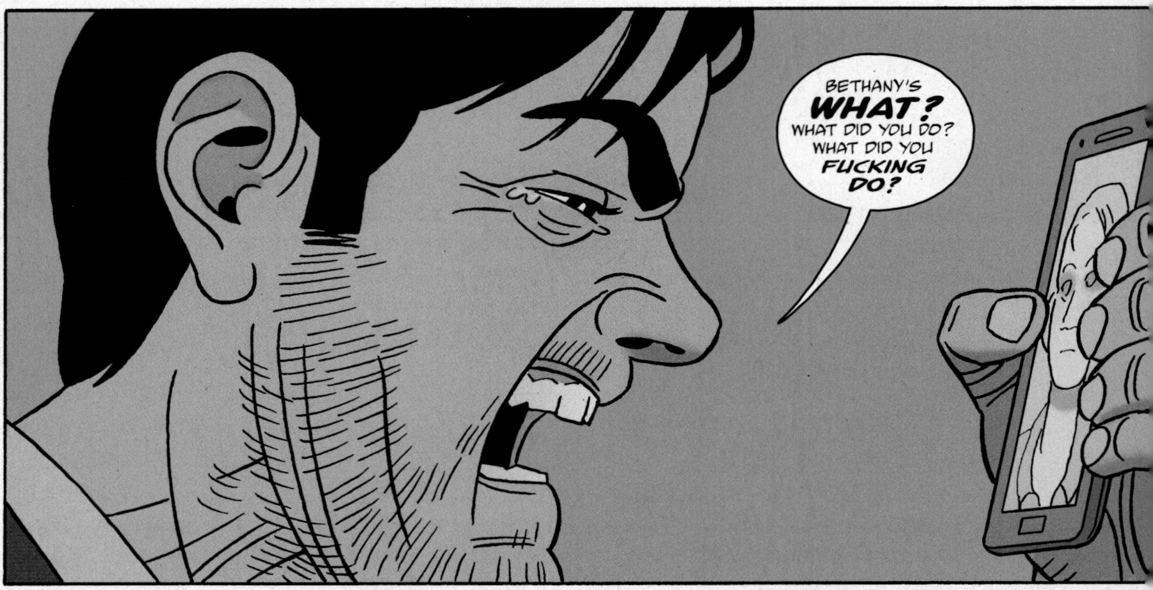
BETHANY'S WHAT? WHAT DID YOU DO? WHAT DID YOU FUCKING DO?

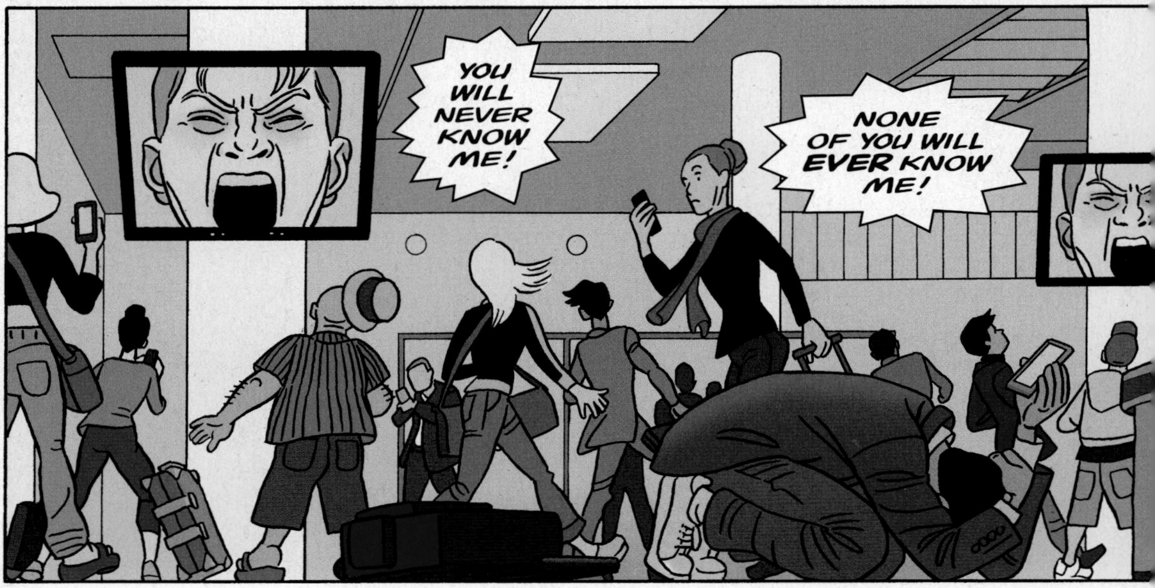
YOU WILL NEVER KNOW ME!
NONE OF YOU WILL EVER KNOW ME!

MY NAME IS LARRY FERRELL.

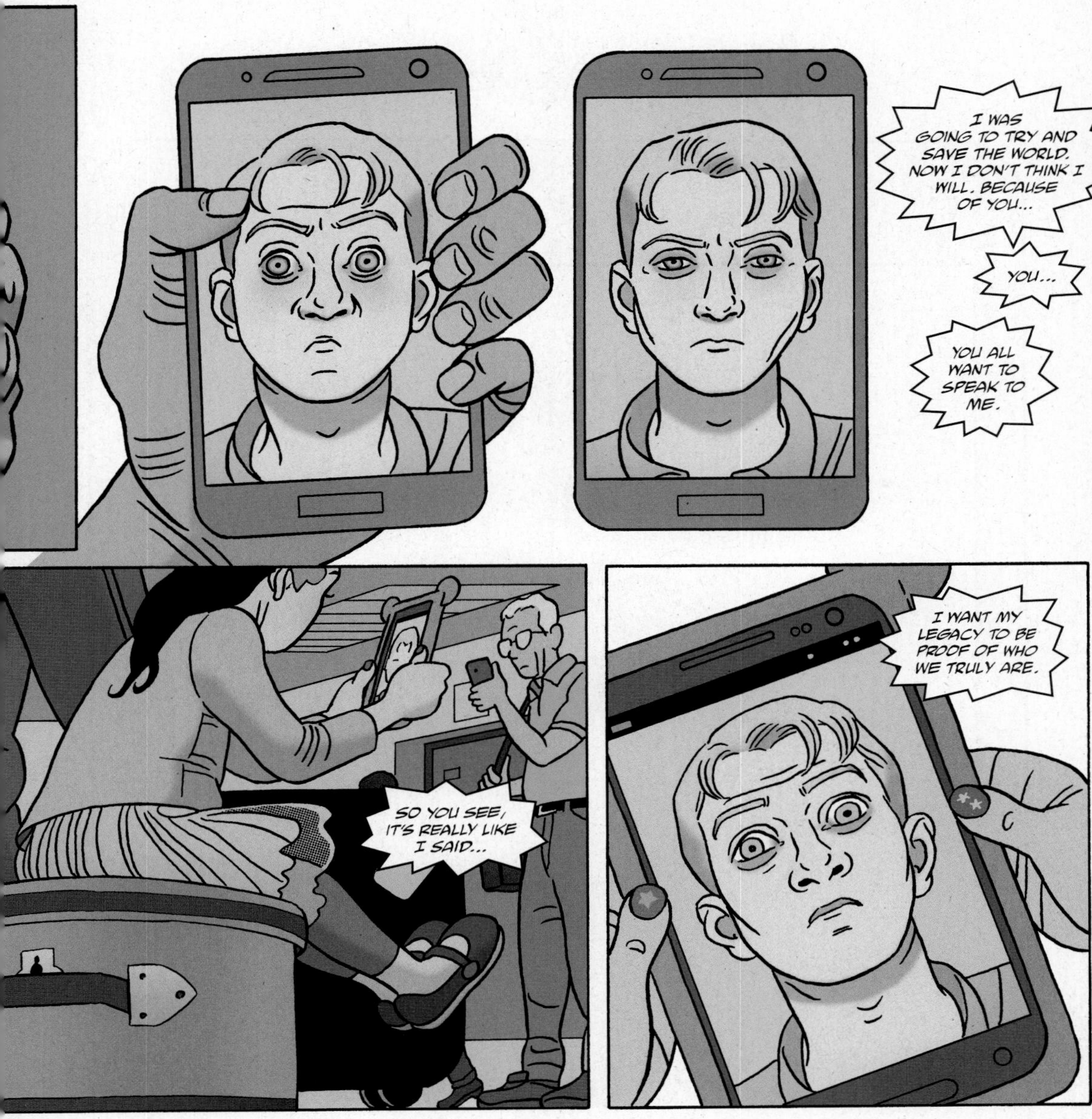

I WAS GOING TO TRY AND SAVE THE WORLD. NOW I DON'T THINK I WILL. BECAUSE OF YOU...
YOU...
YOU ALL WANT TO SPEAK TO ME.
SO YOU SEE, IT'S REALLY LIKE I SAID...
I WANT MY LEGACY TO BE PROOF OF WHO WE TRULY ARE.

AND I THINK, A LONG TIME AGO...

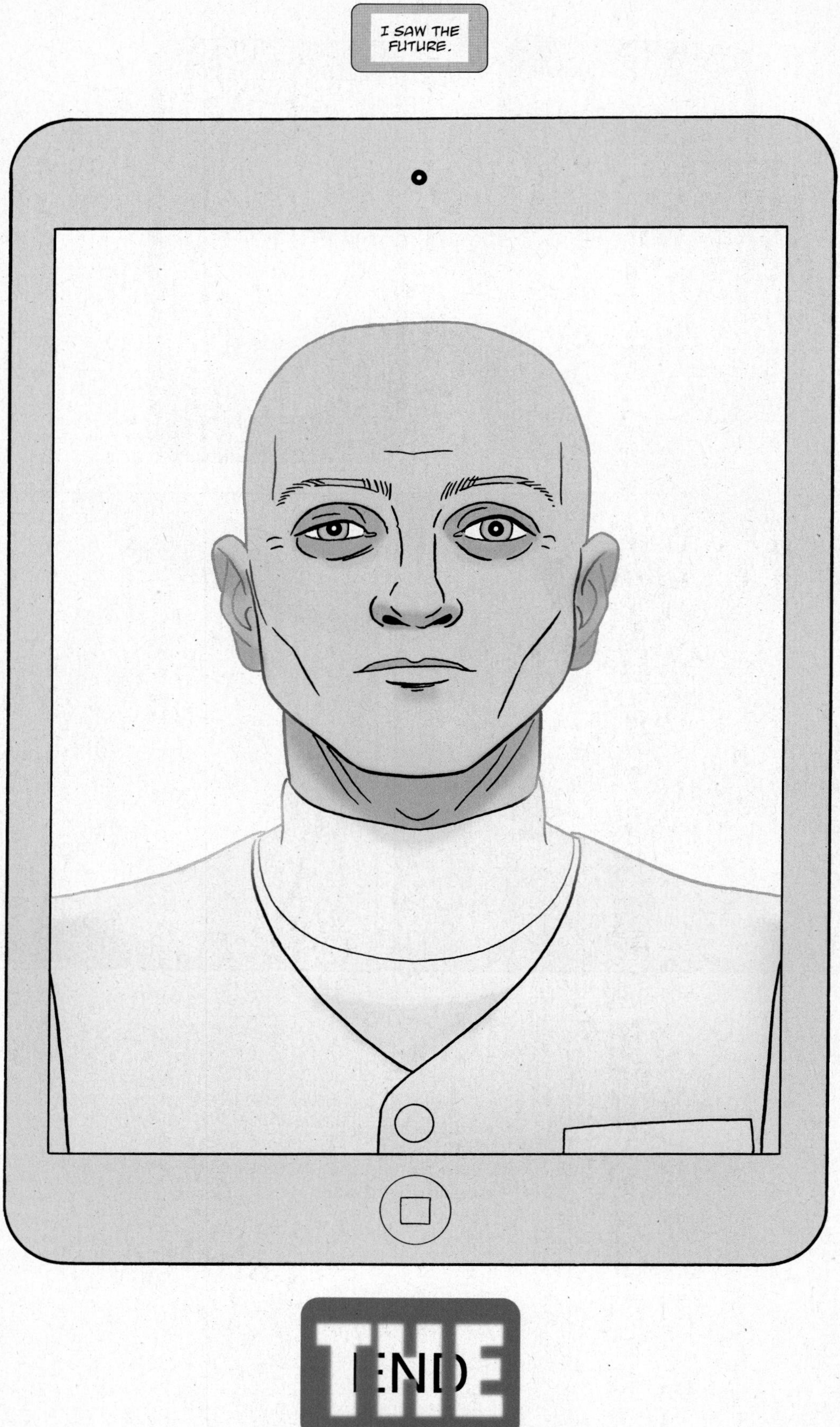
I SAW THE FUTURE.
THE
END

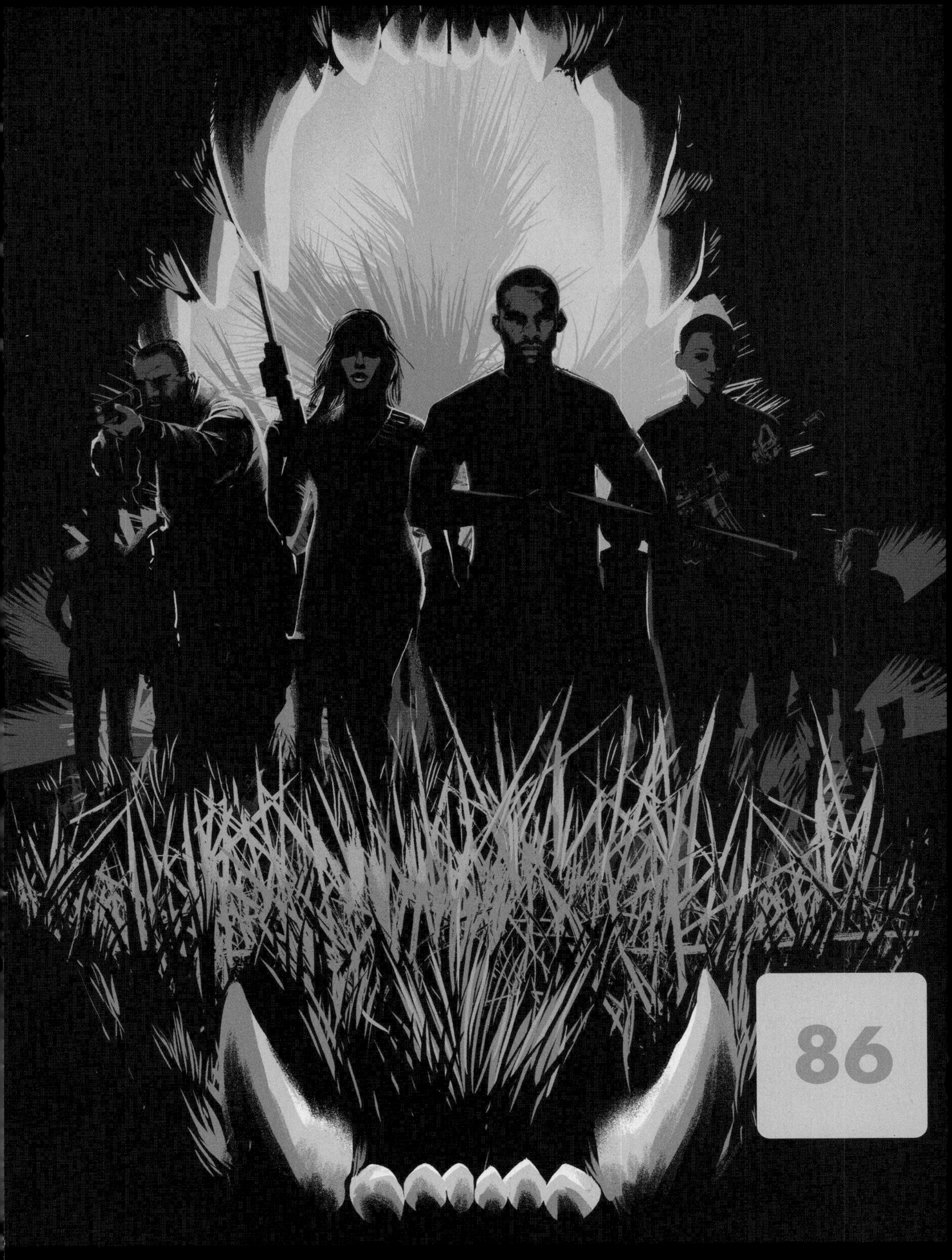
86

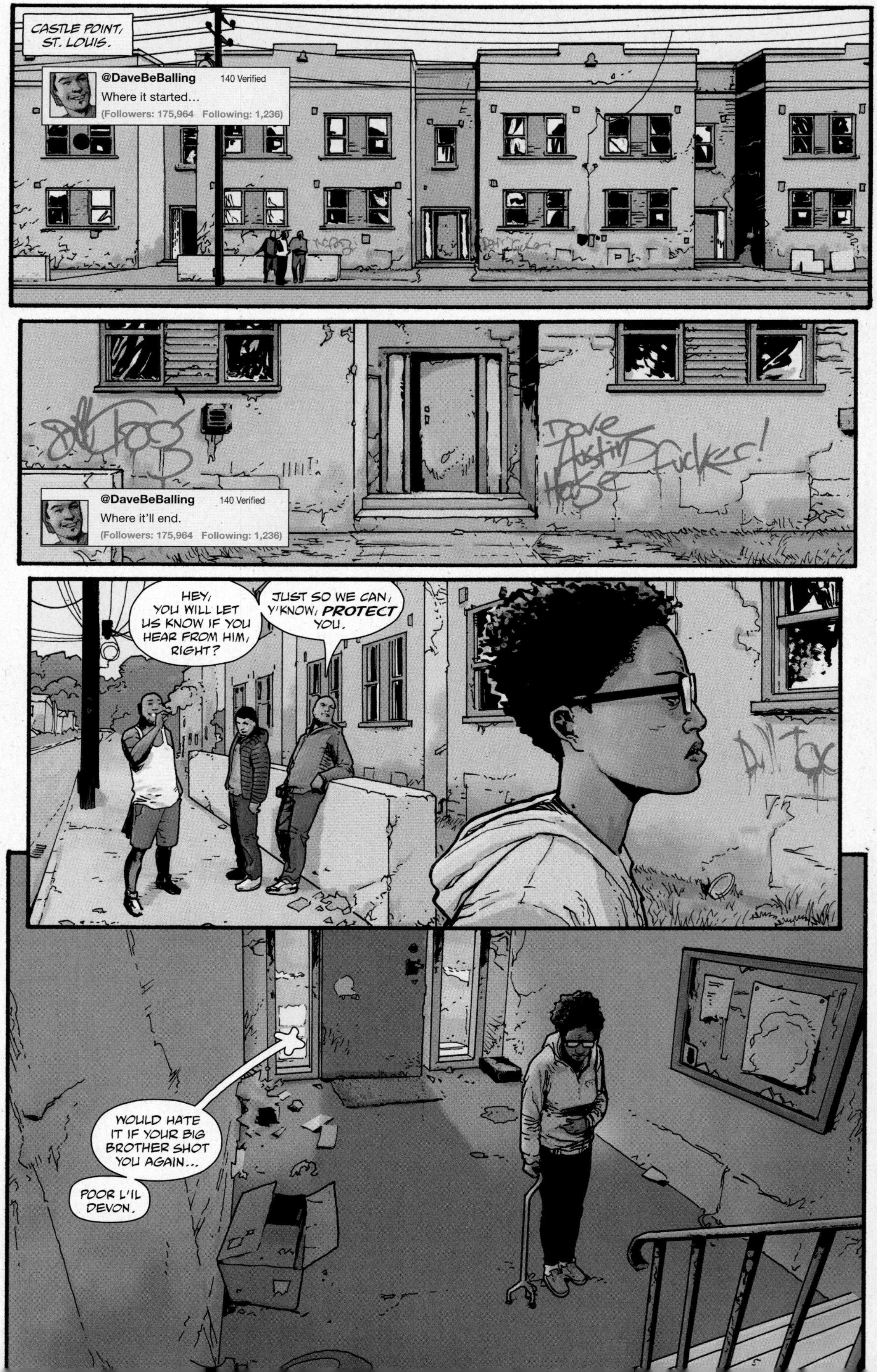

CASTLE POINT, ST. LOUIS.
@DaveBeBalling 140 Verified
Where it started…
(Followers: 175,964 Following: 1,236)
Dave Austins House
Fucker!
@DaveBeBalling 140 Verified
Where it'll end.
(Followers: 175,964 Following: 1,236)
HEY, YOU WILL LET US KNOW IF YOU HEAR FROM HIM, RIGHT?
JUST SO WE CAN, Y'KNOW, PROTECT YOU.
WOULD HATE IT IF YOUR BIG BROTHER SHOT YOU AGAIN...
POOR L'IL DEVON.

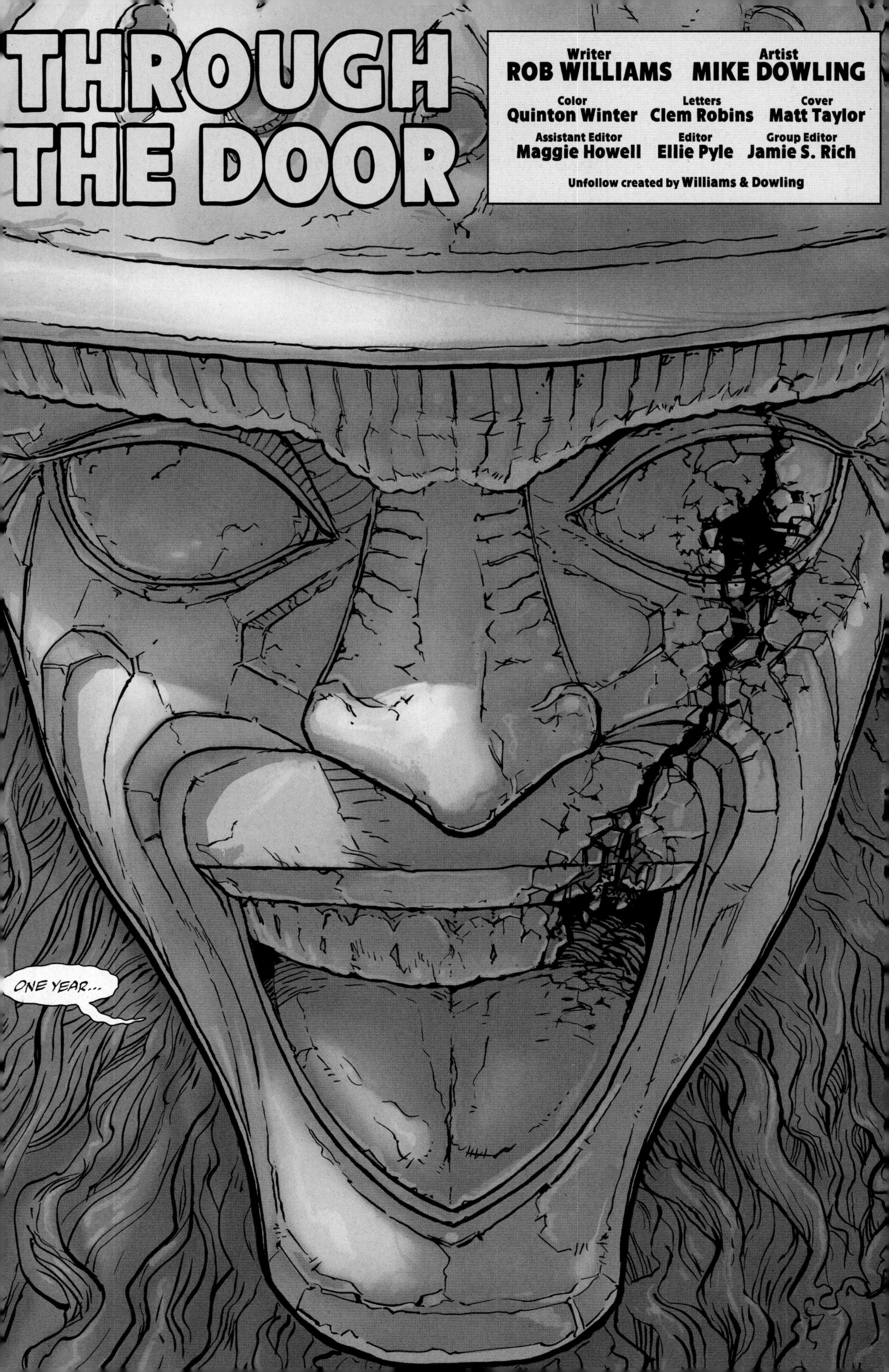
THROUGH THE DOOR
Writer ROB WILLIAMS
Artist MIKE DOWLING
Color Quinton Winter
Letters Clem Robins
Cover Matt Taylor
Assistant Editor Maggie Howell
Editor Ellie Pyle
Group Editor Jamie S. Rich
Unfollow created by Williams & Dowling
ONE YEAR...

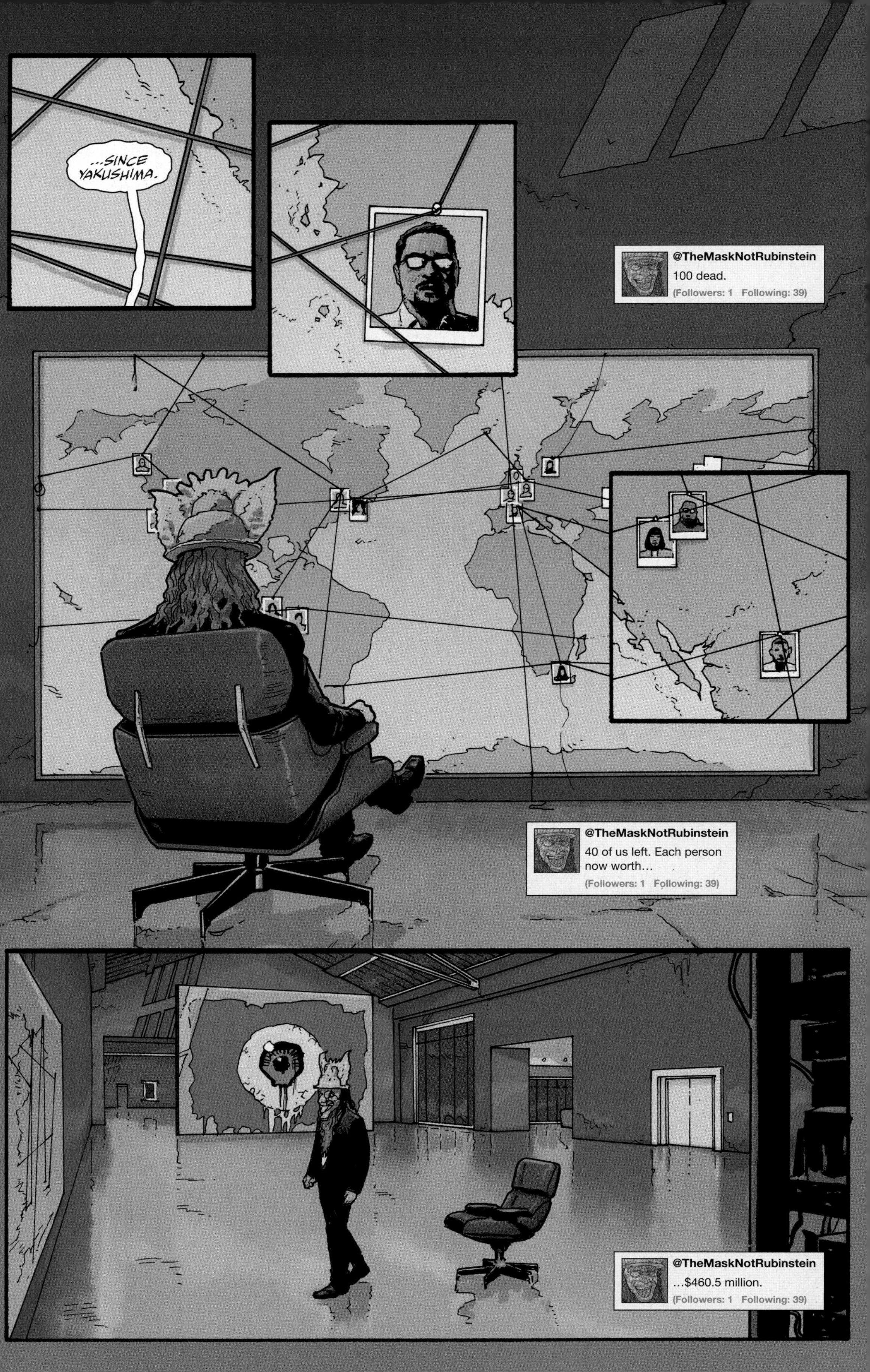
...SINCE YAKUSHIMA.
@TheMaskNotRubinstein
100 dead.
(Followers: 1 Following: 39)
@TheMaskNotRubinstein
40 of us left. Each person now worth...
(Followers: 1 Following: 39)
@TheMaskNotRubinstein
...$460.5 million.
(Followers: 1 Following: 39)

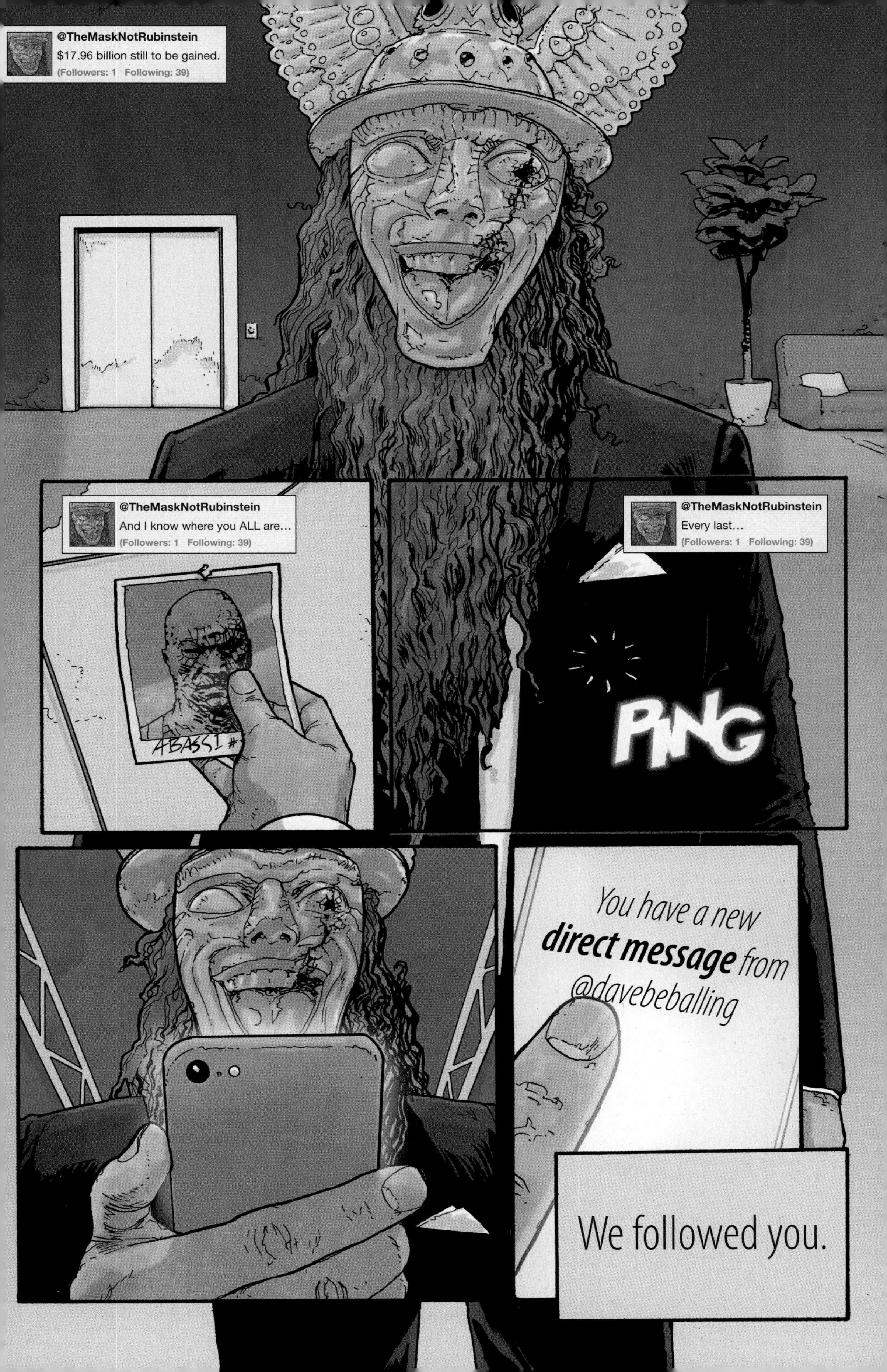
@TheMaskNotRubinstein
$17.96 billion still to be gained.
(Followers: 1 Following: 39)
@TheMaskNotRubinstein
And I know where you ALL are...
(Followers: 1 Following: 39)
ABASSI #
@TheMaskNotRubinstein
Every last...
(Followers: 1 Following: 39)
PING
You have a new direct message from @davebeballing
We followed you.

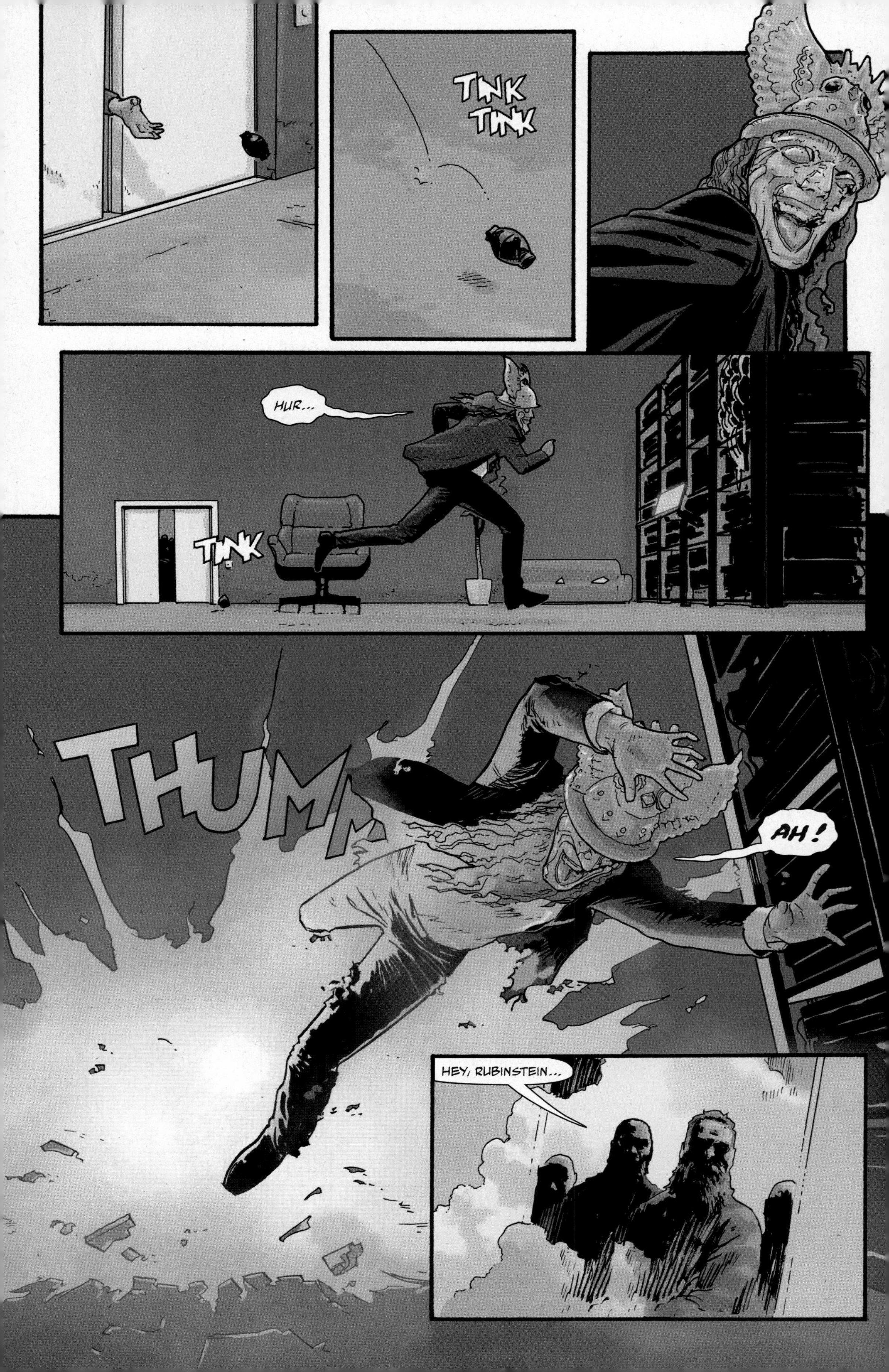
TINK TINK
HUR...
TINK
THUMM
AH!
HEY, RUBINSTEIN...

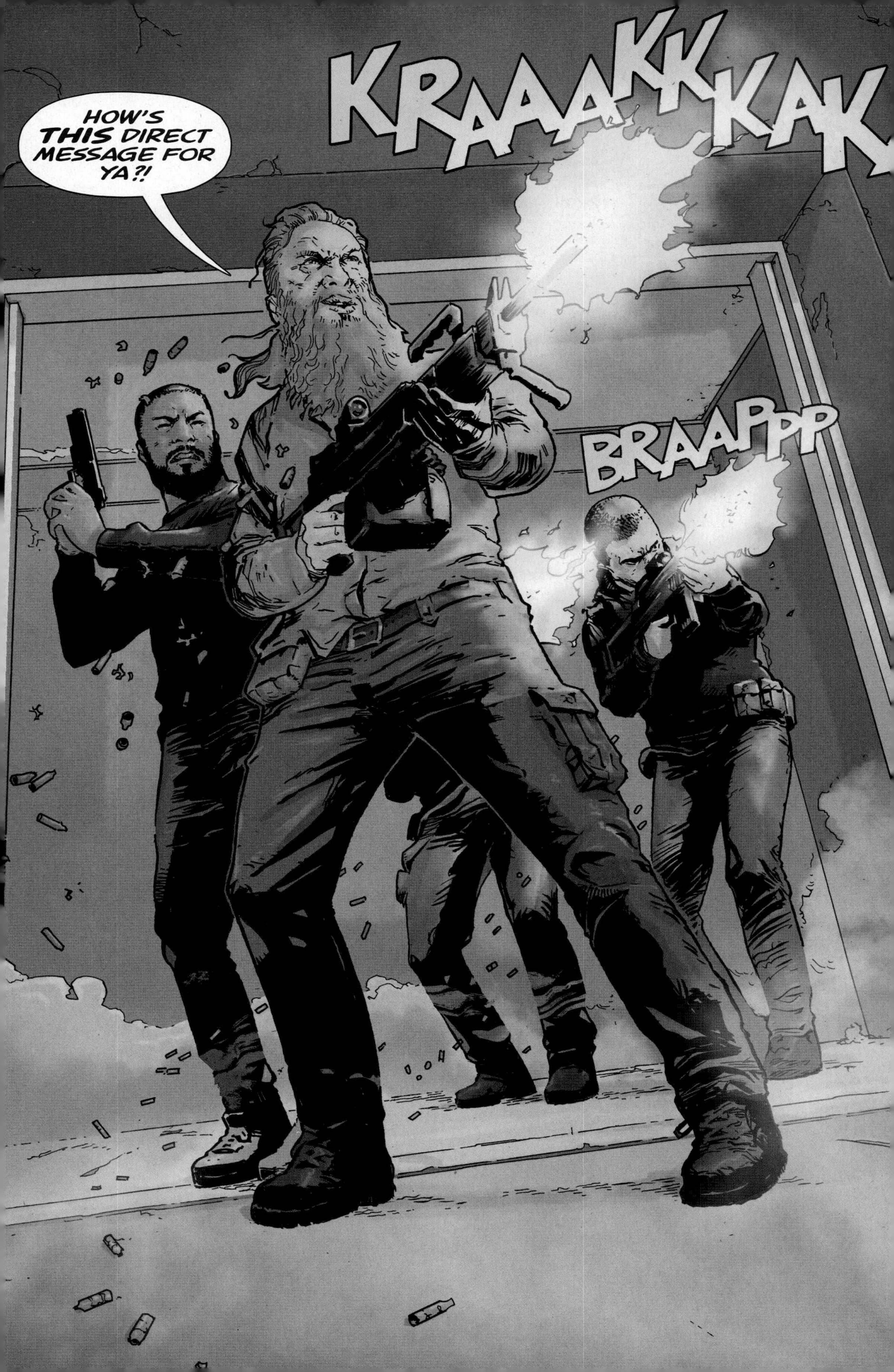
HOW'S THIS DIRECT MESSAGE FOR YA?!
KRAAAKKKAK
BRAAPPP

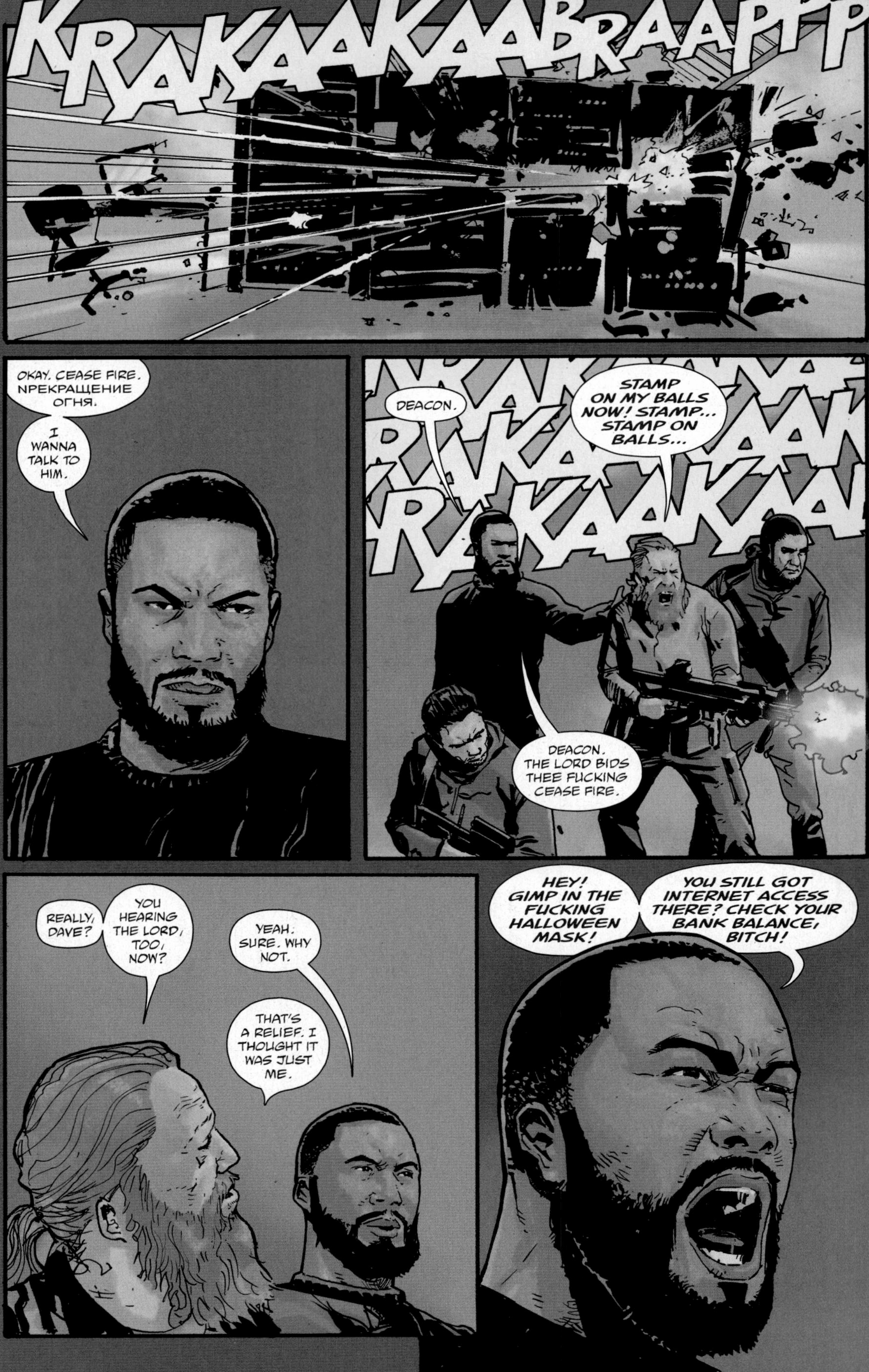
KRAKAAKAABRAAPPP
OKAY. CEASE FIRE. ПРЕКРАЩЕНИЕ ОГНЯ.
I WANNA TALK TO HIM.
DEACON.
STAMP ON MY BALLS NOW! STAMP... STAMP ON BALLS...
DEACON. THE LORD BIDS THEE FUCKING CEASE FIRE.
REALLY, DAVE?
YOU HEARING THE LORD, TOO, NOW?
YEAH. SURE. WHY NOT.
THAT'S A RELIEF. I THOUGHT IT WAS JUST ME.
HEY! GIMP IN THE FUCKING HALLOWEEN MASK!
YOU STILL GOT INTERNET ACCESS THERE? CHECK YOUR BANK BALANCE, BITCH!

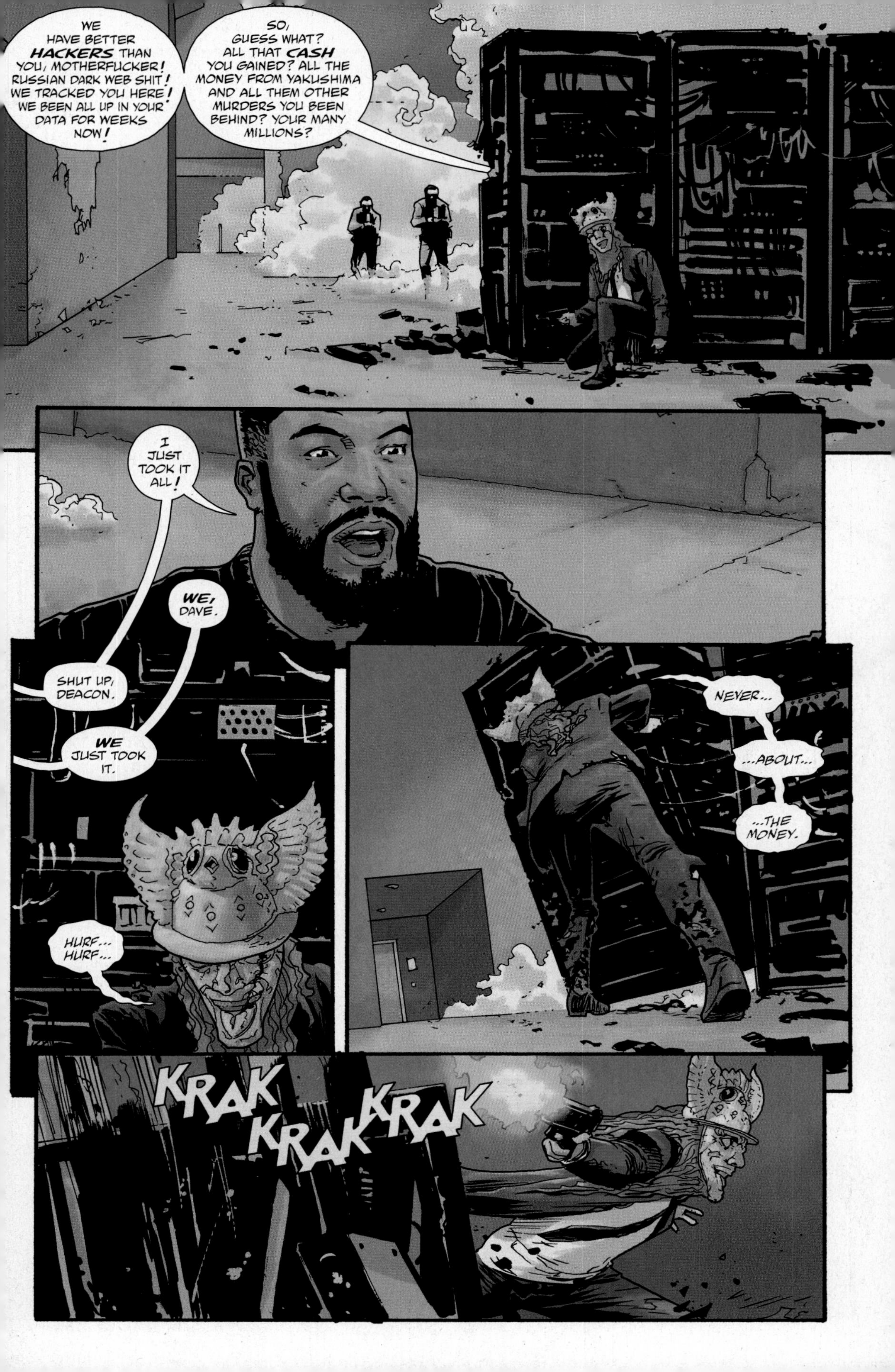
WE HAVE BETTER HACKERS THAN YOU, MOTHERFUCKER! RUSSIAN DARK WEB SHIT! WE TRACKED YOU HERE! WE BEEN ALL UP IN YOUR DATA FOR WEEKS NOW!
SO, GUESS WHAT? ALL THAT CASH YOU GAINED? ALL THE MONEY FROM YAKUSHIMA AND ALL THEM OTHER MURDERS YOU BEEN BEHIND? YOUR MANY MILLIONS?
I JUST TOOK IT ALL!
WE, DAVE.
SHUT UP, DEACON.
WE JUST TOOK IT.
HURF... HURF...
NEVER...
...ABOUT...
...THE MONEY.
KRAK KRAK KRAK KRAK

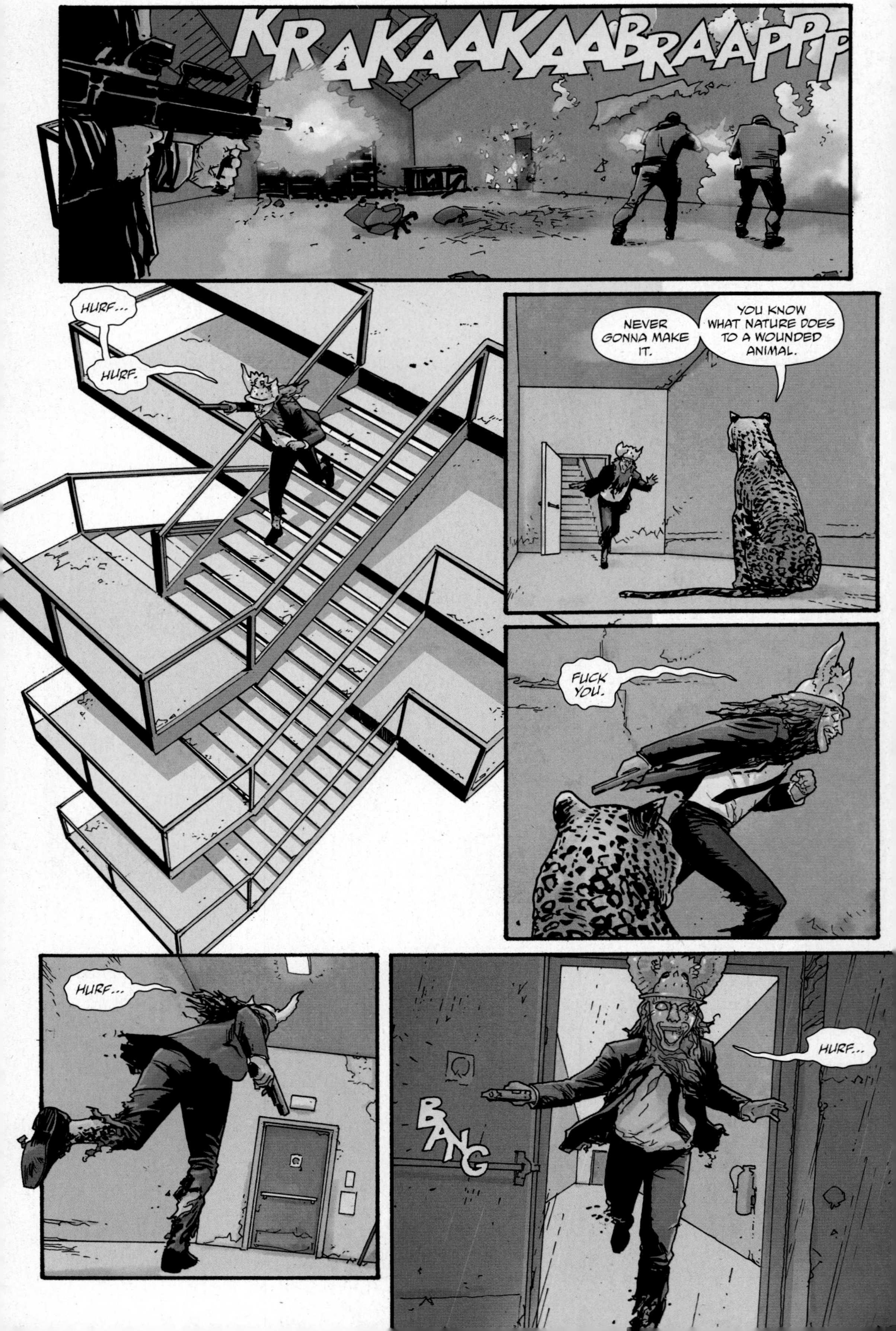
KRAKAAKAABRAAPPP
HURF...
HURF.
NEVER GONNA MAKE IT.
YOU KNOW WHAT NATURE DOES TO A WOUNDED ANIMAL.
FUCK YOU.
HURF...
HURF...
BANG

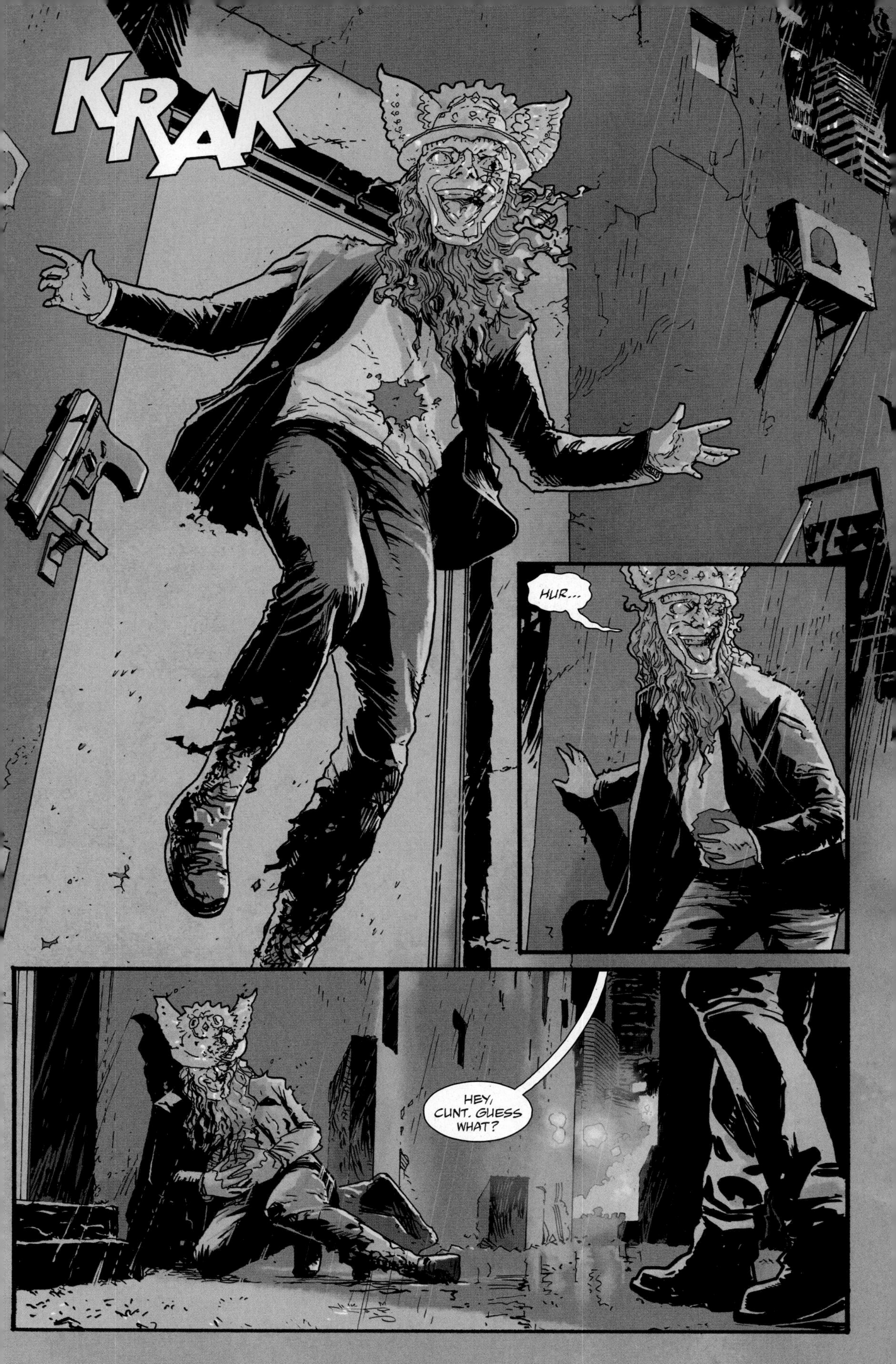
KRAK
HUR...
HEY, CUNT. GUESS WHAT?

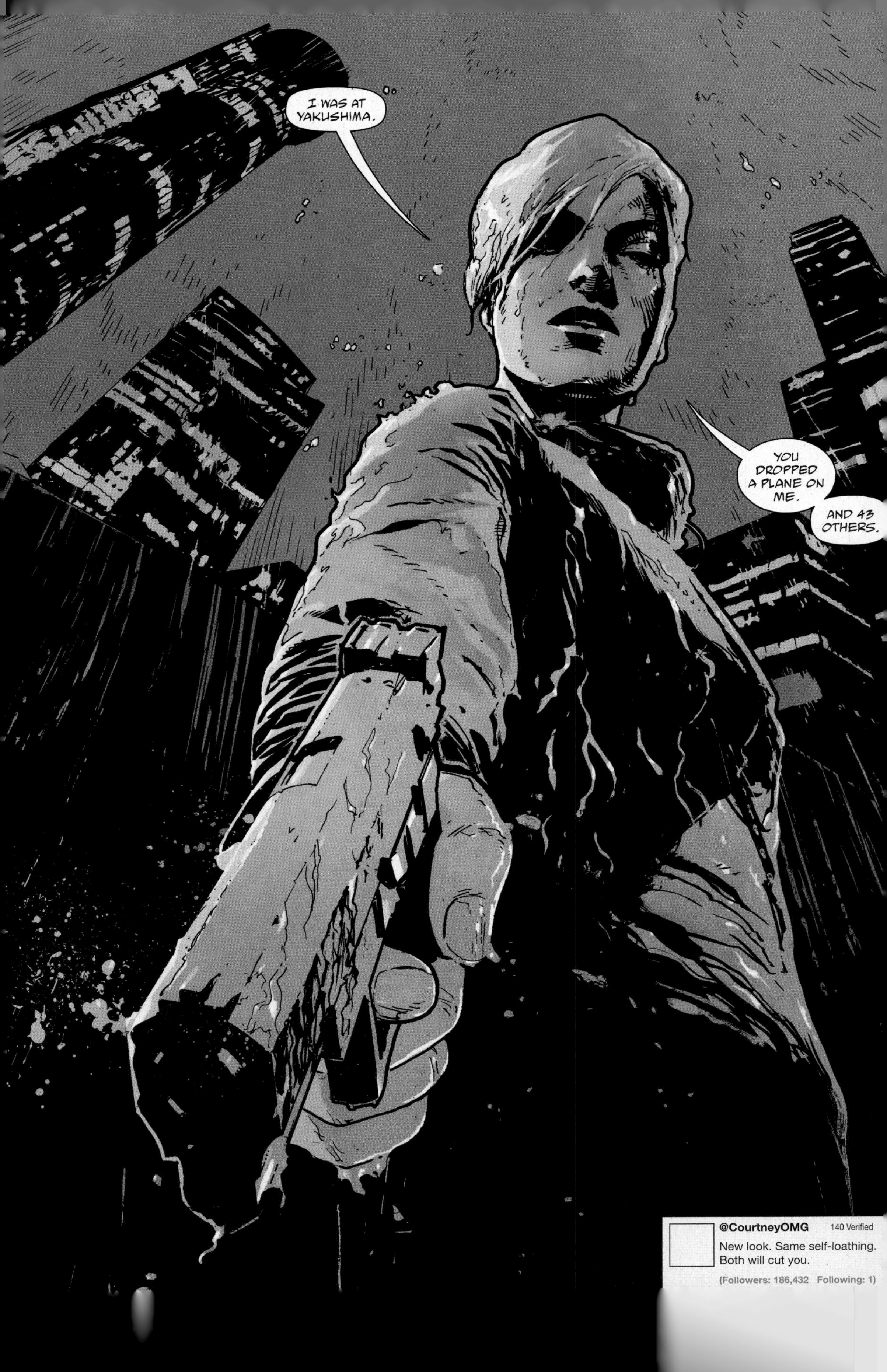
I WAS AT YAKUSHIMA.
YOU DROPPED A PLANE ON ME.
AND 43 OTHERS.
@CourtneyOMG 140 Verified
New look. Same self-loathing. Both will cut you.
(Followers: 186,432 Following: 1)

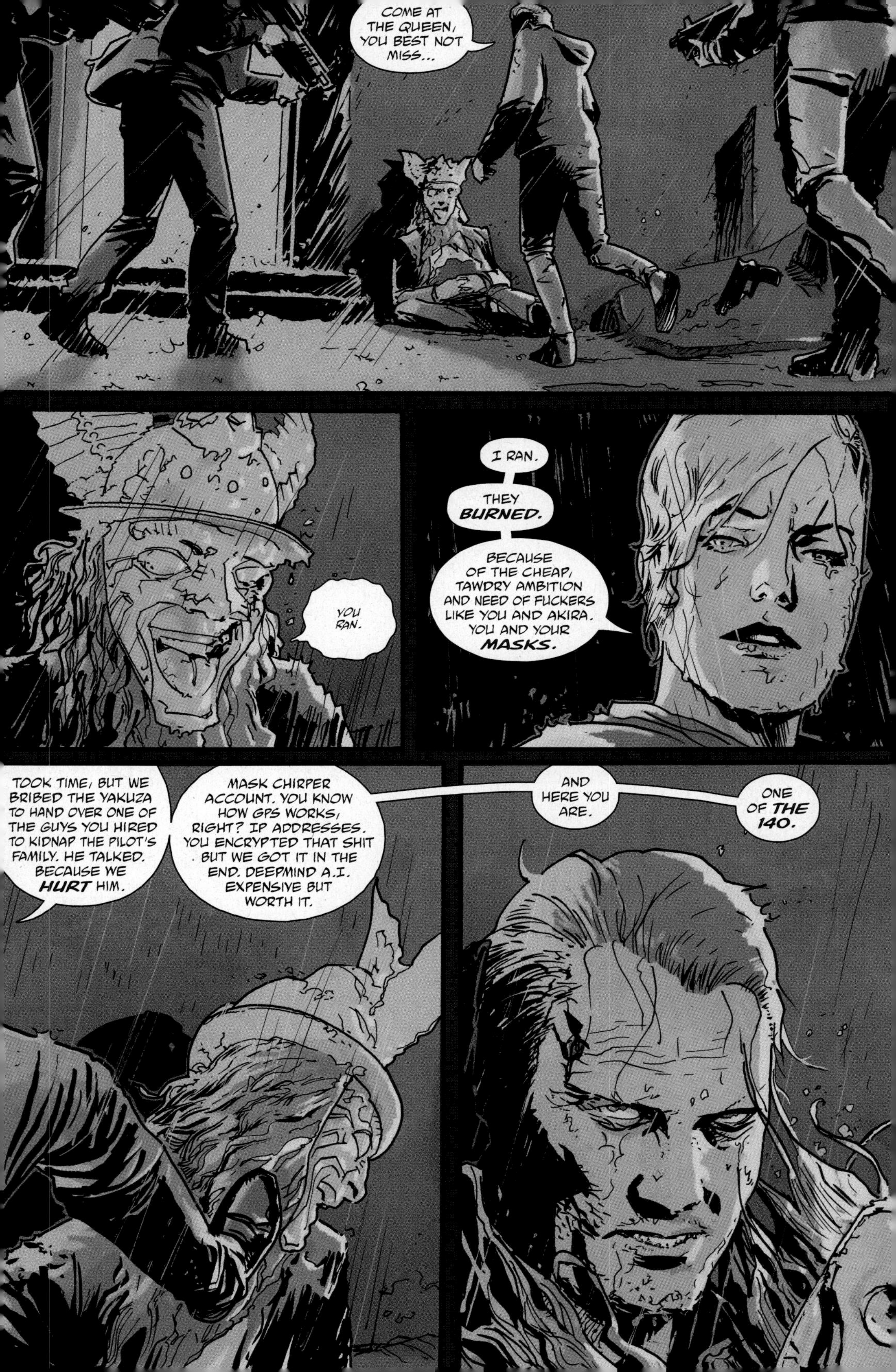
COME AT THE QUEEN, YOU BEST NOT MISS...
YOU RAN.
I RAN.
THEY BURNED.
BECAUSE OF THE CHEAP, TAWDRY AMBITION AND NEED OF FUCKERS LIKE YOU AND AKIRA. YOU AND YOUR MASKS.
TOOK TIME, BUT WE BRIBED THE YAKUZA TO HAND OVER ONE OF THE GUYS YOU HIRED TO KIDNAP THE PILOT'S FAMILY. HE TALKED. BECAUSE WE HURT HIM.
MASK CHIRPER ACCOUNT. YOU KNOW HOW GPS WORKS, RIGHT? IP ADDRESSES. YOU ENCRYPTED THAT SHIT BUT WE GOT IT IN THE END. DEEPMIND A.I. EXPENSIVE BUT WORTH IT.
AND HERE YOU ARE.
ONE OF THE 140.

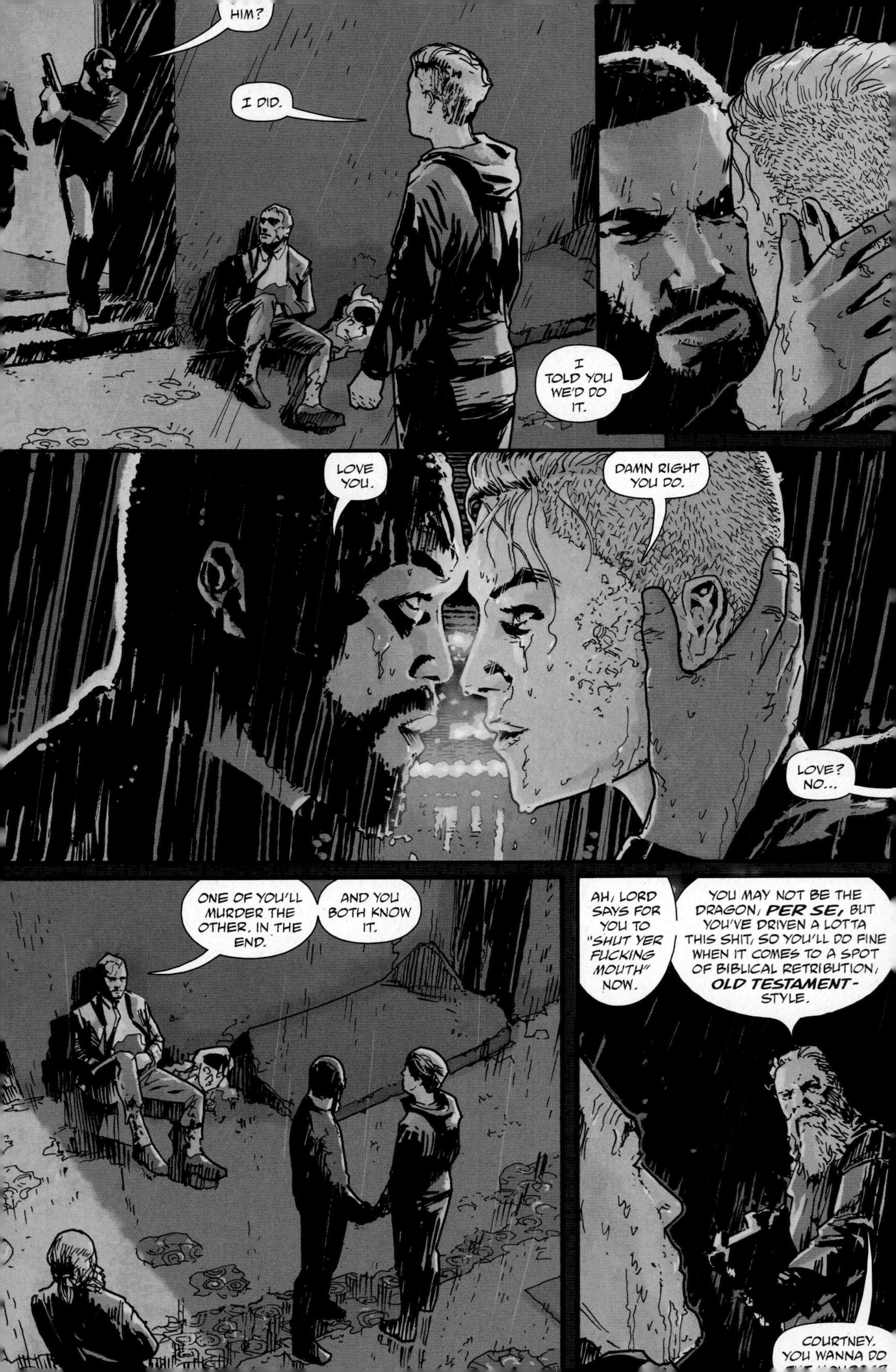
HIM?
I DID.
I TOLD YOU WE'D DO IT.
LOVE YOU.
DAMN RIGHT YOU DO.
LOVE? NO...
ONE OF YOU'LL MURDER THE OTHER. IN THE END.
AND YOU BOTH KNOW IT.
AH, LORD SAYS FOR YOU TO "SHUT YER FUCKING MOUTH" NOW.
YOU MAY NOT BE THE DRAGON, **PER SE,** BUT YOU'VE DRIVEN A LOTTA THIS SHIT, SO YOU'LL DO FINE WHEN IT COMES TO A SPOT OF BIBLICAL RETRIBUTION, **OLD TESTAMENT**-STYLE.
COURTNEY. YOU WANNA DO

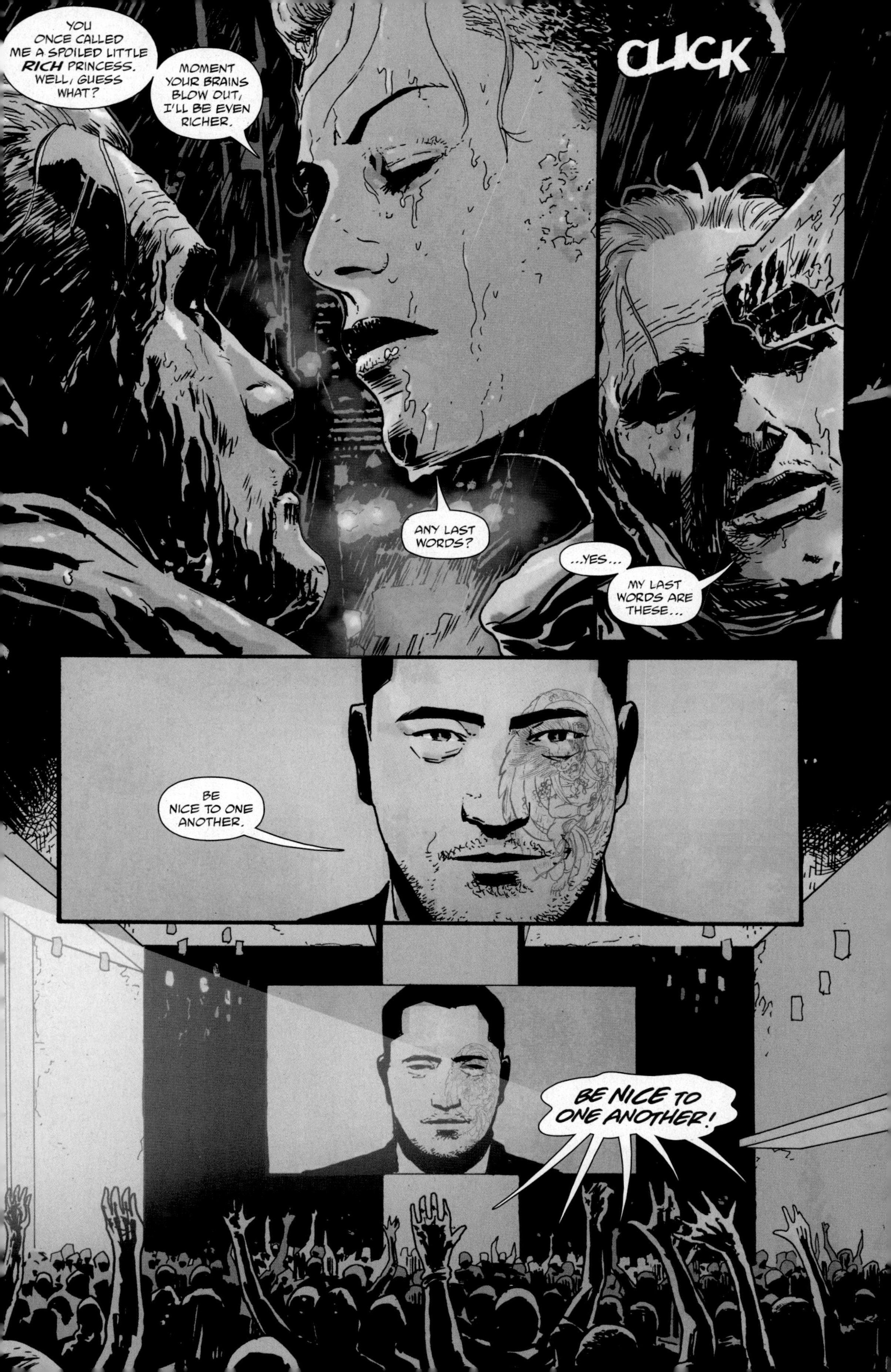
CLICK
YOU ONCE CALLED ME A SPOILED LITTLE RICH PRINCESS. WELL, GUESS WHAT?
MOMENT YOUR BRAINS BLOW OUT, I'LL BE EVEN RICHER.
ANY LAST WORDS?
...YES...
MY LAST WORDS ARE THESE...
BE NICE TO ONE ANOTHER.
BE NICE TO ONE ANOTHER!

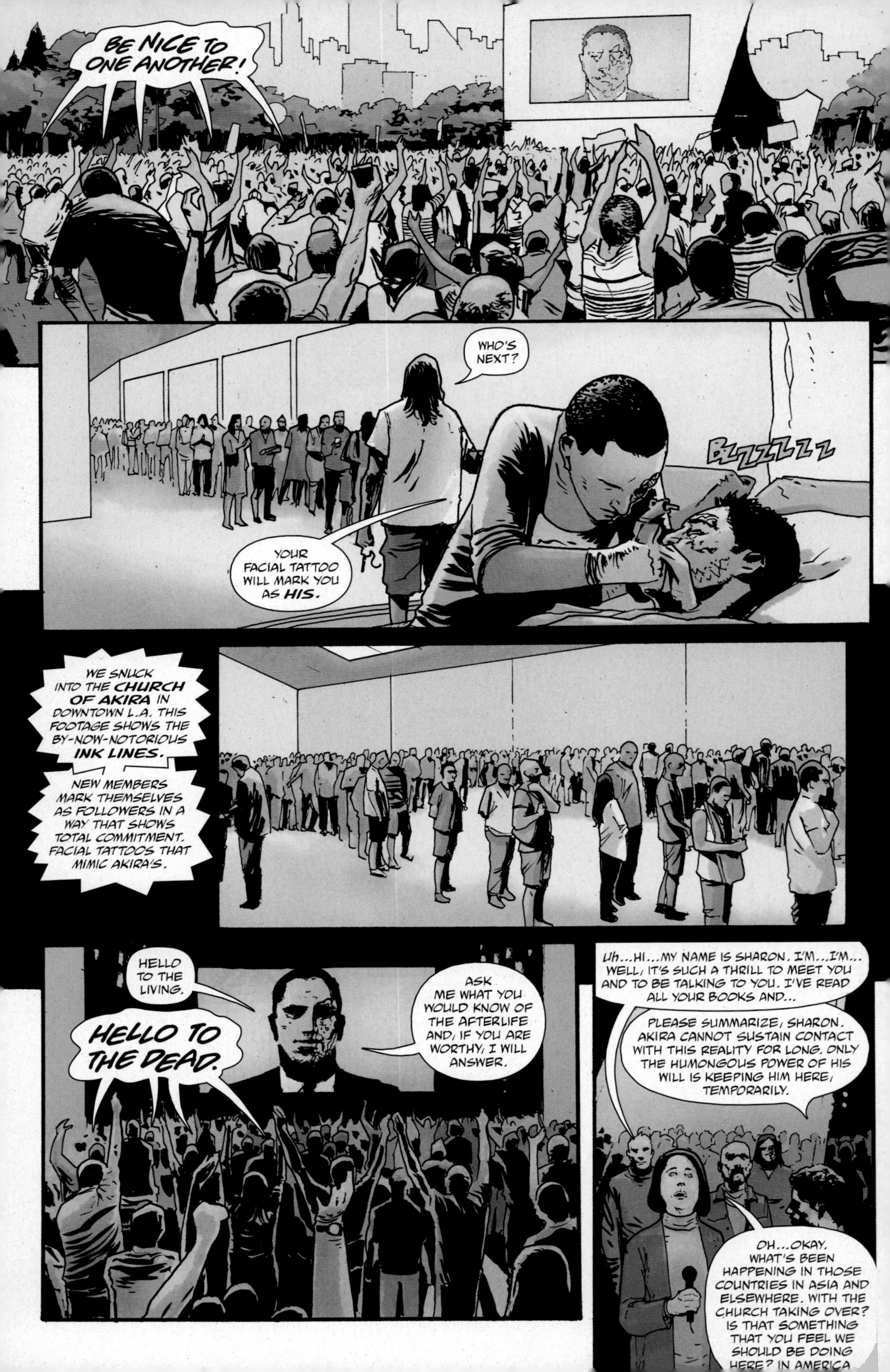
BE NICE TO ONE ANOTHER!
WHO'S NEXT?
BZZZZZZ
YOUR FACIAL TATTOO WILL MARK YOU AS HIS.
WE SNUCK INTO THE CHURCH OF AKIRA IN DOWNTOWN L.A. THIS FOOTAGE SHOWS THE BY-NOW-NOTORIOUS INK LINES.
NEW MEMBERS MARK THEMSELVES AS FOLLOWERS IN A WAY THAT SHOWS TOTAL COMMITMENT. FACIAL TATTOOS THAT MIMIC AKIRA'S.
HELLO TO THE LIVING.
HELLO TO THE DEAD.
ASK ME WHAT YOU WOULD KNOW OF THE AFTERLIFE AND, IF YOU ARE WORTHY, I WILL ANSWER.
UH...HI...MY NAME IS SHARON. I'M...I'M... WELL, IT'S SUCH A THRILL TO MEET YOU AND TO BE TALKING TO YOU. I'VE READ ALL YOUR BOOKS AND...
PLEASE SUMMARIZE, SHARON. AKIRA CANNOT SUSTAIN CONTACT WITH THIS REALITY FOR LONG. ONLY THE HUMONGOUS POWER OF HIS WILL IS KEEPING HIM HERE, TEMPORARILY.
OH...OKAY. WHAT'S BEEN HAPPENING IN THOSE COUNTRIES IN ASIA AND ELSEWHERE. WITH THE CHURCH TAKING OVER? IS THAT SOMETHING THAT YOU FEEL WE SHOULD BE DOING HERE? IN AMERICA

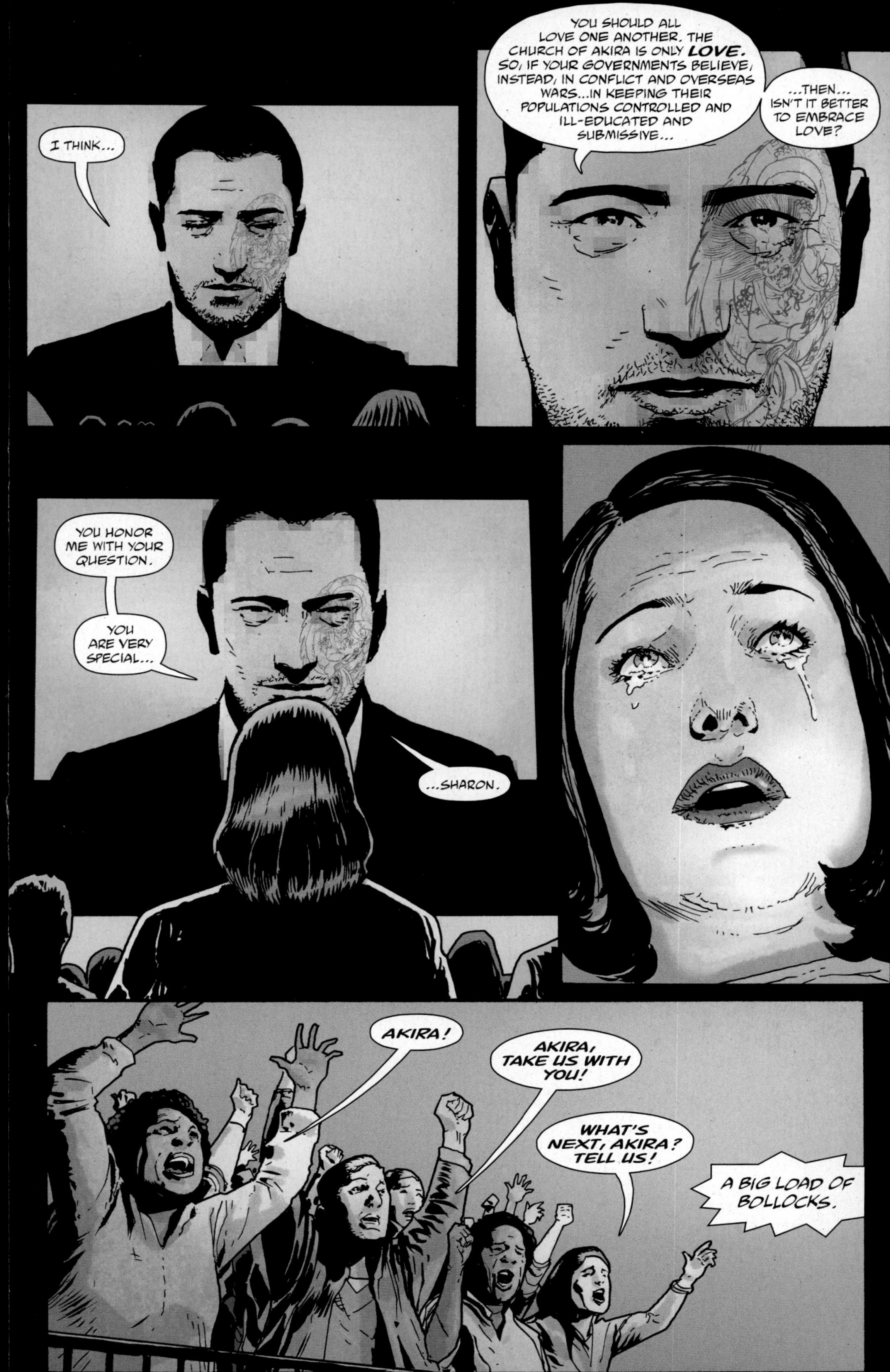
I THINK...
YOU SHOULD ALL LOVE ONE ANOTHER. THE CHURCH OF AKIRA IS ONLY LOVE. SO, IF YOUR GOVERNMENTS BELIEVE, INSTEAD, IN CONFLICT AND OVERSEAS WARS...IN KEEPING THEIR POPULATIONS CONTROLLED AND ILL-EDUCATED AND SUBMISSIVE...
...THEN... ISN'T IT BETTER TO EMBRACE LOVE?
YOU HONOR ME WITH YOUR QUESTION.
YOU ARE VERY SPECIAL...
...SHARON.
AKIRA!
AKIRA, TAKE US WITH YOU!
WHAT'S NEXT, AKIRA? TELL US!
A BIG LOAD OF BOLLOCKS.

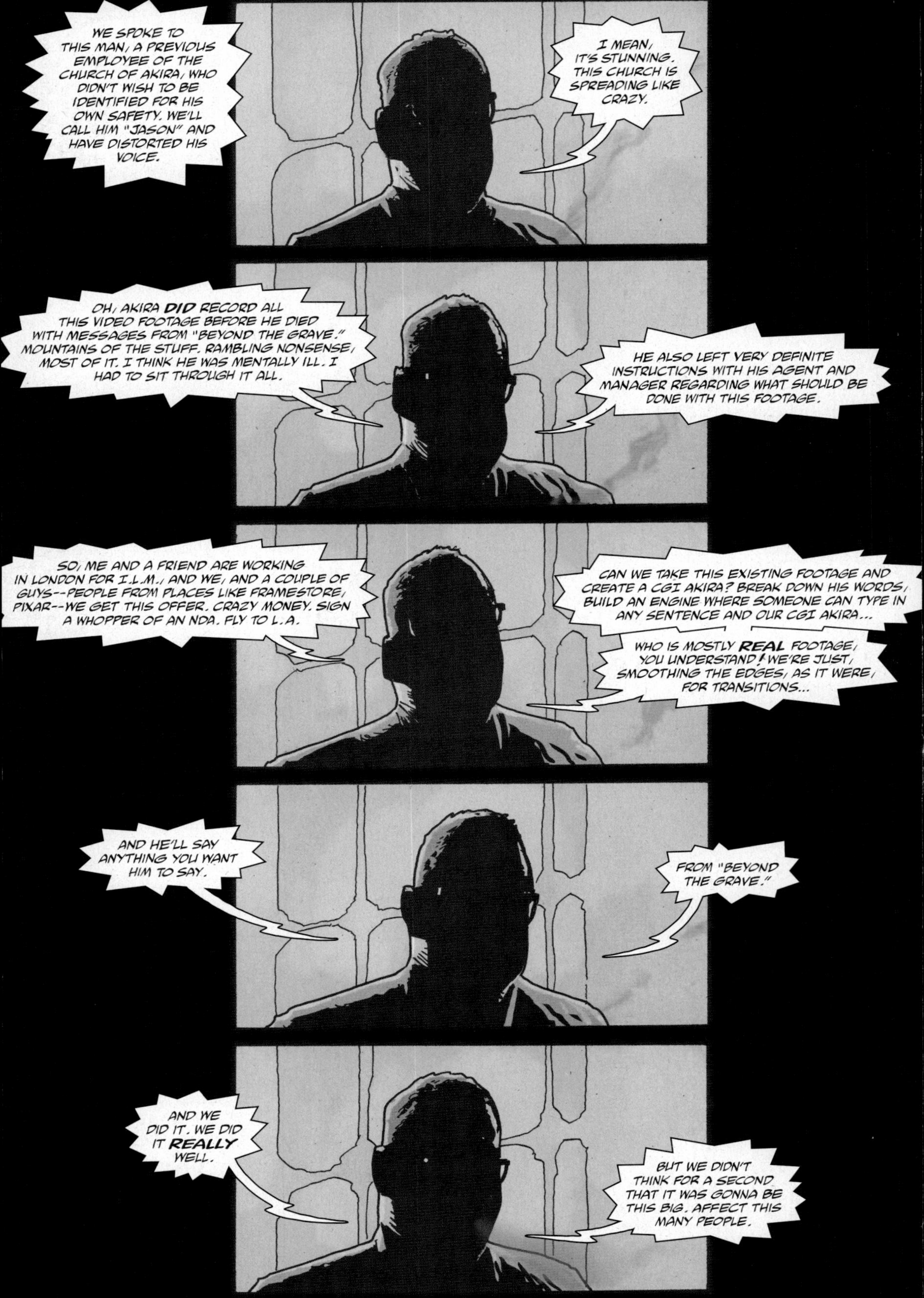
WE SPOKE TO THIS MAN, A PREVIOUS EMPLOYEE OF THE CHURCH OF AKIRA, WHO DIDN'T WISH TO BE IDENTIFIED FOR HIS OWN SAFETY. WE'LL CALL HIM "JASON" AND HAVE DISTORTED HIS VOICE.
I MEAN, IT'S STUNNING. THIS CHURCH IS SPREADING LIKE CRAZY.
OH, AKIRA **DID** RECORD ALL THIS VIDEO FOOTAGE BEFORE HE DIED WITH MESSAGES FROM "BEYOND THE GRAVE." MOUNTAINS OF THE STUFF. RAMBLING NONSENSE, MOST OF IT. I THINK HE WAS MENTALLY ILL. I HAD TO SIT THROUGH IT ALL.
HE ALSO LEFT VERY DEFINITE INSTRUCTIONS WITH HIS AGENT AND MANAGER REGARDING WHAT SHOULD BE DONE WITH THIS FOOTAGE.
SO, ME AND A FRIEND ARE WORKING IN LONDON FOR I.L.M., AND WE, AND A COUPLE OF GUYS--PEOPLE FROM PLACES LIKE FRAMESTORE, PIXAR--WE GET THIS OFFER. CRAZY MONEY. SIGN A WHOPPER OF AN NDA. FLY TO L.A.
CAN WE TAKE THIS EXISTING FOOTAGE AND CREATE A CGI AKIRA? BREAK DOWN HIS WORDS, BUILD AN ENGINE WHERE SOMEONE CAN TYPE IN ANY SENTENCE AND OUR CGI AKIRA...
WHO IS MOSTLY **REAL** FOOTAGE, YOU UNDERSTAND! WE'RE JUST, SMOOTHING THE EDGES, AS IT WERE, FOR TRANSITIONS...
AND HE'LL SAY ANYTHING YOU WANT HIM TO SAY.
FROM "BEYOND THE GRAVE."
AND WE DID IT. WE DID IT **REALLY** WELL.
BUT WE DIDN'T THINK FOR A SECOND THAT IT WAS GONNA BE THIS BIG. AFFECT THIS MANY PEOPLE.

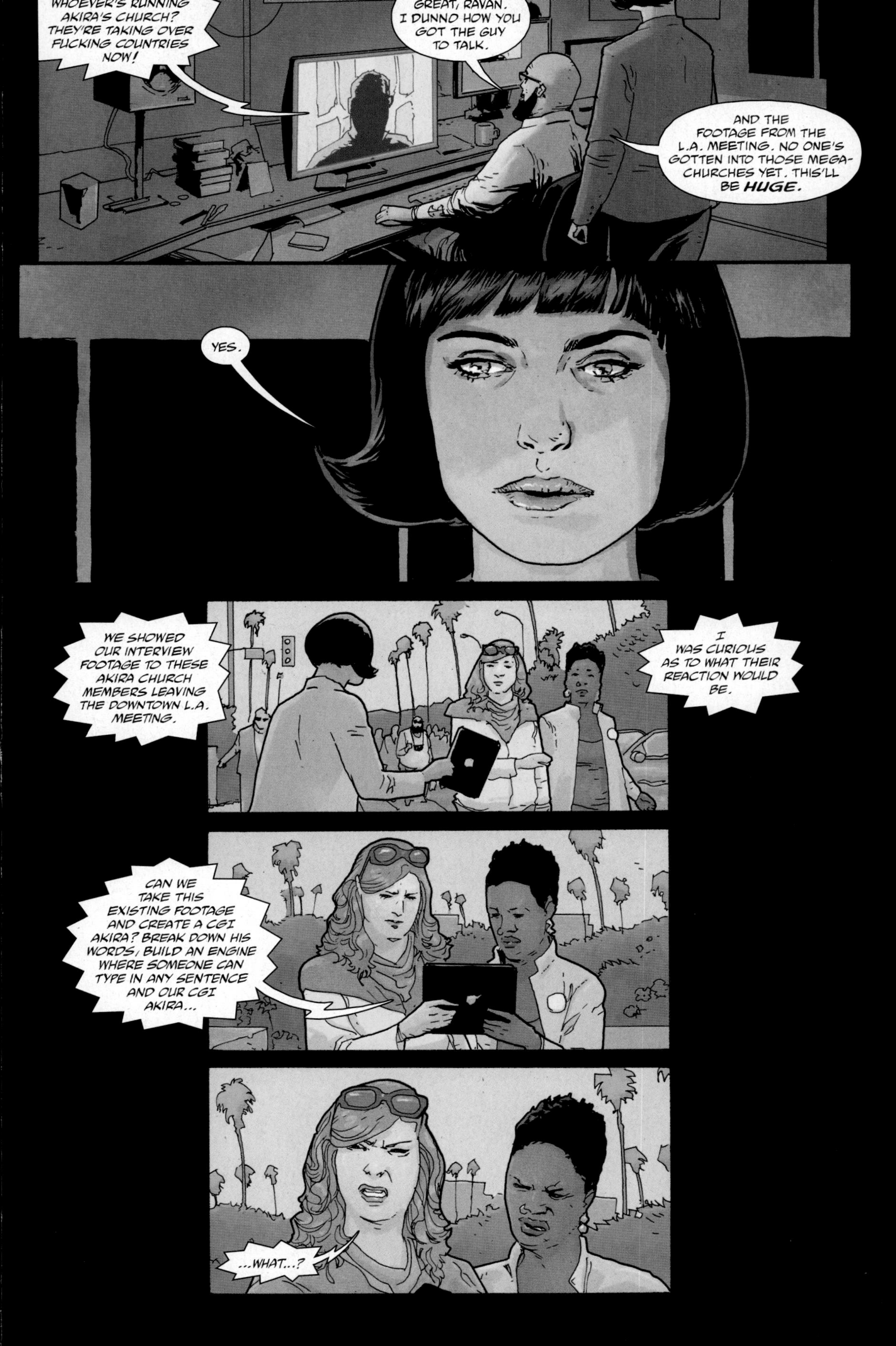
WHOEVER'S RUNNING AKIRA'S CHURCH? THEY'RE TAKING OVER FUCKING COUNTRIES NOW!
GREAT, RAVAN. I DUNNO HOW YOU GOT THE GUY TO TALK.
AND THE FOOTAGE FROM THE L.A. MEETING. NO ONE'S GOTTEN INTO THOSE MEGA-CHURCHES YET. THIS'LL BE HUGE.
YES.
WE SHOWED OUR INTERVIEW FOOTAGE TO THESE AKIRA CHURCH MEMBERS LEAVING THE DOWNTOWN L.A. MEETING.
I WAS CURIOUS AS TO WHAT THEIR REACTION WOULD BE.
CAN WE TAKE THIS EXISTING FOOTAGE AND CREATE A CGI AKIRA? BREAK DOWN HIS WORDS, BUILD AN ENGINE WHERE SOMEONE CAN TYPE IN ANY SENTENCE AND OUR CGI AKIRA...
...WHAT...?

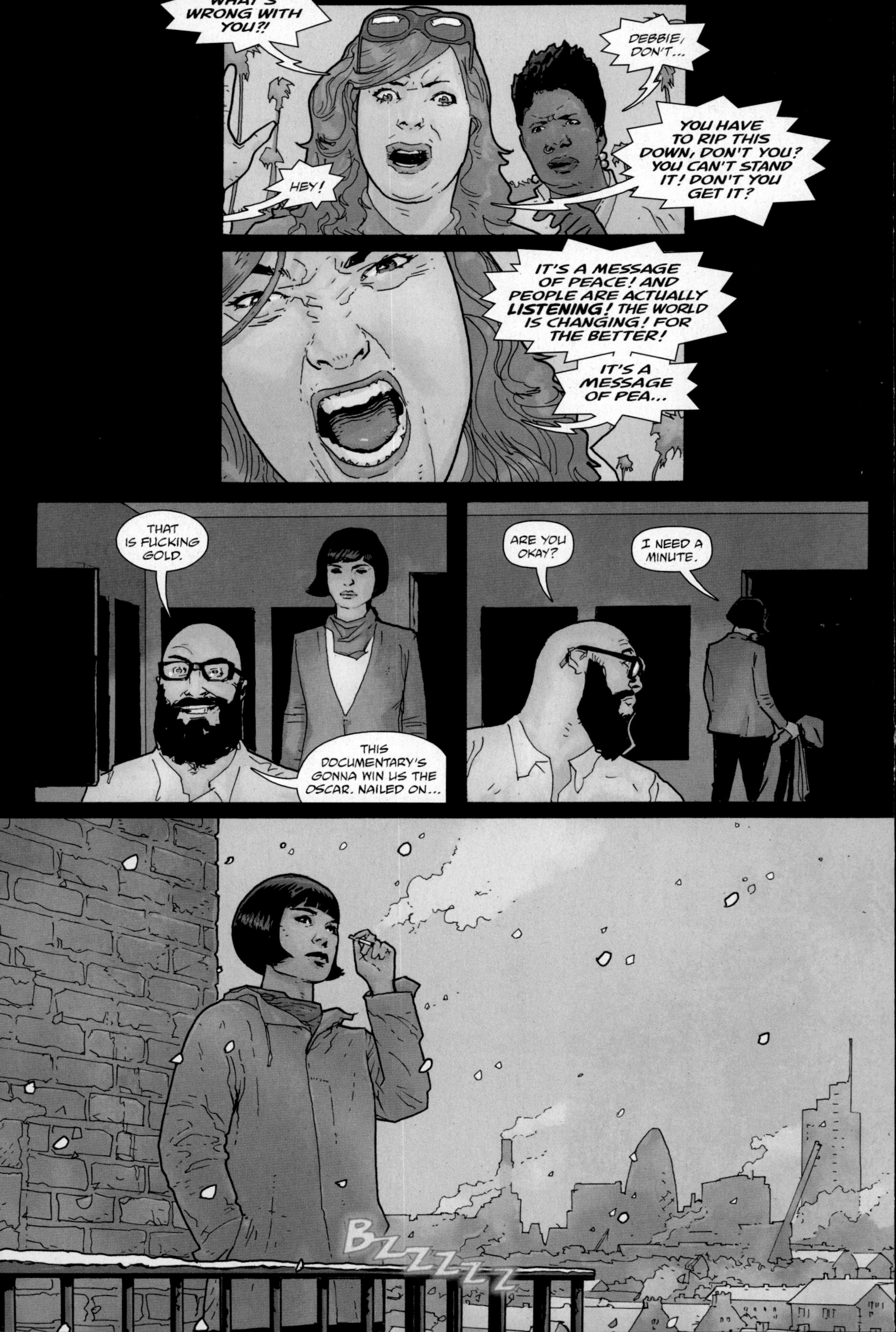
WHAT'S WRONG WITH YOU?!
DEBBIE, DON'T...
HEY!
YOU HAVE TO RIP THIS DOWN, DON'T YOU? YOU CAN'T STAND IT! DON'T YOU GET IT?
IT'S A MESSAGE OF PEACE! AND PEOPLE ARE ACTUALLY LISTENING! THE WORLD IS CHANGING! FOR THE BETTER!
IT'S A MESSAGE OF PEA...
THAT IS FUCKING GOLD.
THIS DOCUMENTARY'S GONNA WIN US THE OSCAR. NAILED ON...
ARE YOU OKAY?
I NEED A MINUTE.
BZZZZZZ

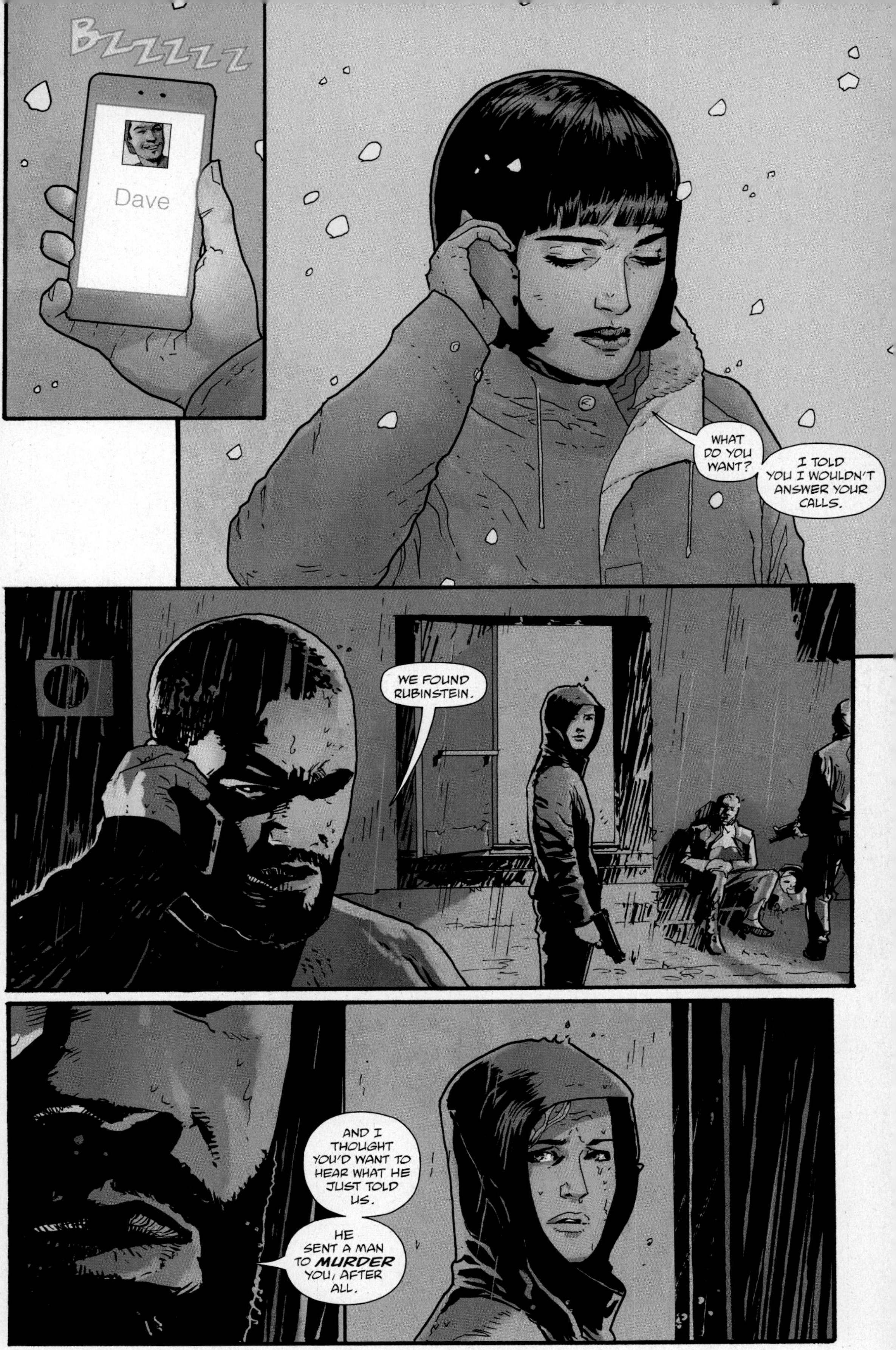
BZZZZZ
Dave
WHAT DO YOU WANT?
I TOLD YOU I WOULDN'T ANSWER YOUR CALLS.
WE FOUND RUBINSTEIN.
AND I THOUGHT YOU'D WANT TO HEAR WHAT HE JUST TOLD US.
HE SENT A MAN TO MURDER YOU, AFTER ALL.

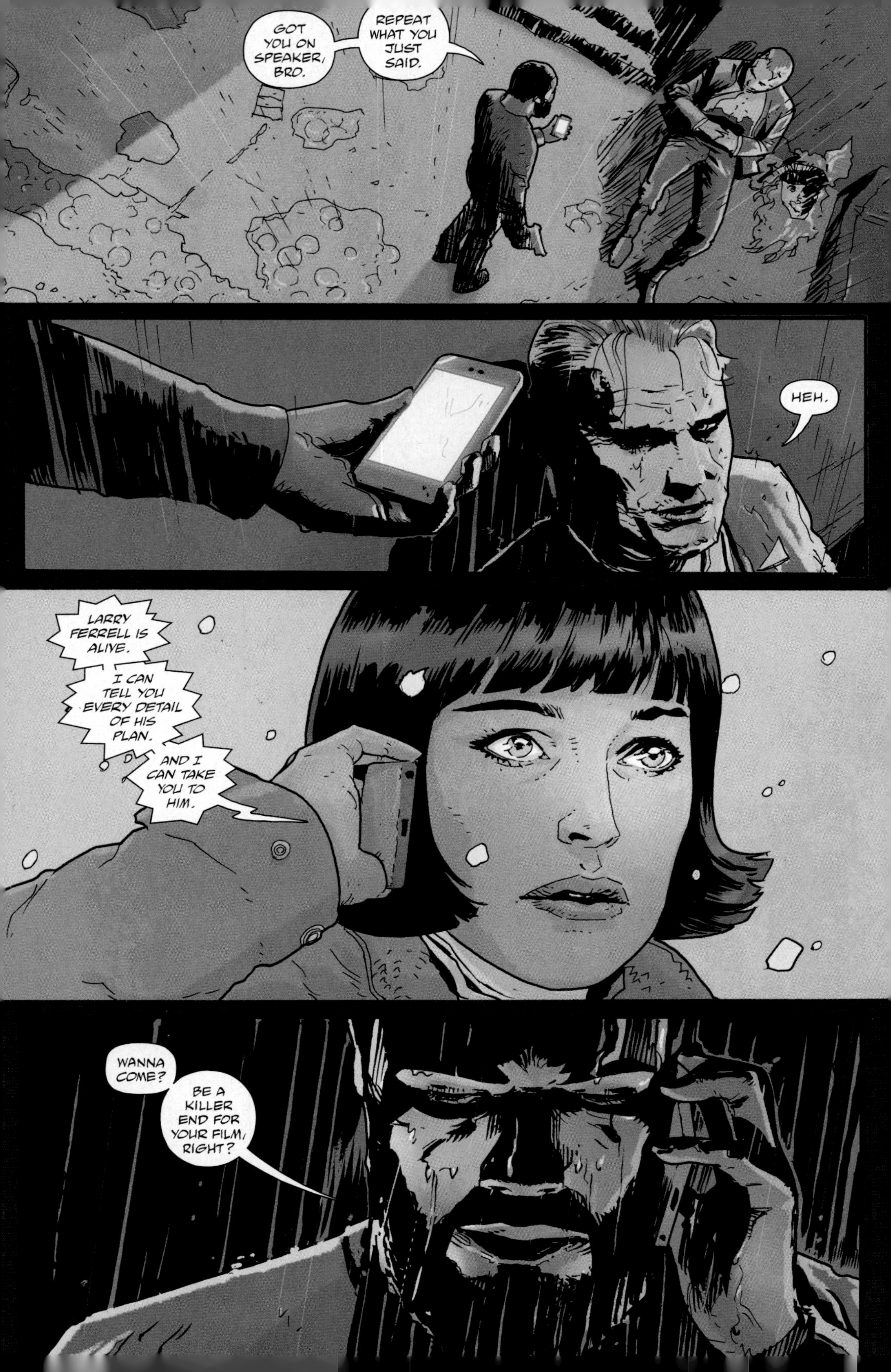

GOT YOU ON SPEAKER, BRO.
REPEAT WHAT YOU JUST SAID.
HEH.
LARRY FERRELL IS ALIVE.
I CAN TELL YOU EVERY DETAIL OF HIS PLAN.
AND I CAN TAKE YOU TO HIM.
WANNA COME?
BE A KILLER END FOR YOUR FILM, RIGHT?

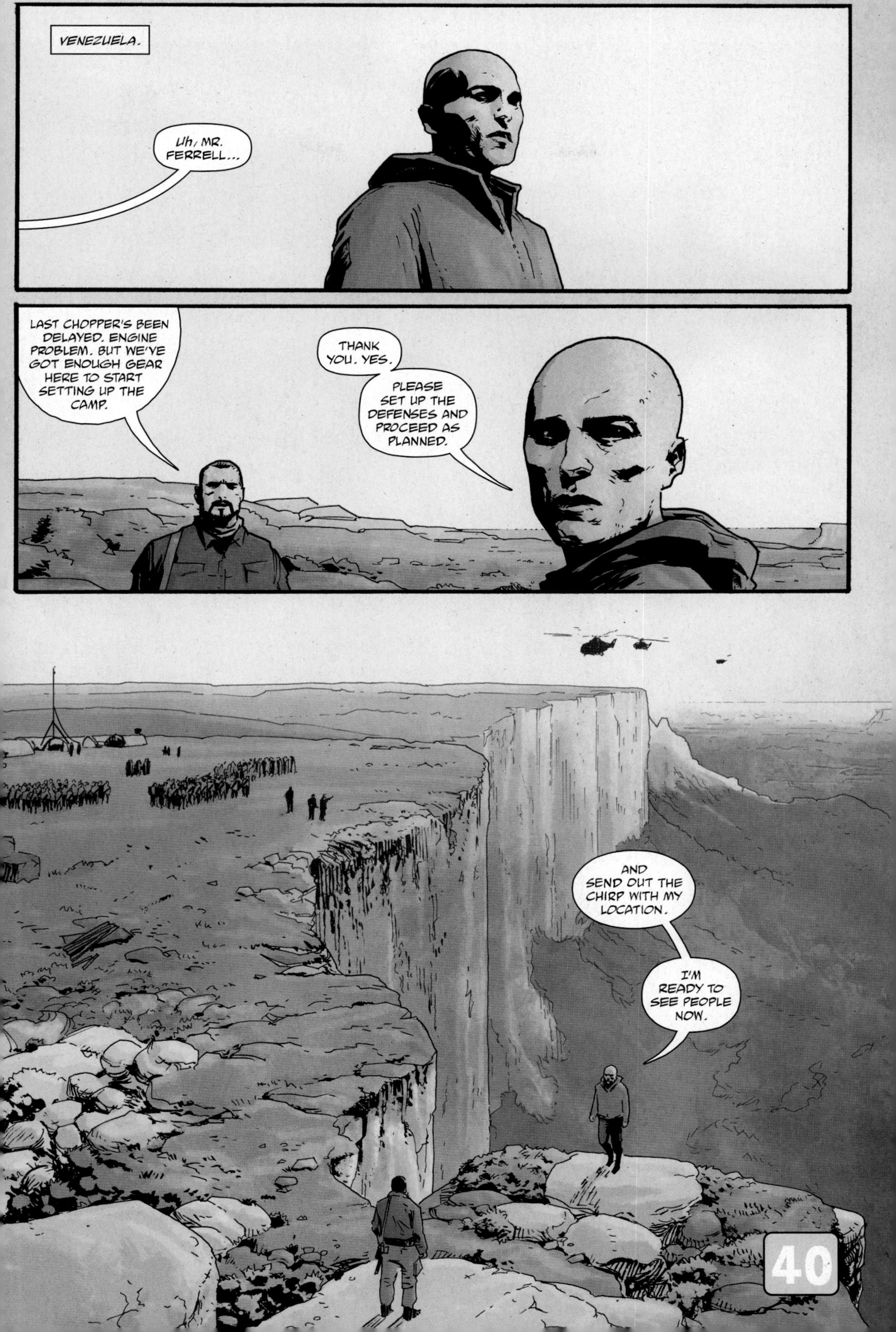
VENEZUELA.
UH, MR. FERRELL...
LAST CHOPPER'S BEEN DELAYED. ENGINE PROBLEM. BUT WE'VE GOT ENOUGH GEAR HERE TO START SETTING UP THE CAMP.
THANK YOU. YES.
PLEASE SET UP THE DEFENSES AND PROCEED AS PLANNED.
AND SEND OUT THE CHIRP WITH MY LOCATION.
I'M READY TO SEE PEOPLE NOW.

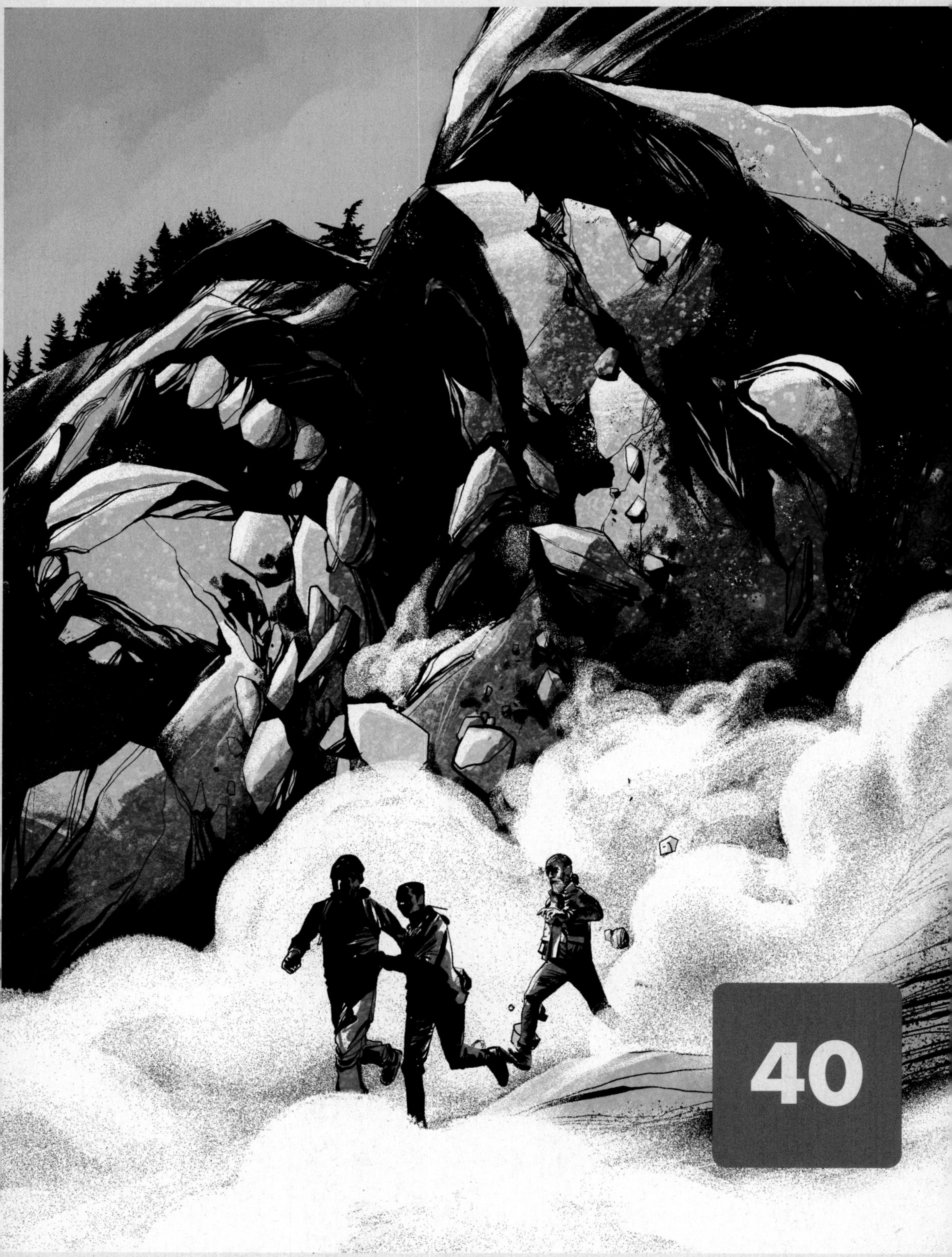
40

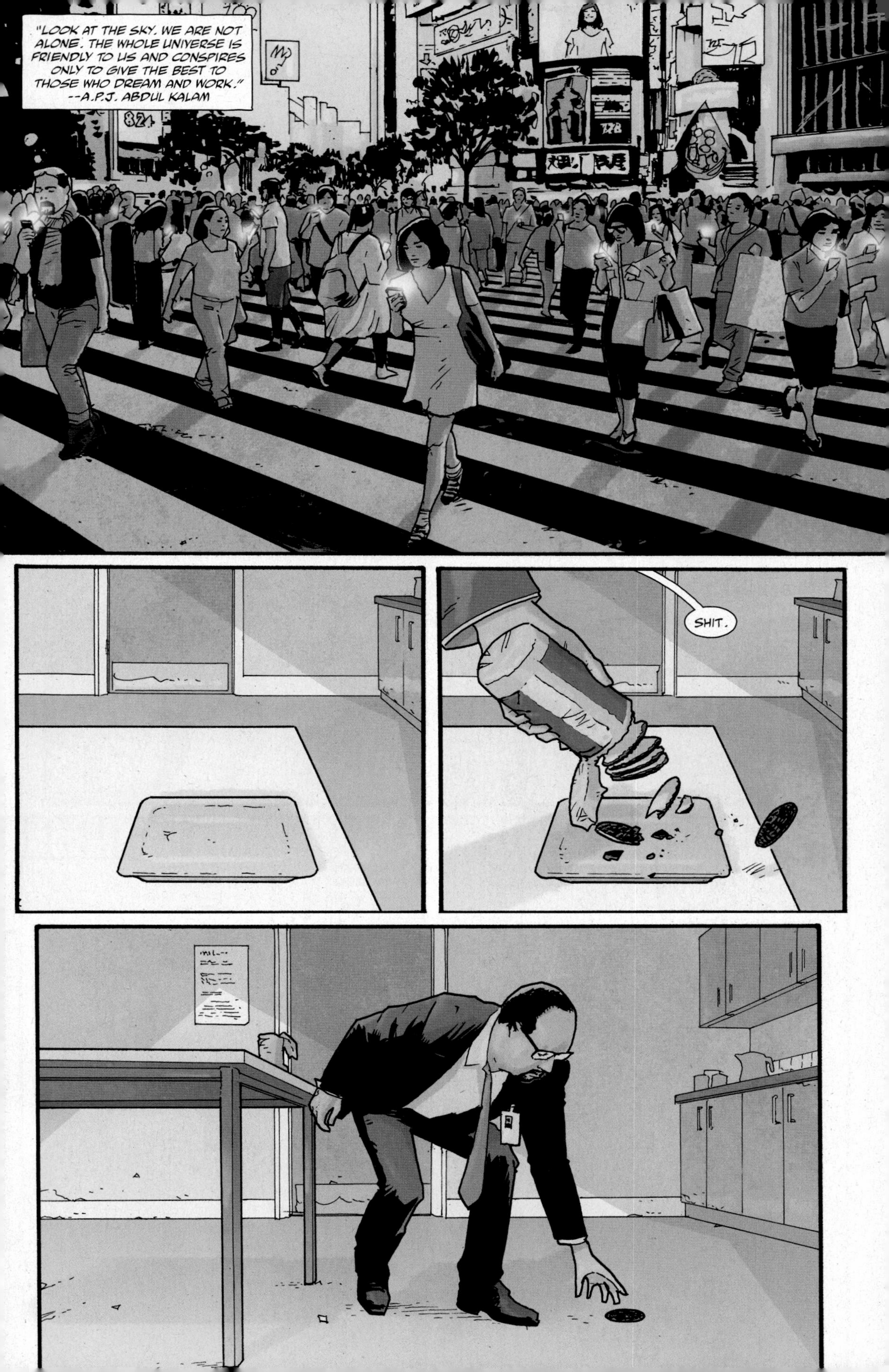
"LOOK AT THE SKY. WE ARE NOT ALONE. THE WHOLE UNIVERSE IS FRIENDLY TO US AND CONSPIRES ONLY TO GIVE THE BEST TO THOSE WHO DREAM AND WORK."
--A.P.J. ABDUL KALAM
SHIT.

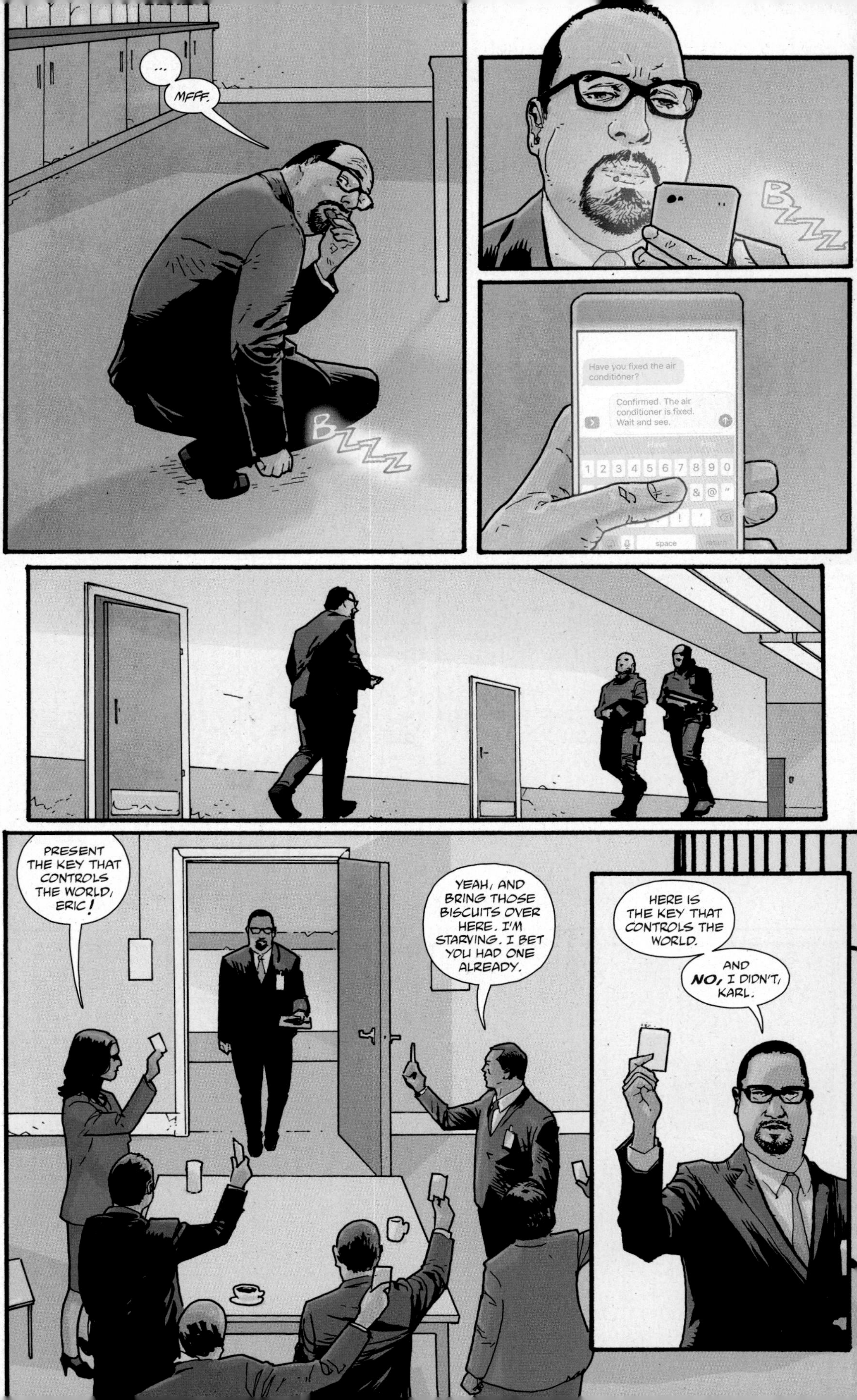
...
MFFF.
BZZZ
BZZZ
Have you fixed the air conditioner?
Confirmed. The air conditioner is fixed. Wait and see.
PRESENT THE KEY THAT CONTROLS THE WORLD, ERIC!
YEAH, AND BRING THOSE BISCUITS OVER HERE. I'M STARVING. I BET YOU HAD ONE ALREADY.
HERE IS THE KEY THAT CONTROLS THE WORLD.
AND NO, I DIDN'T, KARL.

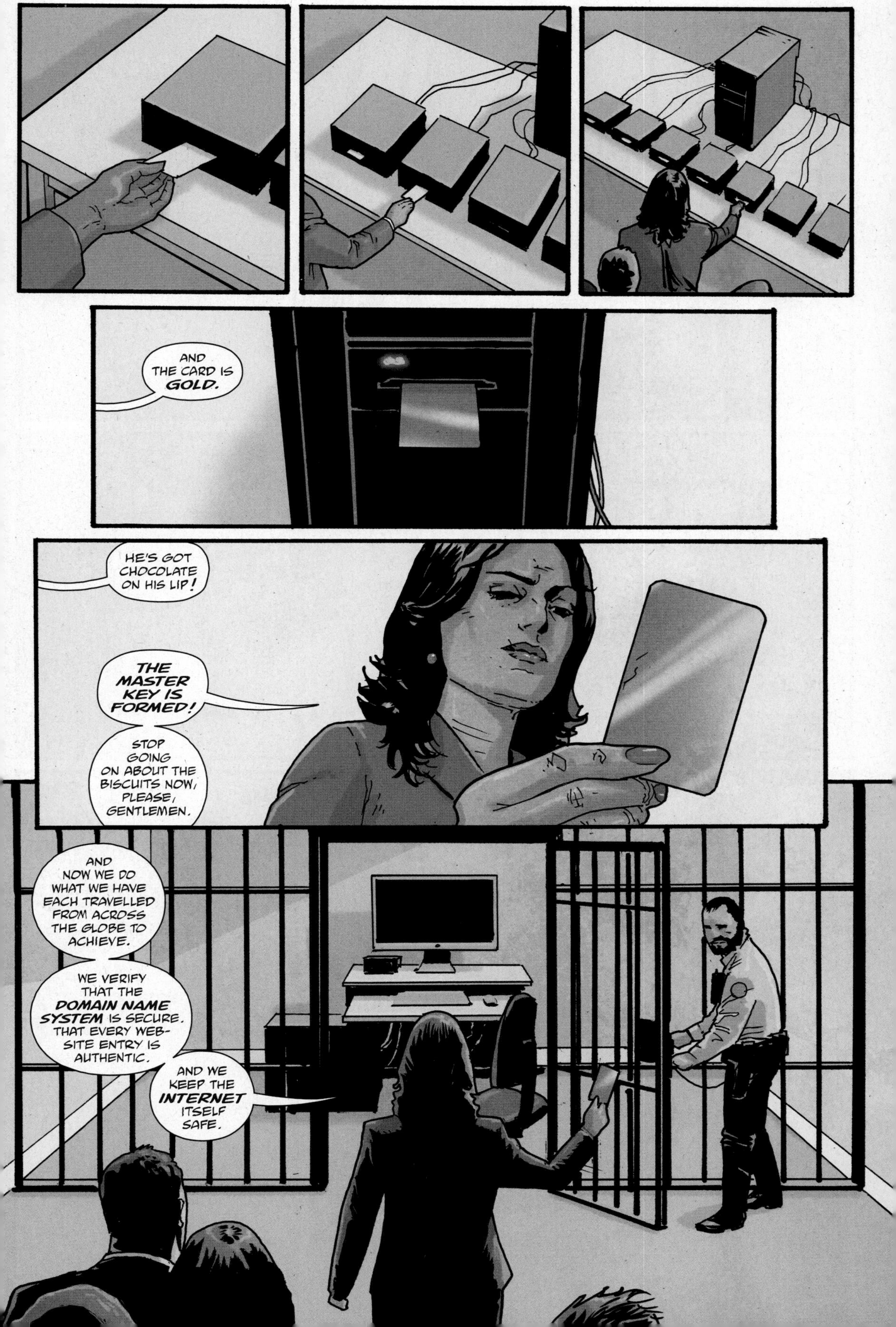
AND THE CARD IS GOLD.
HE'S GOT CHOCOLATE ON HIS LIP!
THE MASTER KEY IS FORMED!
STOP GOING ON ABOUT THE BISCUITS NOW, PLEASE, GENTLEMEN.
AND NOW WE DO WHAT WE HAVE EACH TRAVELLED FROM ACROSS THE GLOBE TO ACHIEVE.
WE VERIFY THAT THE DOMAIN NAME SYSTEM IS SECURE. THAT EVERY WEB-SITE ENTRY IS AUTHENTIC.
AND WE KEEP THE INTERNET ITSELF SAFE.

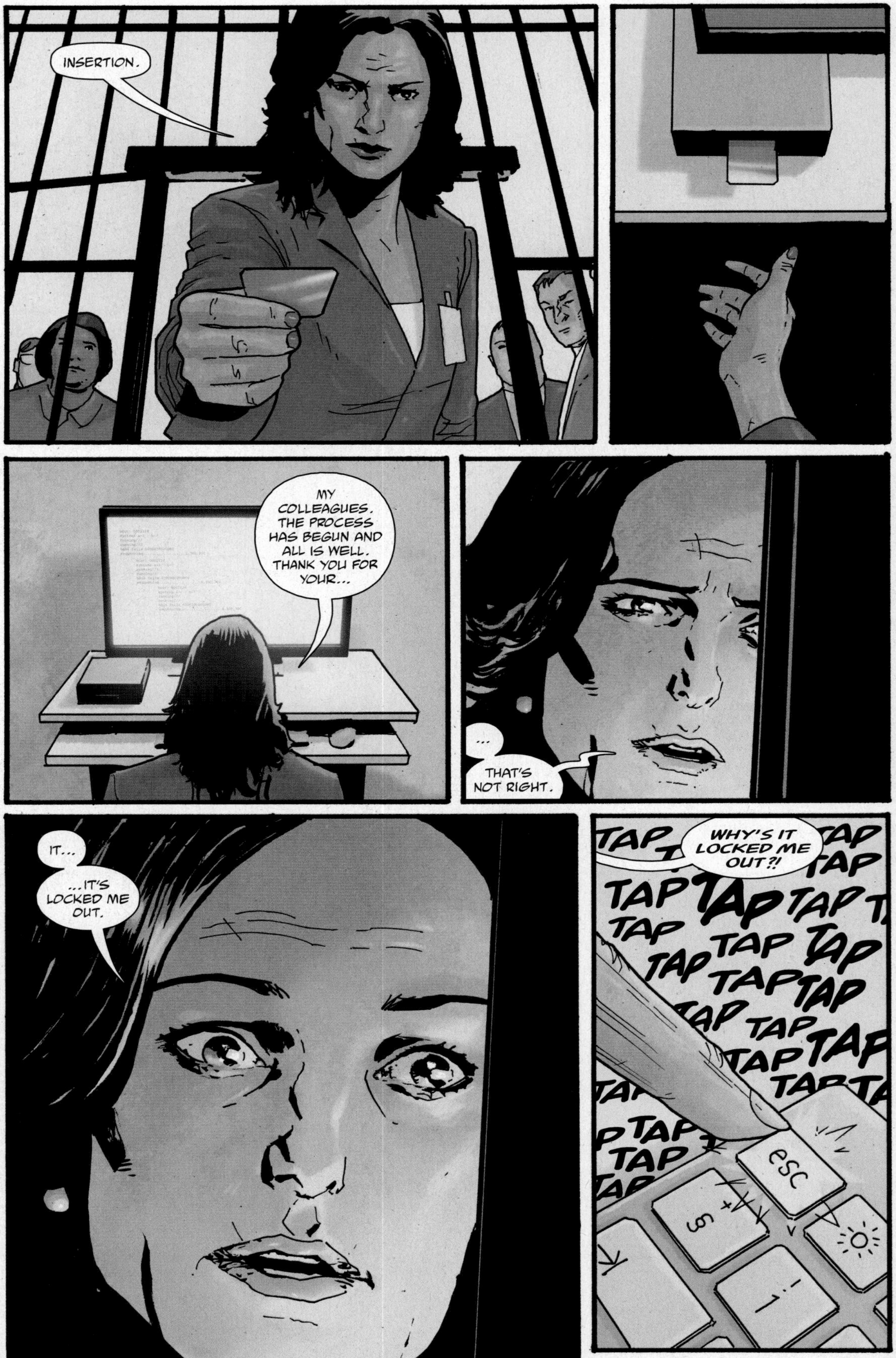
INSERTION.
MY COLLEAGUES. THE PROCESS HAS BEGUN AND ALL IS WELL. THANK YOU FOR YOUR...
...
THAT'S NOT RIGHT.
IT...
...IT'S LOCKED ME OUT.
WHY'S IT LOCKED ME OUT?!
TAP TAP TAP TAP TAP TAP TAP TAP TAP TAP TAP TAP TAP TAP TAP TAP TAP TAP TAP TAP TAP TAP
esc

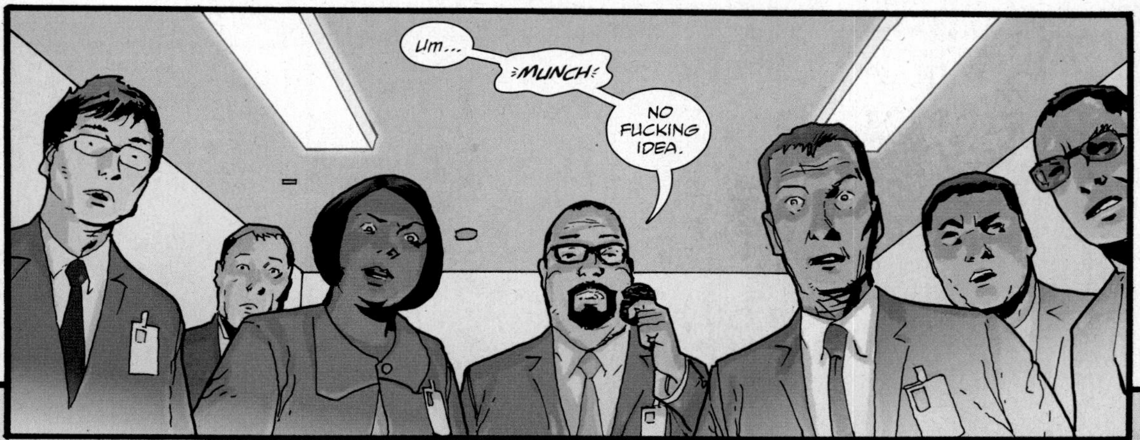
UM...
MUNCH
NO FUCKING IDEA.

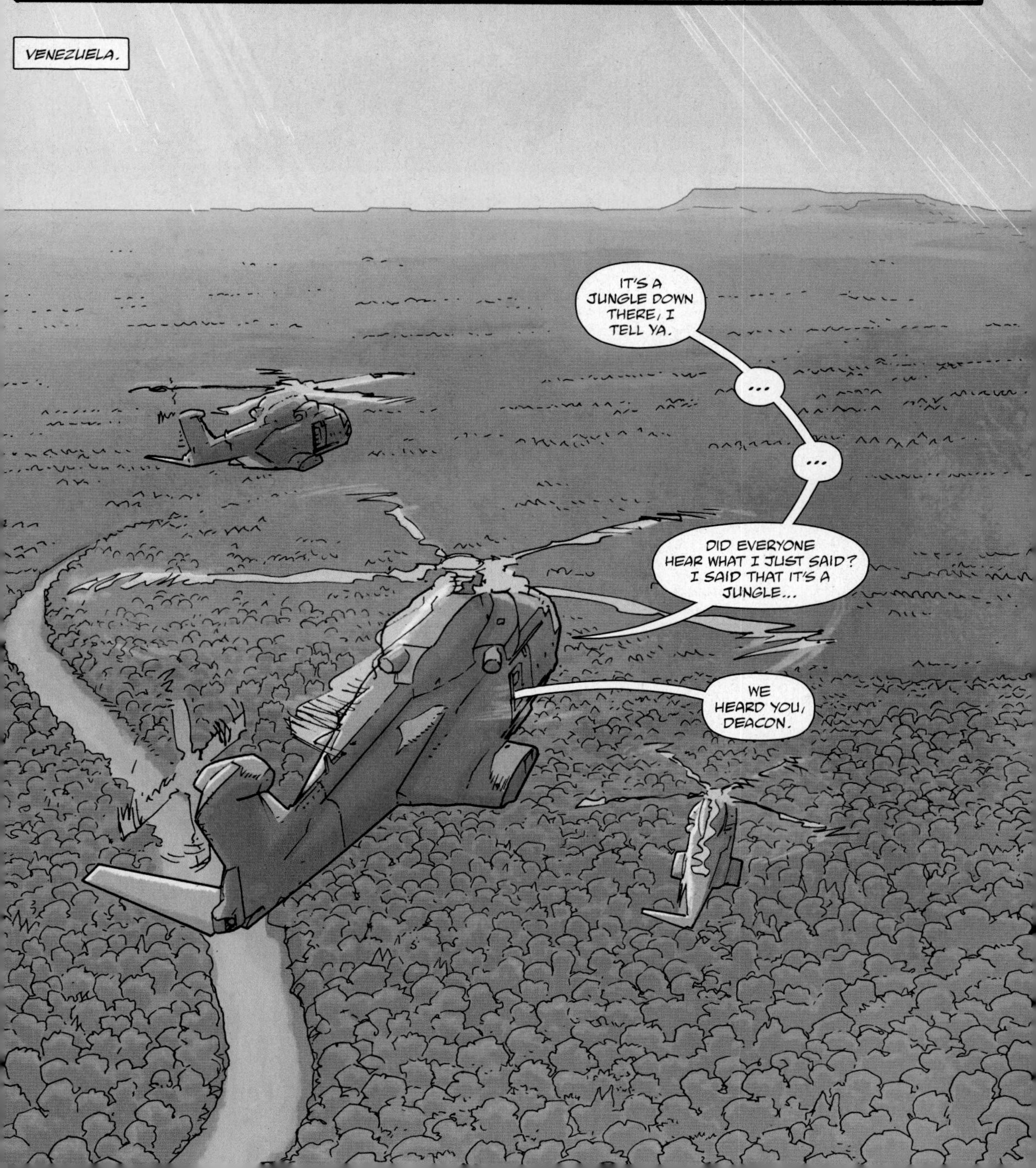
VENEZUELA.
IT'S A JUNGLE DOWN THERE, I TELL YA.
...
...
DID EVERYONE HEAR WHAT I JUST SAID? I SAID THAT IT'S A JUNGLE...
WE HEARD YOU, DEACON.

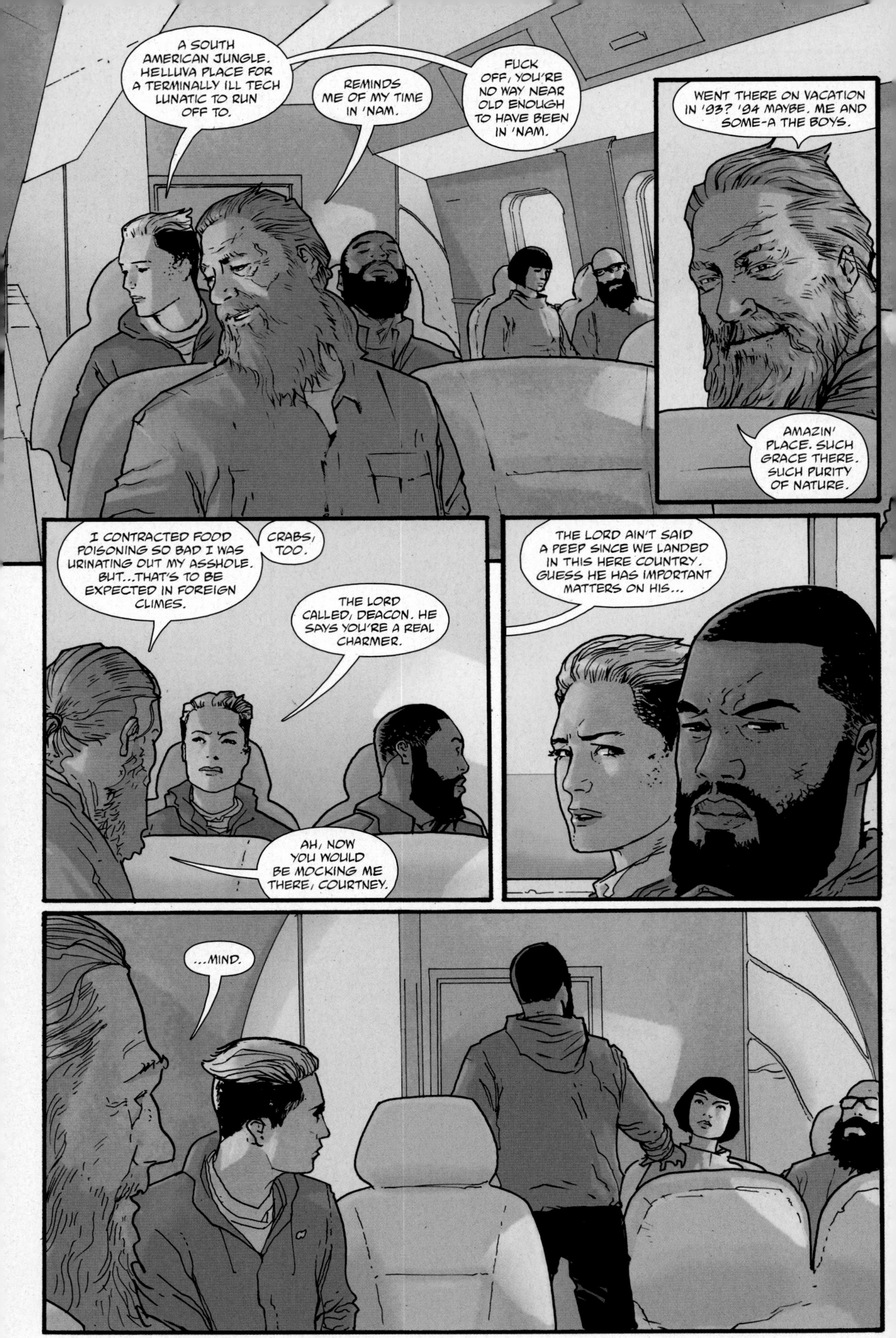
A SOUTH AMERICAN JUNGLE. HELLUVA PLACE FOR A TERMINALLY ILL TECH LUNATIC TO RUN OFF TO.
REMINDS ME OF MY TIME IN 'NAM.
FUCK OFF, YOU'RE NO WAY NEAR OLD ENOUGH TO HAVE BEEN IN 'NAM.
WENT THERE ON VACATION IN '93? '94 MAYBE. ME AND SOME-A THE BOYS.
AMAZIN' PLACE. SUCH GRACE THERE. SUCH PURITY OF NATURE.
I CONTRACTED FOOD POISONING SO BAD I WAS URINATING OUT MY ASSHOLE. BUT...THAT'S TO BE EXPECTED IN FOREIGN CLIMES.
CRABS, TOO.
THE LORD CALLED, DEACON. HE SAYS YOU'RE A REAL CHARMER.
AH, NOW YOU WOULD BE MOCKING ME THERE, COURTNEY.
THE LORD AIN'T SAID A PEEP SINCE WE LANDED IN THIS HERE COUNTRY. GUESS HE HAS IMPORTANT MATTERS ON HIS...
...MIND.

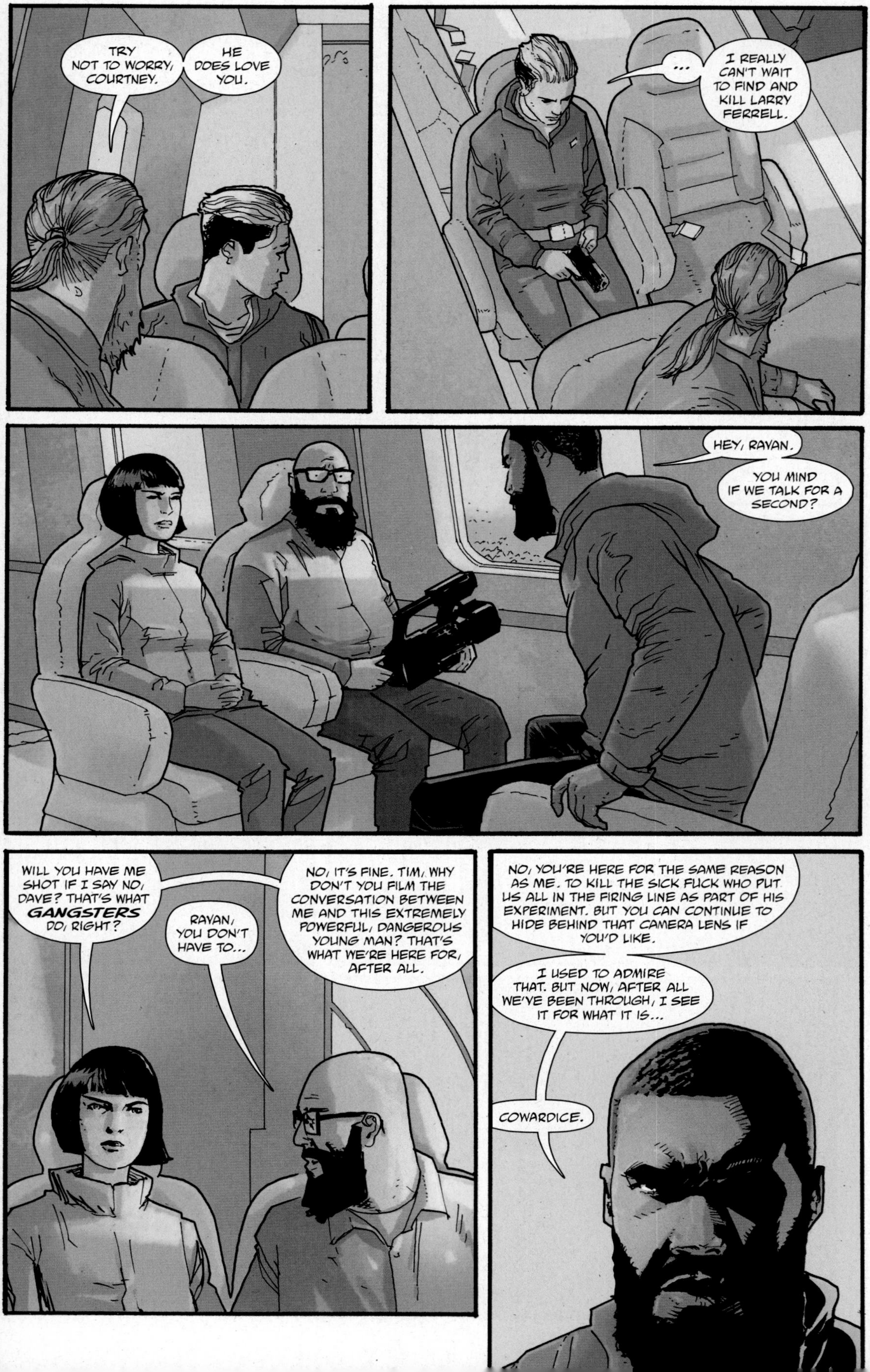
TRY NOT TO WORRY, COURTNEY.
HE DOES LOVE YOU.
...
I REALLY CAN'T WAIT TO FIND AND KILL LARRY FERRELL.
HEY, RAVAN.
YOU MIND IF WE TALK FOR A SECOND?
WILL YOU HAVE ME SHOT IF I SAY NO, DAVE? THAT'S WHAT GANGSTERS DO, RIGHT?
RAVAN, YOU DON'T HAVE TO...
NO, IT'S FINE. TIM, WHY DON'T YOU FILM THE CONVERSATION BETWEEN ME AND THIS EXTREMELY POWERFUL, DANGEROUS YOUNG MAN? THAT'S WHAT WE'RE HERE FOR, AFTER ALL.
NO, YOU'RE HERE FOR THE SAME REASON AS ME. TO KILL THE SICK FUCK WHO PUT US ALL IN THE FIRING LINE AS PART OF HIS EXPERIMENT. BUT YOU CAN CONTINUE TO HIDE BEHIND THAT CAMERA LENS IF YOU'D LIKE.
I USED TO ADMIRE THAT. BUT NOW, AFTER ALL WE'VE BEEN THROUGH, I SEE IT FOR WHAT IT IS...
COWARDICE.

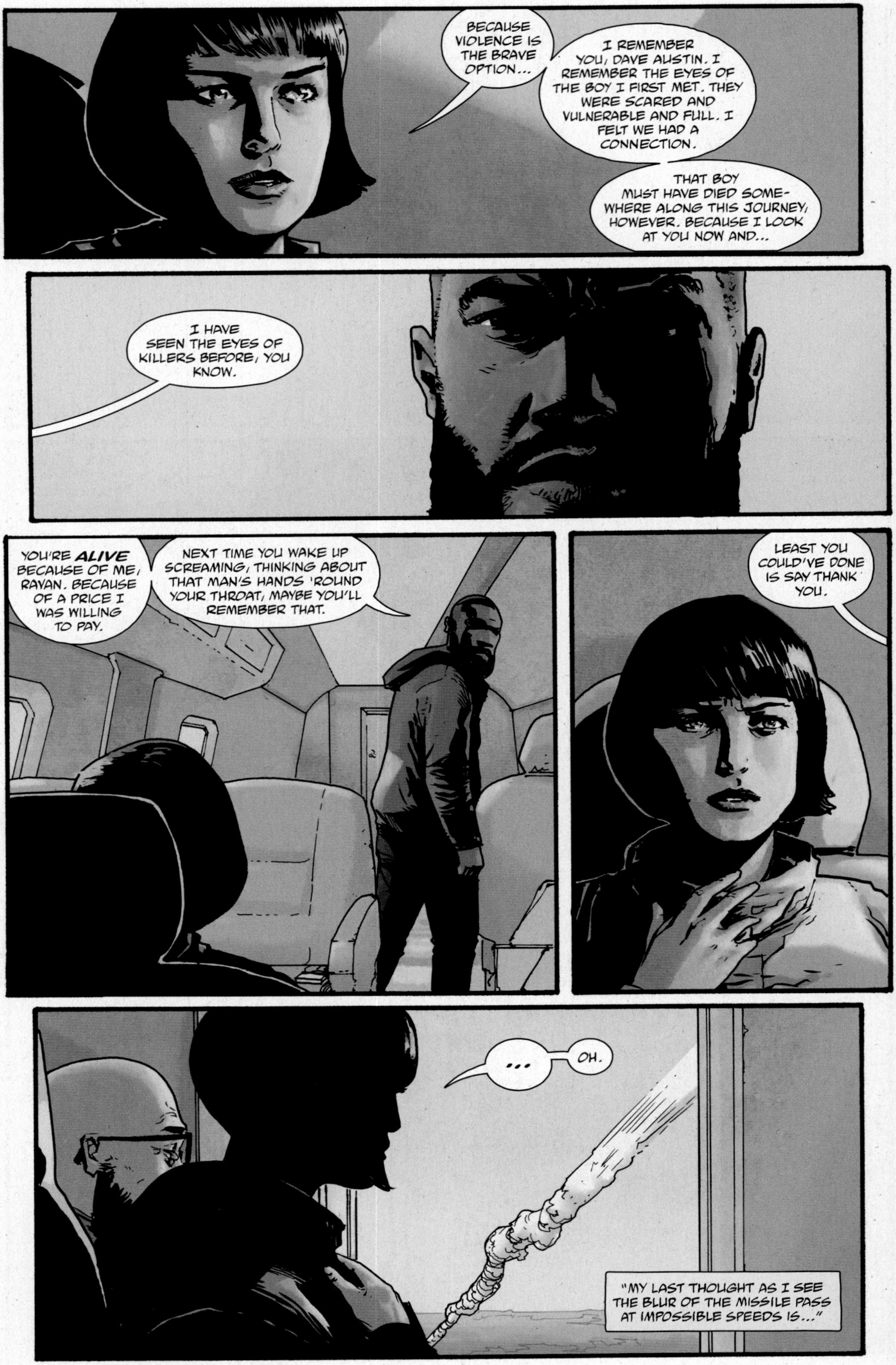
BECAUSE VIOLENCE IS THE BRAVE OPTION...
I REMEMBER YOU, DAVE AUSTIN. I REMEMBER THE EYES OF THE BOY I FIRST MET. THEY WERE SCARED AND VULNERABLE AND FULL. I FELT WE HAD A CONNECTION.
THAT BOY MUST HAVE DIED SOME-WHERE ALONG THIS JOURNEY, HOWEVER. BECAUSE I LOOK AT YOU NOW AND...
I HAVE SEEN THE EYES OF KILLERS BEFORE, YOU KNOW.
YOU'RE ***ALIVE*** BECAUSE OF ME, RAYAN. BECAUSE OF A PRICE I WAS WILLING TO PAY.
NEXT TIME YOU WAKE UP SCREAMING, THINKING ABOUT THAT MAN'S HANDS 'ROUND YOUR THROAT, MAYBE YOU'LL REMEMBER THAT.
LEAST YOU COULD'VE DONE IS SAY THANK YOU.
...
OH.
"MY LAST THOUGHT AS I SEE THE BLUR OF THE MISSILE PASS AT IMPOSSIBLE SPEEDS IS..."

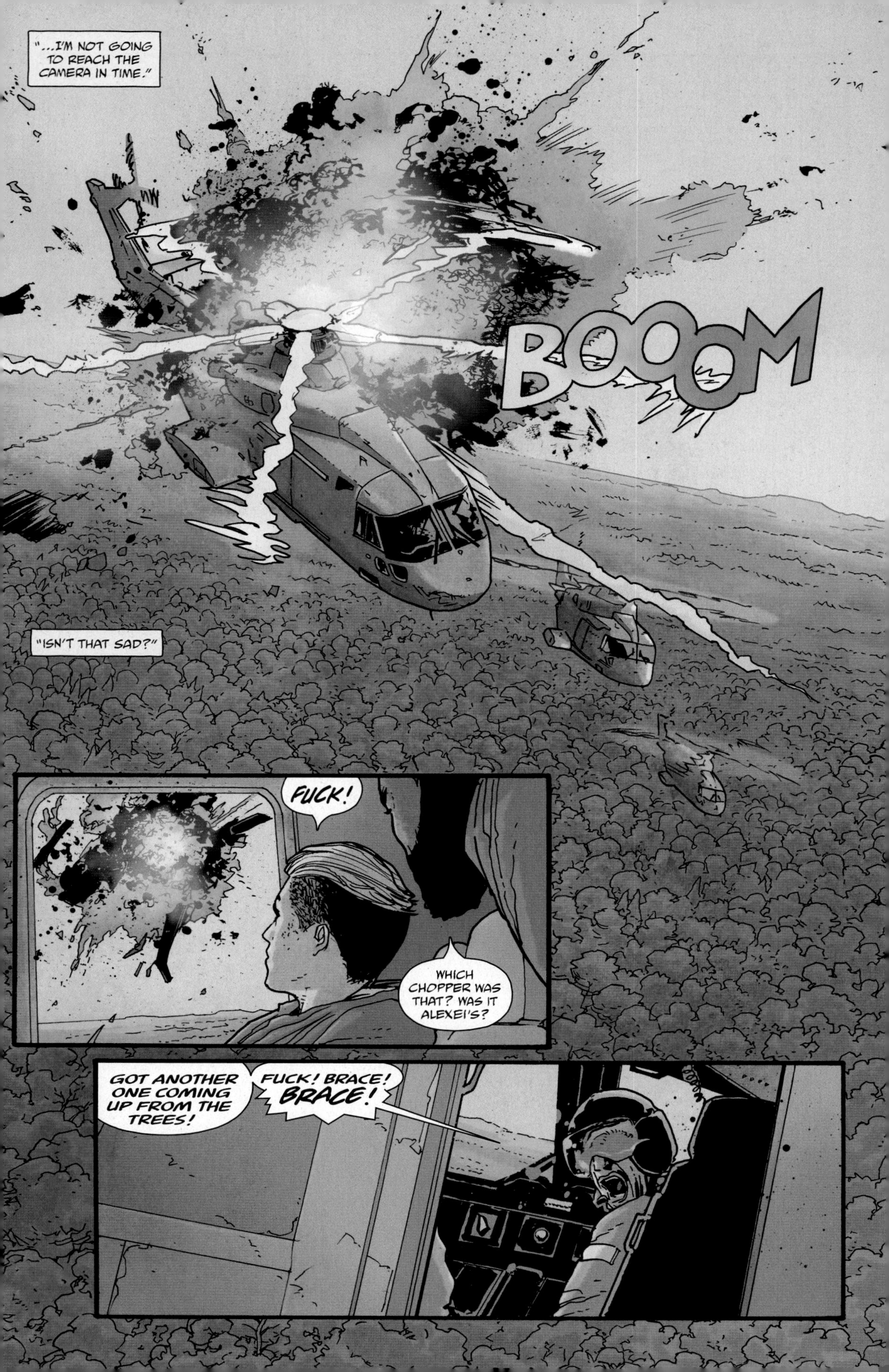
"...I'M NOT GOING TO REACH THE CAMERA IN TIME."
BOOOM
"ISN'T THAT SAD?"
FUCK!
WHICH CHOPPER WAS THAT? WAS IT ALEXEI'S?
GOT ANOTHER ONE COMING UP FROM THE TREES!
FUCK! BRACE! BRACE!

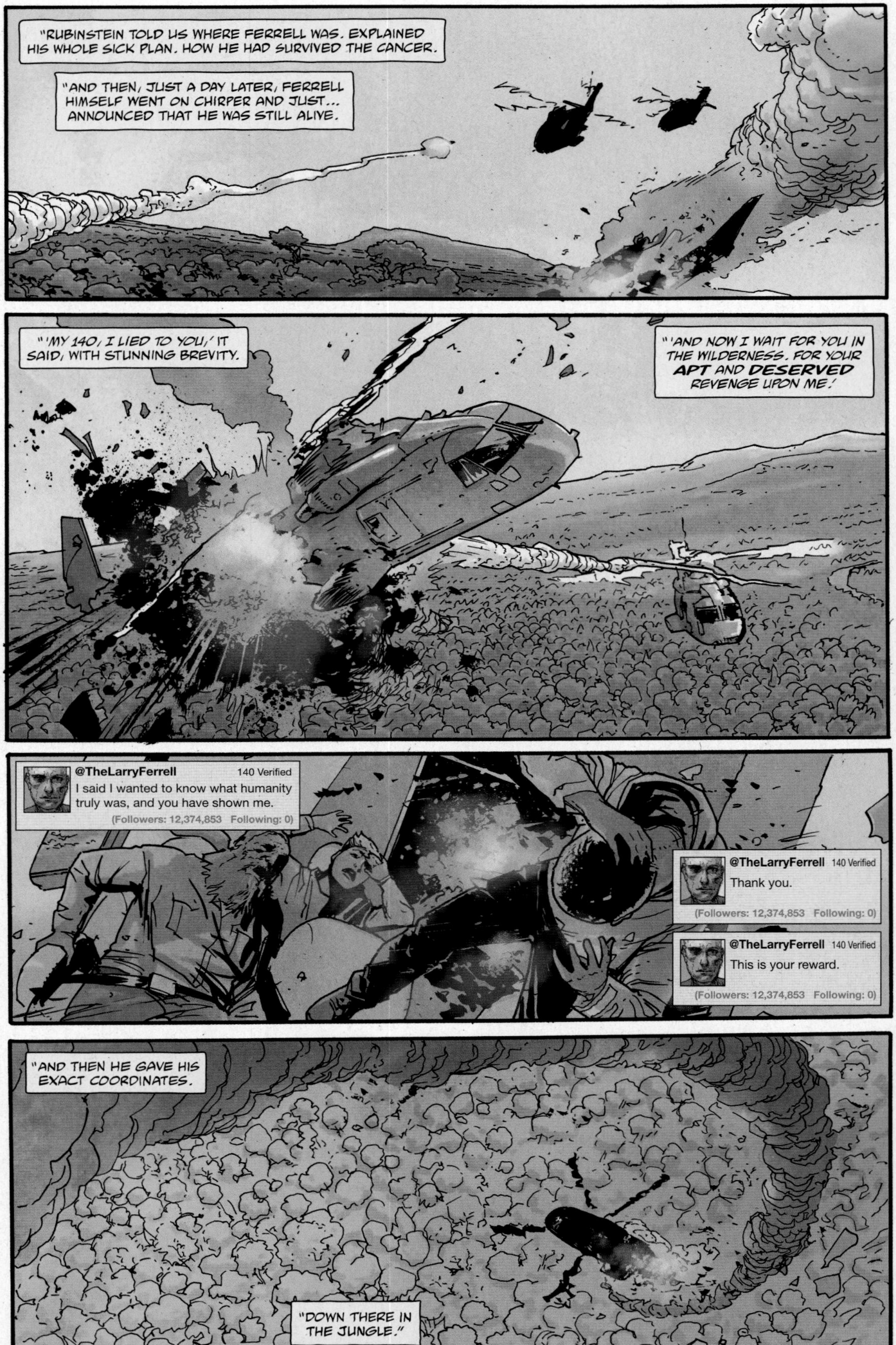
"RUBINSTEIN TOLD US WHERE FERRELL WAS. EXPLAINED HIS WHOLE SICK PLAN. HOW HE HAD SURVIVED THE CANCER.
"AND THEN, JUST A DAY LATER, FERRELL HIMSELF WENT ON CHIRPER AND JUST... ANNOUNCED THAT HE WAS STILL ALIVE.
"'MY 140, I LIED TO YOU,' IT SAID, WITH STUNNING BREVITY.
"'AND NOW I WAIT FOR YOU IN THE WILDERNESS. FOR YOUR APT AND DESERVED REVENGE UPON ME.'
@TheLarryFerrell 140 Verified
I said I wanted to know what humanity truly was, and you have shown me.
(Followers: 12,374,853 Following: 0)
@TheLarryFerrell 140 Verified
Thank you.
(Followers: 12,374,853 Following: 0)
@TheLarryFerrell 140 Verified
This is your reward.
(Followers: 12,374,853 Following: 0)
"AND THEN HE GAVE HIS EXACT COORDINATES.
"DOWN THERE IN THE JUNGLE."

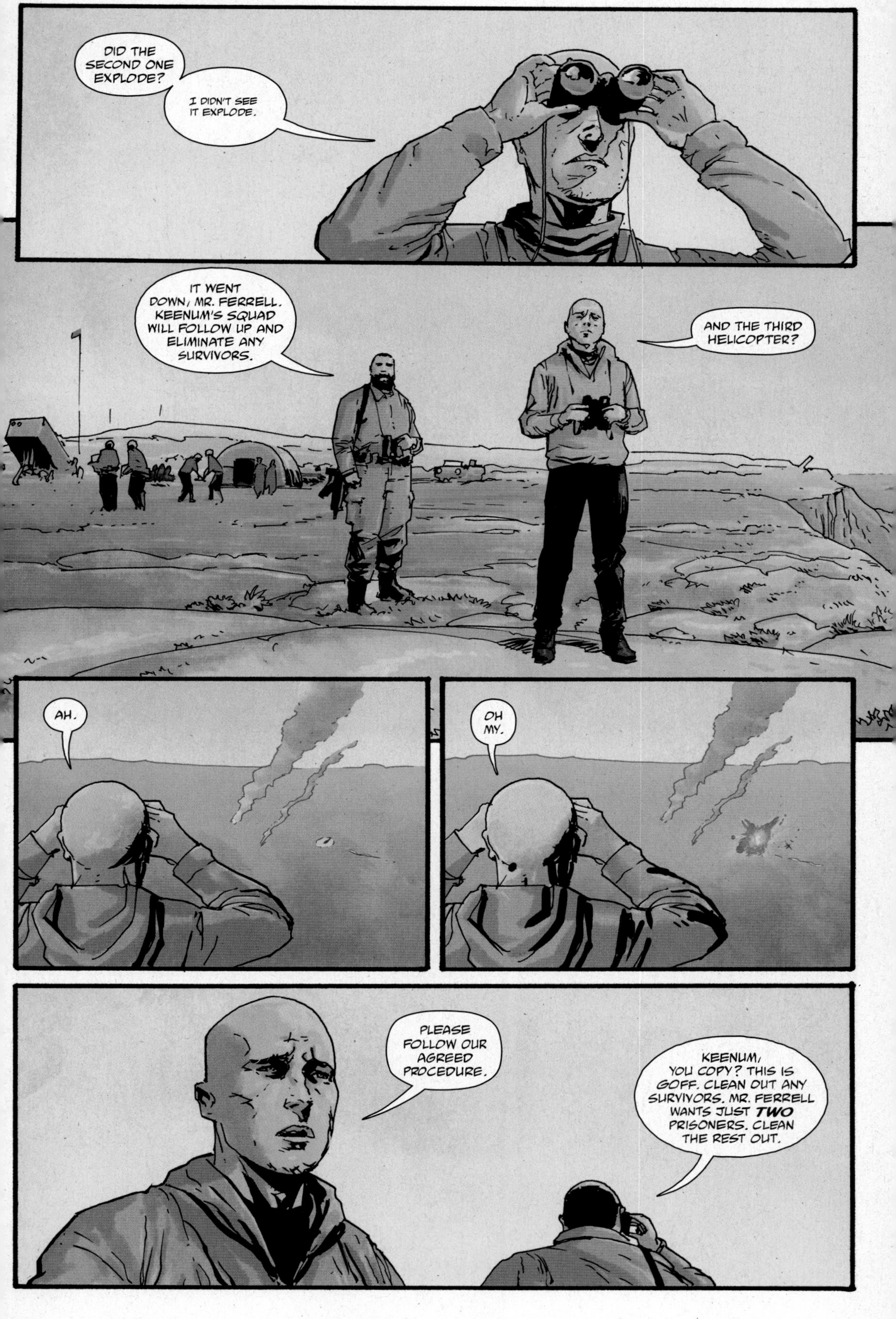
DID THE SECOND ONE EXPLODE?
I DIDN'T SEE IT EXPLODE.
IT WENT DOWN, MR. FERRELL. KEENUM'S SQUAD WILL FOLLOW UP AND ELIMINATE ANY SURVIVORS.
AND THE THIRD HELICOPTER?
AH.
OH MY.
PLEASE FOLLOW OUR AGREED PROCEDURE.
KEENUM, YOU COPY? THIS IS GOFF. CLEAN OUT ANY SURVIVORS. MR. FERRELL WANTS JUST **TWO** PRISONERS. CLEAN THE REST OUT.

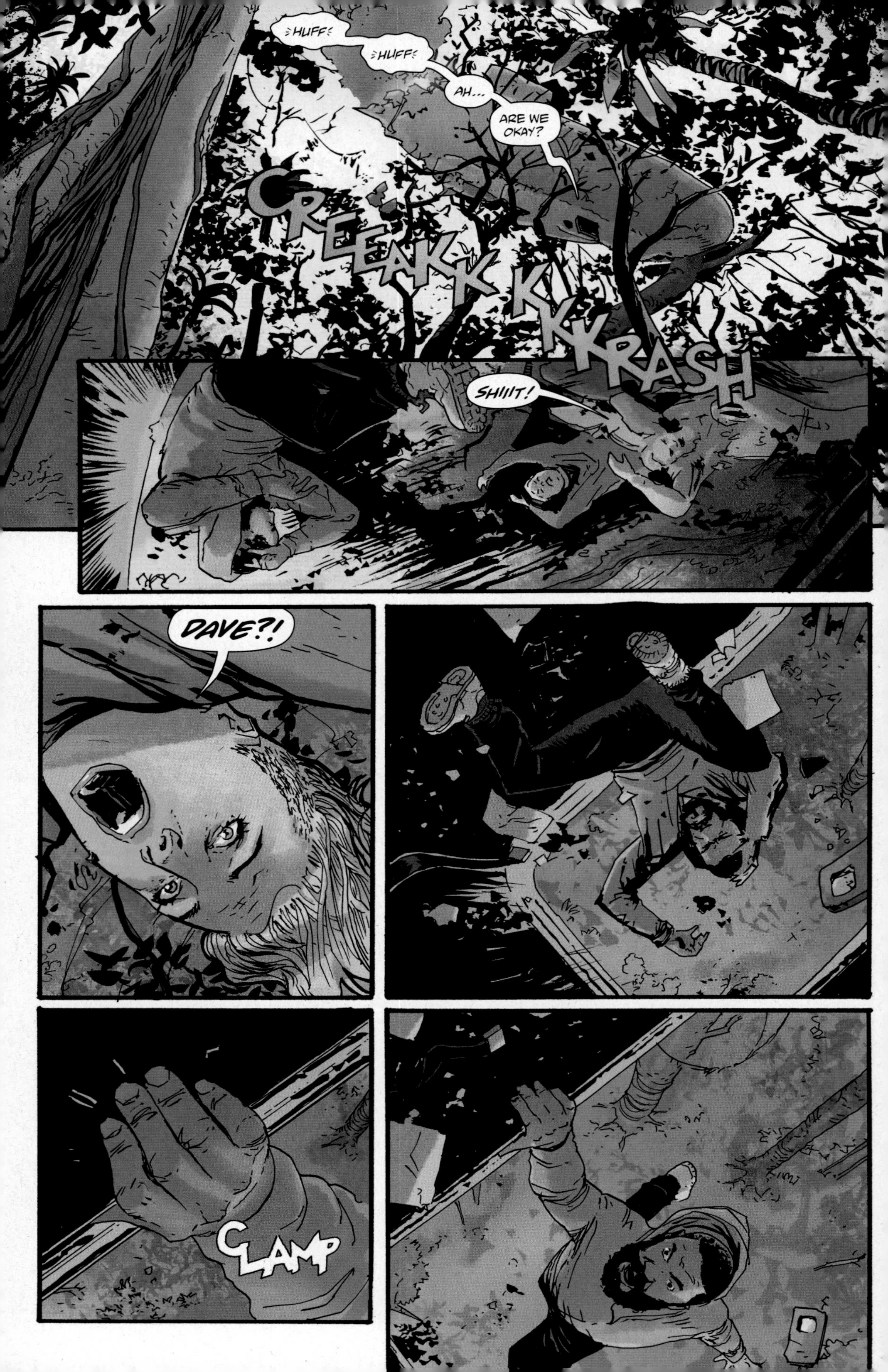
HUFF
HUFF
AH...
ARE WE OKAY?
CREEAKK KKKRASH
SHIIIT!
DAVE?!
CLAMP

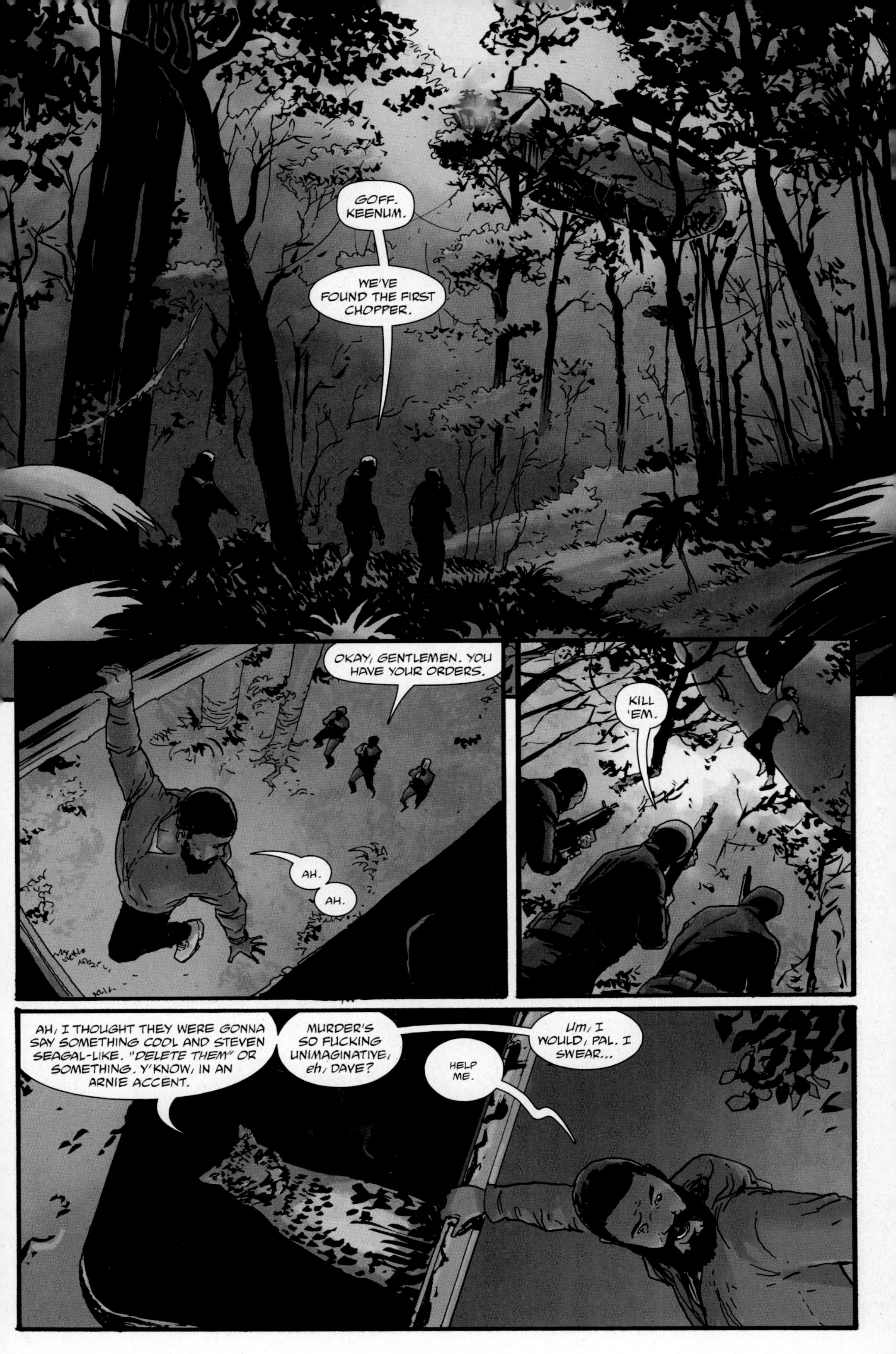
GOFF. KEENUM.
WE'VE FOUND THE FIRST CHOPPER.
OKAY, GENTLEMEN. YOU HAVE YOUR ORDERS.
AH.
AH.
KILL 'EM.
AH, I THOUGHT THEY WERE GONNA SAY SOMETHING COOL AND STEVEN SEAGAL-LIKE. "DELETE THEM" OR SOMETHING. Y'KNOW, IN AN ARNIE ACCENT.
MURDER'S SO FUCKING UNIMAGINATIVE, eh, DAVE?
HELP ME.
Um, I WOULD, PAL. I SWEAR...

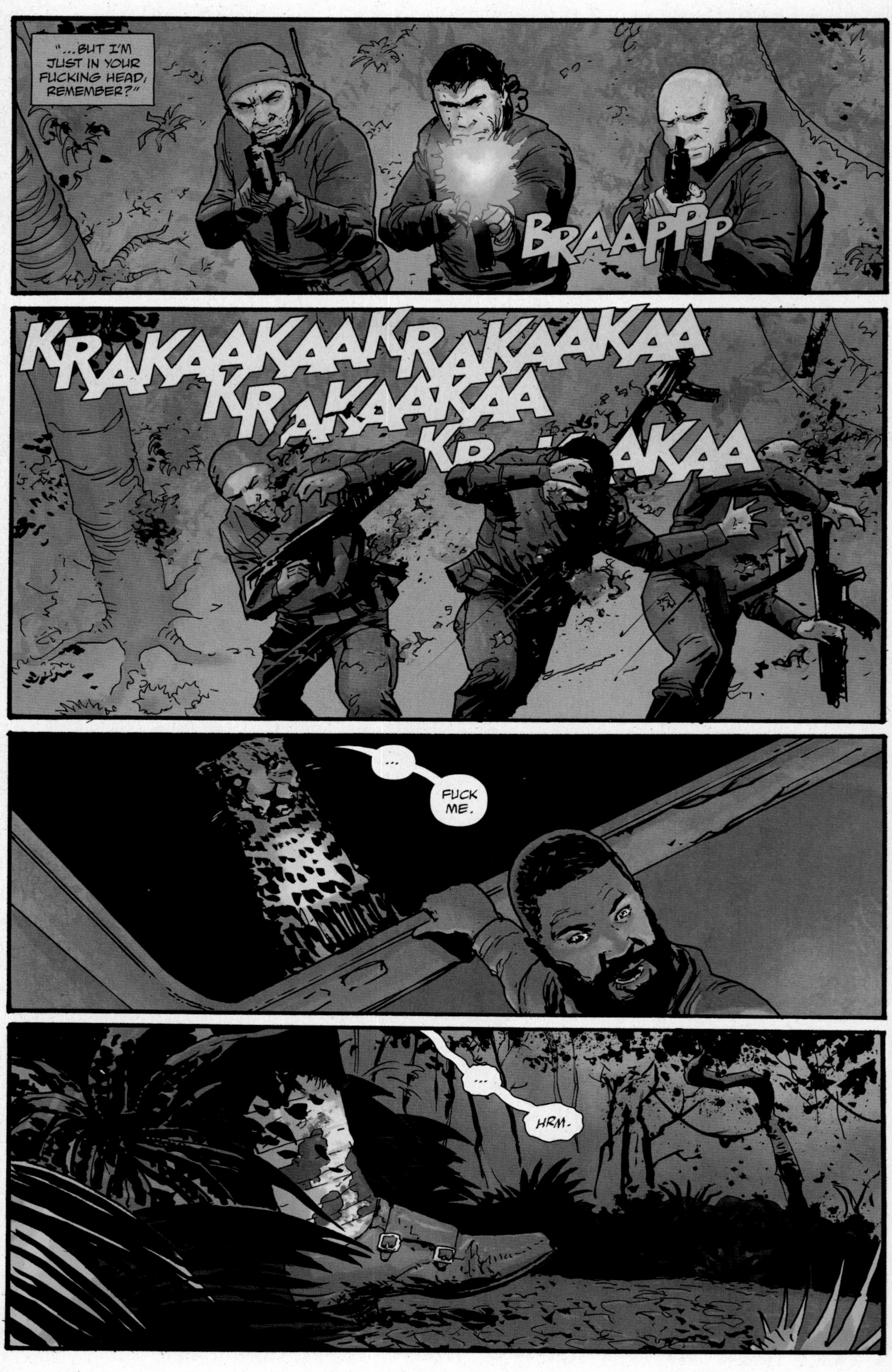
"...BUT I'M JUST IN YOUR FUCKING HEAD, REMEMBER?"
BRAAPPP
KRAKAAKAAKRAKAAKAA
KRAKAAKAA
...
FUCK ME.
...
HRM.

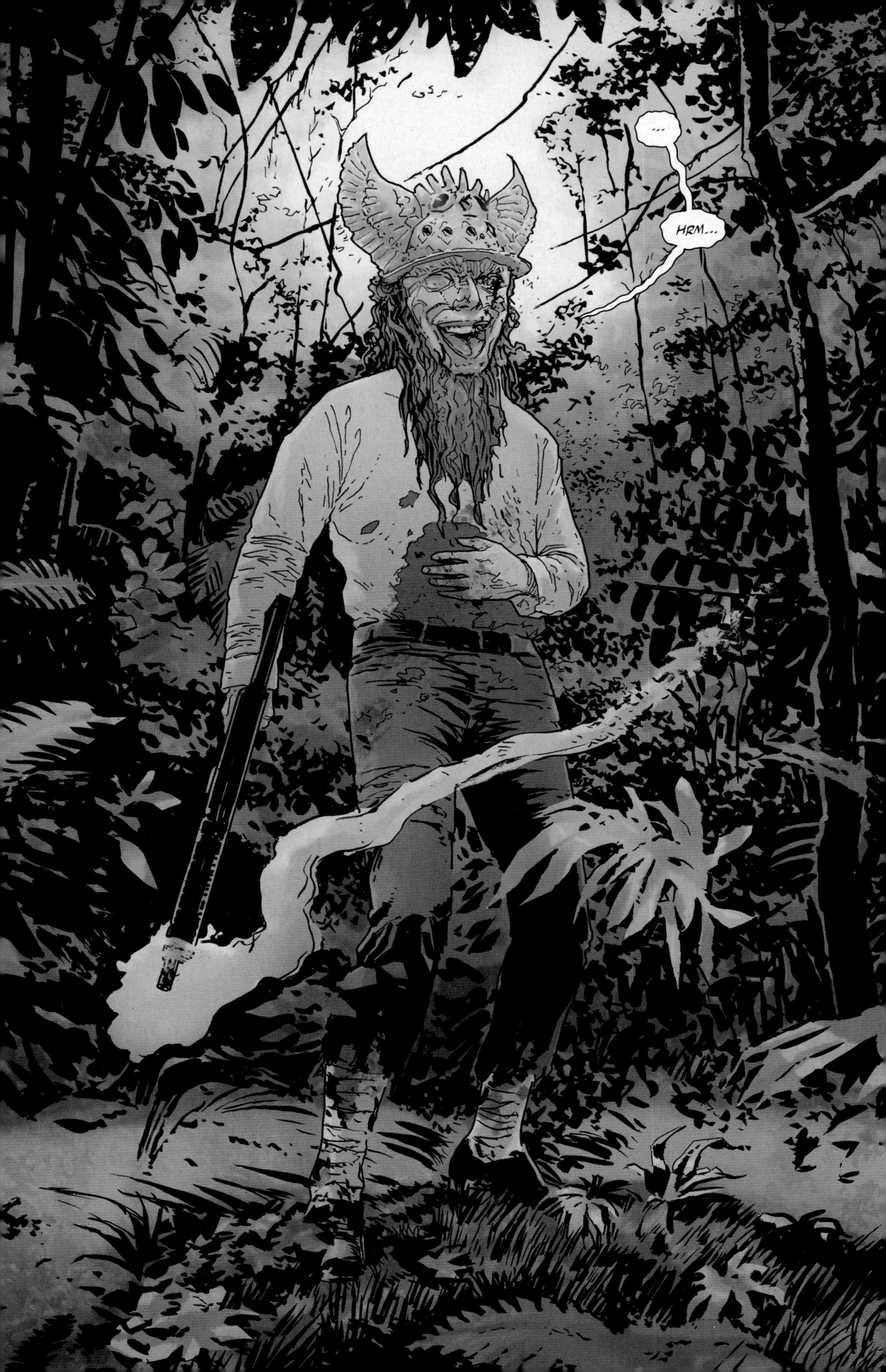
...
HRM...

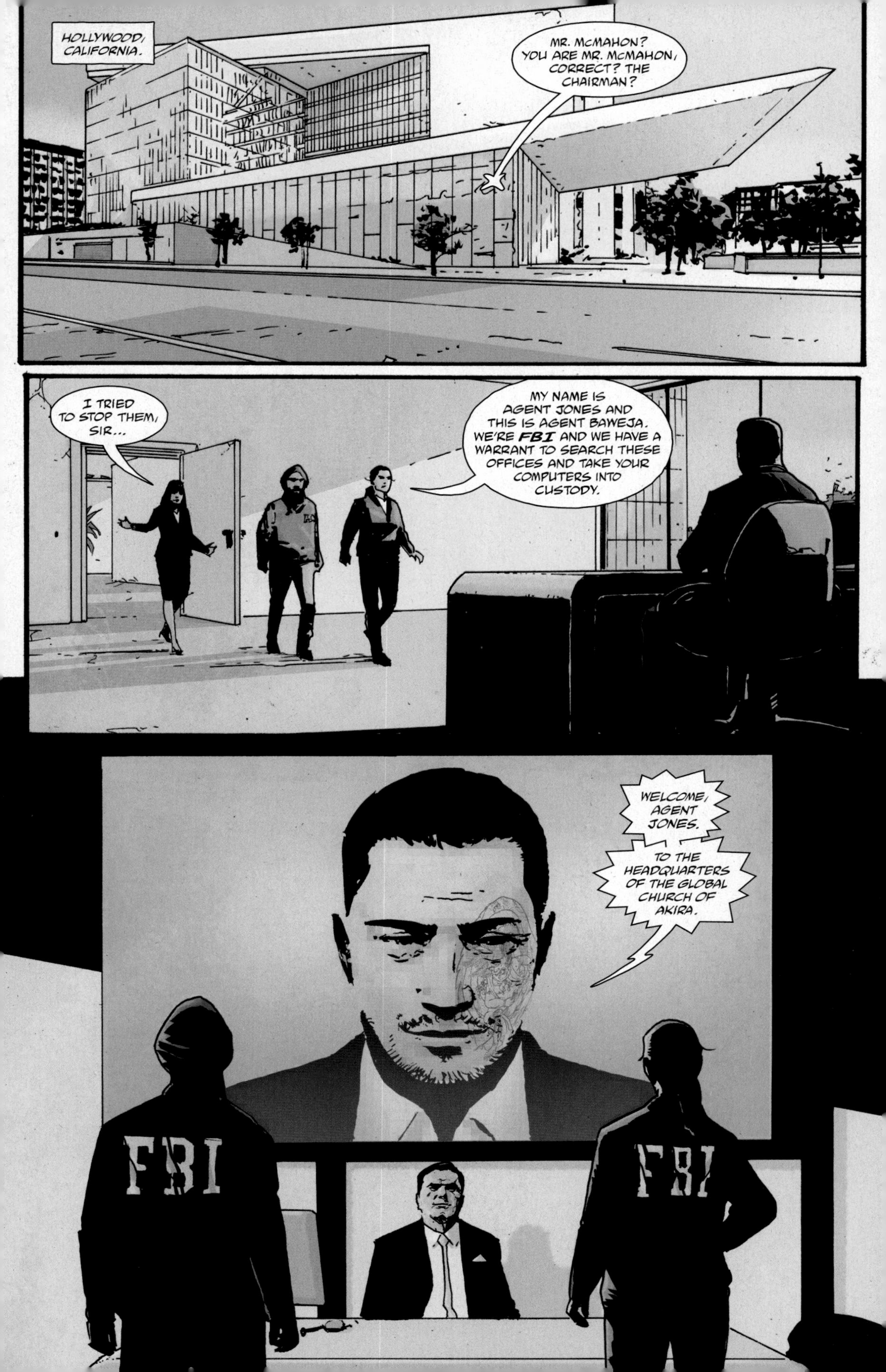
HOLLYWOOD, CALIFORNIA.
MR. McMAHON? YOU ARE MR. McMAHON, CORRECT? THE CHAIRMAN?
I TRIED TO STOP THEM, SIR...
MY NAME IS AGENT JONES AND THIS IS AGENT BAWEJA. WE'RE FBI AND WE HAVE A WARRANT TO SEARCH THESE OFFICES AND TAKE YOUR COMPUTERS INTO CUSTODY.
WELCOME, AGENT JONES.
TO THE HEADQUARTERS OF THE GLOBAL CHURCH OF AKIRA.
FBI
FBI

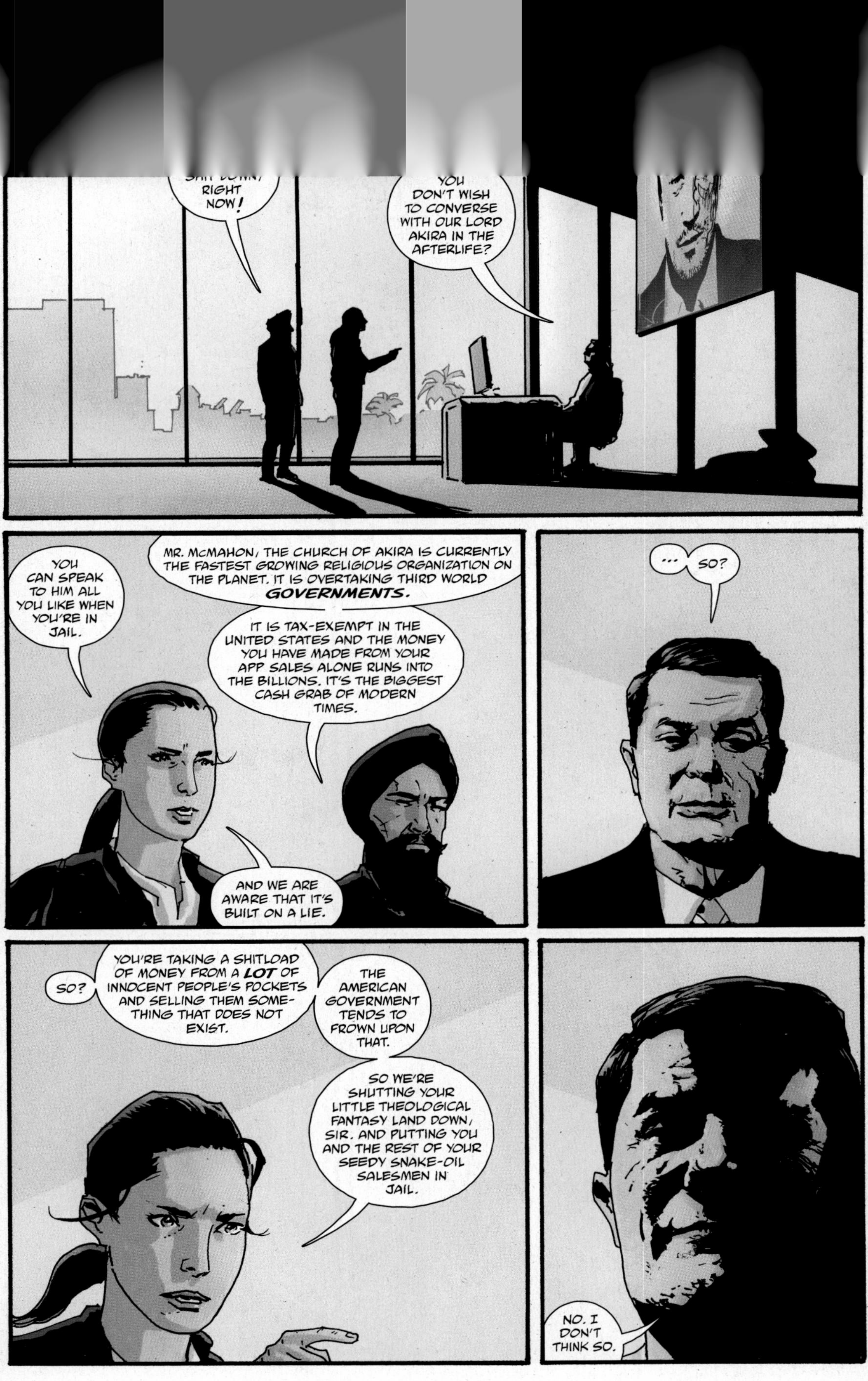
RIGHT NOW!
YOU DON'T WISH TO CONVERSE WITH OUR LORD AKIRA IN THE AFTERLIFE?
MR. McMAHON, THE CHURCH OF AKIRA IS CURRENTLY THE FASTEST GROWING RELIGIOUS ORGANIZATION ON THE PLANET. IT IS OVERTAKING THIRD WORLD GOVERNMENTS.
YOU CAN SPEAK TO HIM ALL YOU LIKE WHEN YOU'RE IN JAIL.
IT IS TAX-EXEMPT IN THE UNITED STATES AND THE MONEY YOU HAVE MADE FROM YOUR APP SALES ALONE RUNS INTO THE BILLIONS. IT'S THE BIGGEST CASH GRAB OF MODERN TIMES.
AND WE ARE AWARE THAT IT'S BUILT ON A LIE.
...
SO?
YOU'RE TAKING A SHITLOAD OF MONEY FROM A LOT OF INNOCENT PEOPLE'S POCKETS AND SELLING THEM SOMETHING THAT DOES NOT EXIST.
SO?
THE AMERICAN GOVERNMENT TENDS TO FROWN UPON THAT.
SO WE'RE SHUTTING YOUR LITTLE THEOLOGICAL FANTASY LAND DOWN, SIR. AND PUTTING YOU AND THE REST OF YOUR SEEDY SNAKE-OIL SALESMEN IN JAIL.
NO. I DON'T THINK SO.

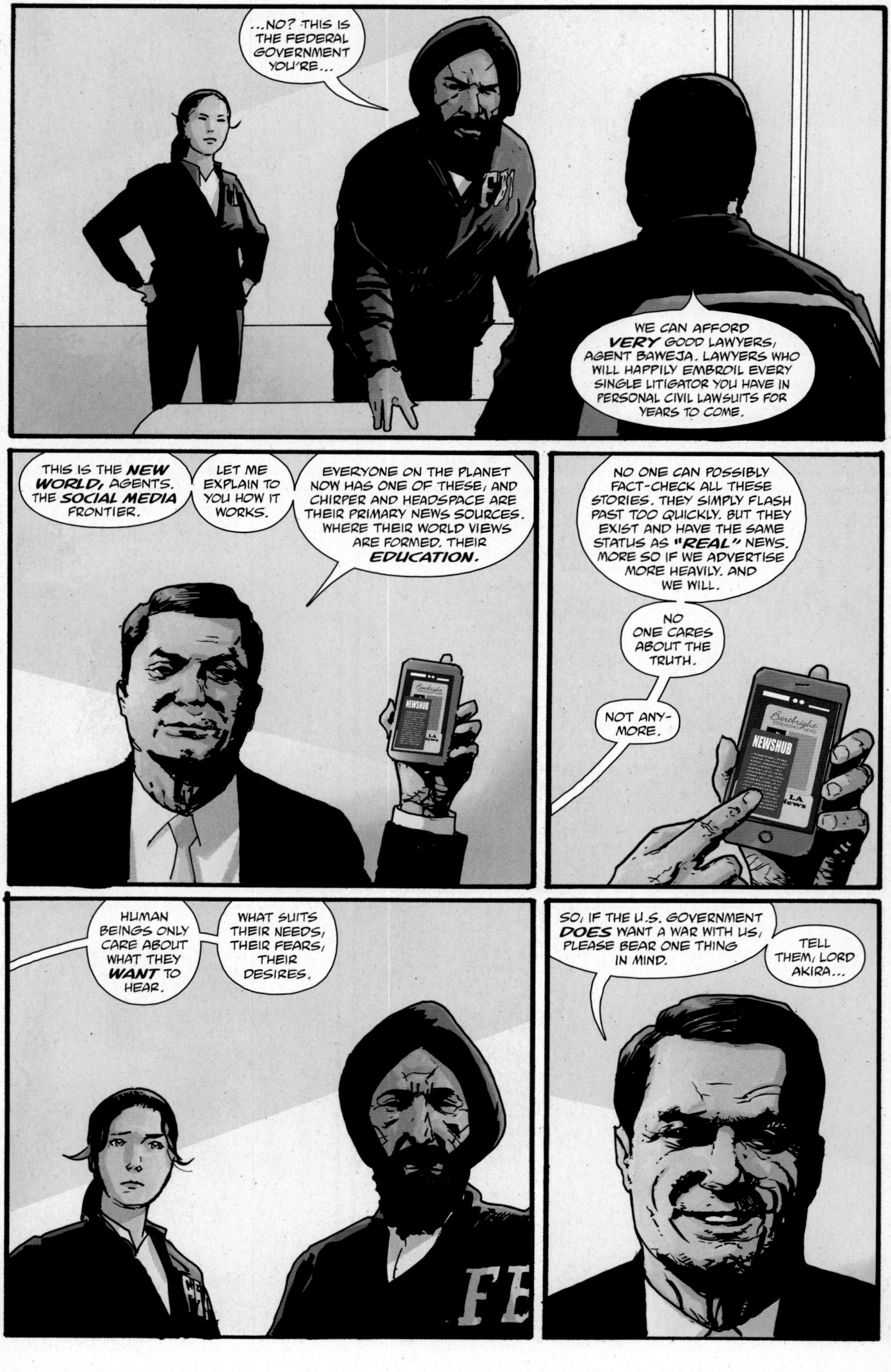
...NO? THIS IS THE FEDERAL GOVERNMENT YOU'RE...
WE CAN AFFORD VERY GOOD LAWYERS, AGENT BAWEJA. LAWYERS WHO WILL HAPPILY EMBROIL EVERY SINGLE LITIGATOR YOU HAVE IN PERSONAL CIVIL LAWSUITS FOR YEARS TO COME.
THIS IS THE NEW WORLD, AGENTS. THE SOCIAL MEDIA FRONTIER.
LET ME EXPLAIN TO YOU HOW IT WORKS.
EVERYONE ON THE PLANET NOW HAS ONE OF THESE, AND CHIRPER AND HEADSPACE ARE THEIR PRIMARY NEWS SOURCES. WHERE THEIR WORLD VIEWS ARE FORMED. THEIR EDUCATION.
NEWSHUB
NO ONE CAN POSSIBLY FACT-CHECK ALL THESE STORIES. THEY SIMPLY FLASH PAST TOO QUICKLY. BUT THEY EXIST AND HAVE THE SAME STATUS AS "REAL" NEWS. MORE SO IF WE ADVERTISE MORE HEAVILY. AND WE WILL.
NO ONE CARES ABOUT THE TRUTH.
NOT ANY-MORE.
Barebright STREAMING NEWS
NEWSHUB
LA News
HUMAN BEINGS ONLY CARE ABOUT WHAT THEY WANT TO HEAR.
WHAT SUITS THEIR NEEDS, THEIR FEARS, THEIR DESIRES.
SO, IF THE U.S. GOVERNMENT DOES WANT A WAR WITH US, PLEASE BEAR ONE THING IN MIND.
TELL THEM, LORD AKIRA...

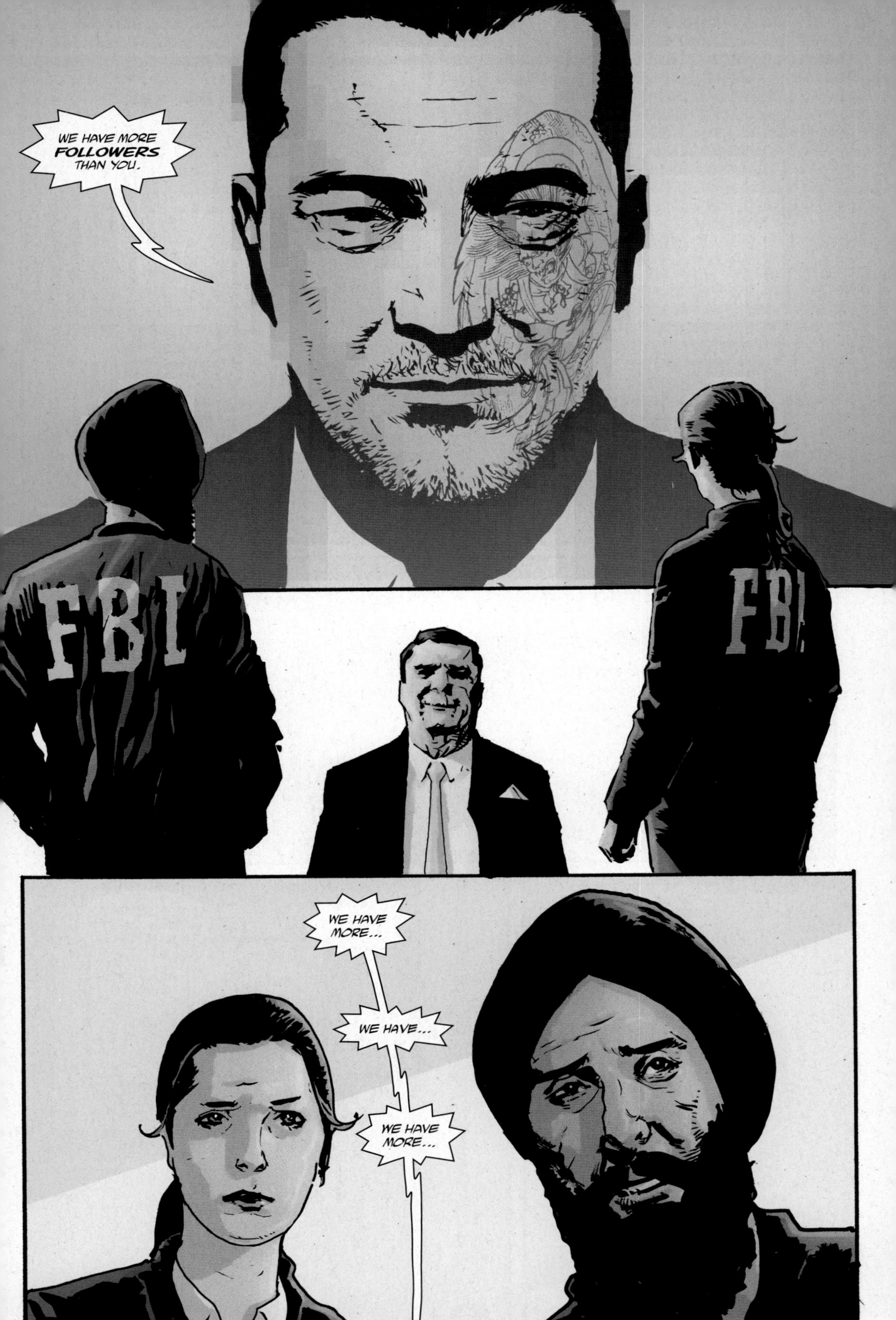
WE HAVE MORE **FOLLOWERS** THAN YOU.
FBI
FBI
WE HAVE MORE...
WE HAVE...
WE HAVE MORE...

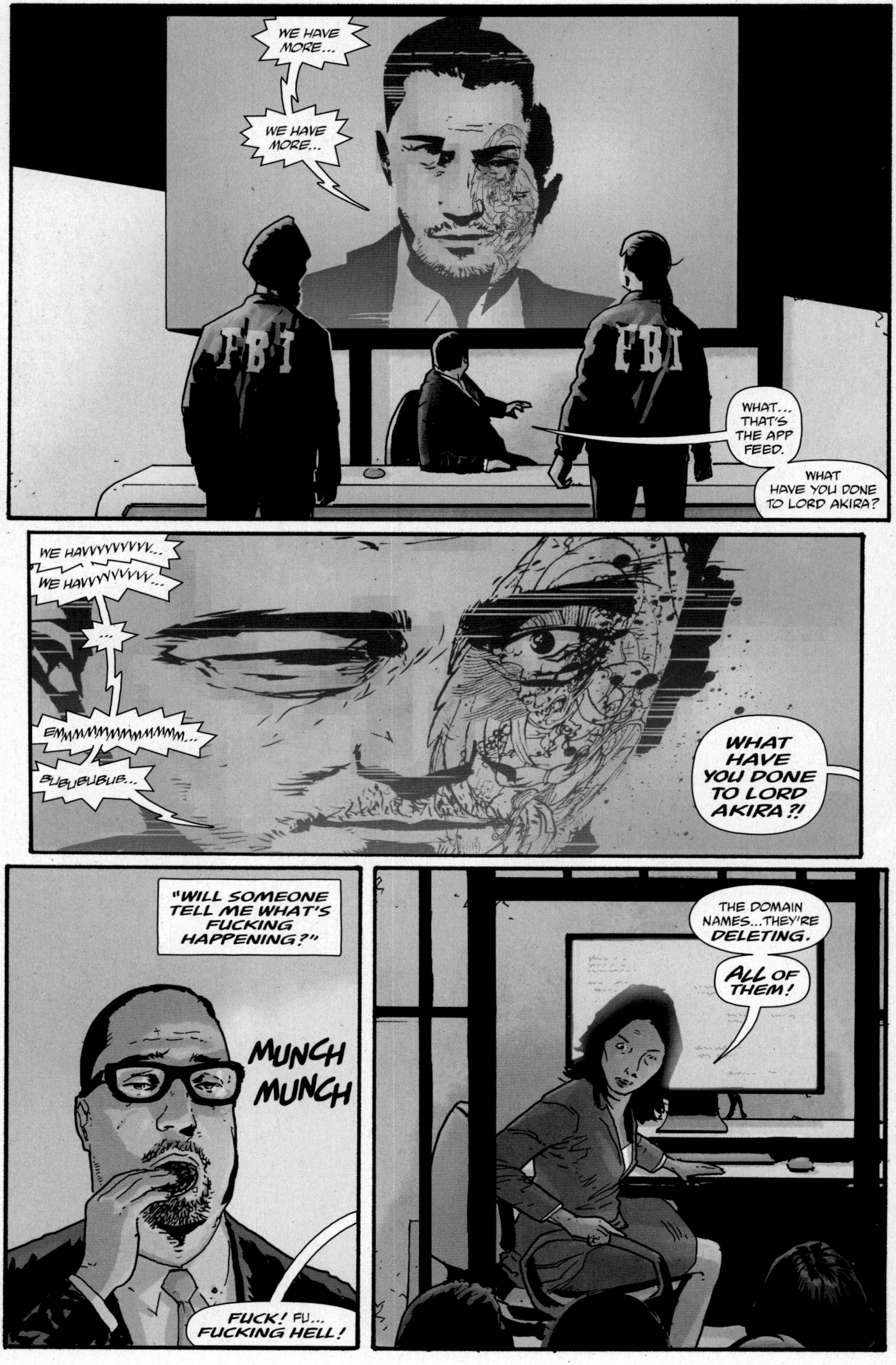
WE HAVE MORE...
WE HAVE MORE...
WHAT... THAT'S THE APP FEED.
WHAT HAVE YOU DONE TO LORD AKIRA?
WE HAVVVVVVVV...
WE HAVVVVVVVV...
...
EMMMMMMMMMMMM...
BUBUBUBUB...
WHAT HAVE YOU DONE TO LORD AKIRA?!
"WILL SOMEONE TELL ME WHAT'S FUCKING HAPPENING?"
MUNCH MUNCH
FUCK! FU... FUCKING HELL!
THE DOMAIN NAMES...THEY'RE DELETING.
ALL OF THEM!

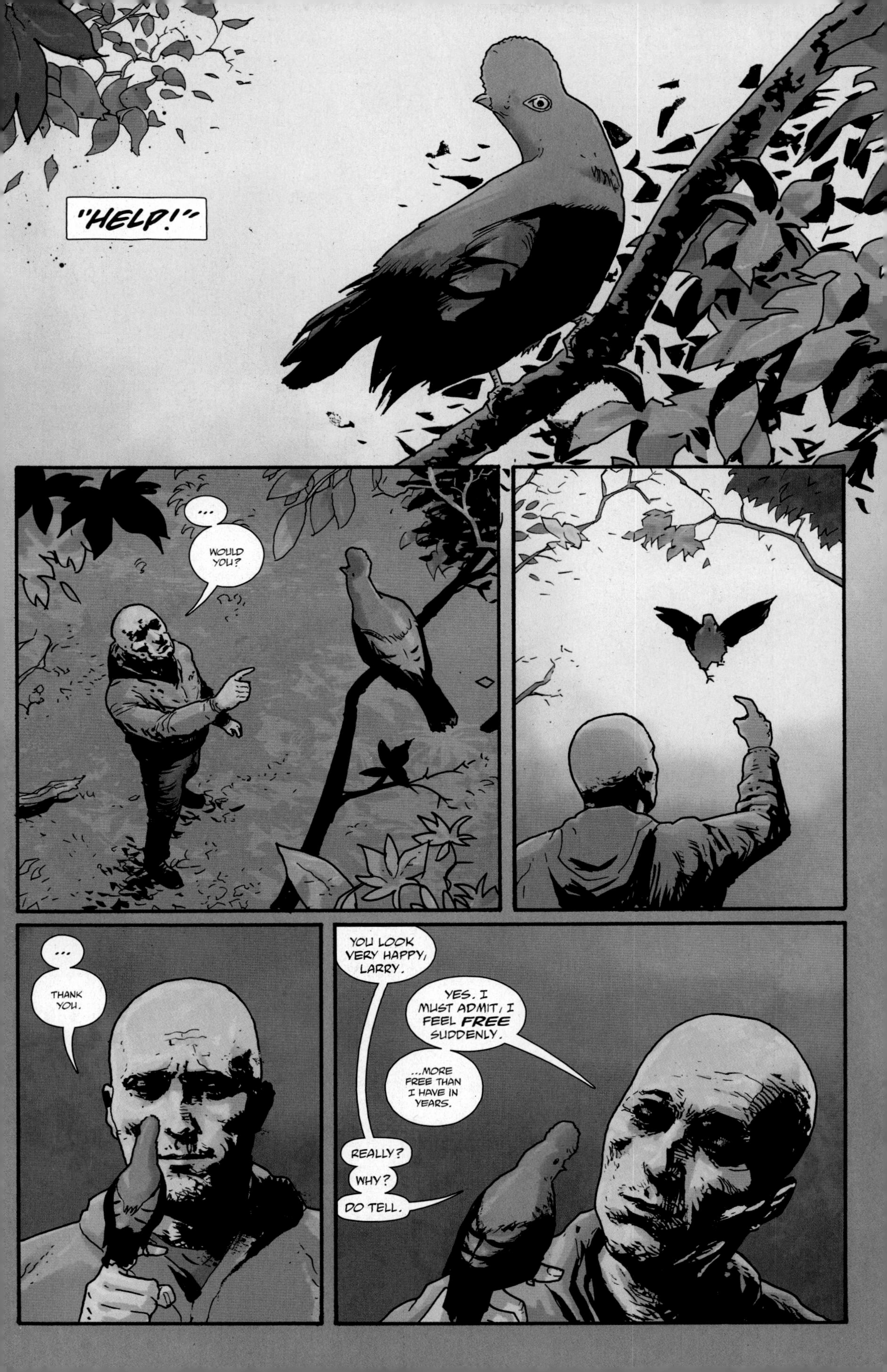
"HELP!"
...
WOULD YOU?
...
THANK YOU.
YOU LOOK VERY HAPPY, LARRY.
YES. I MUST ADMIT, I FEEL FREE SUDDENLY.
...MORE FREE THAN I HAVE IN YEARS.
REALLY?
WHY?
DO TELL.

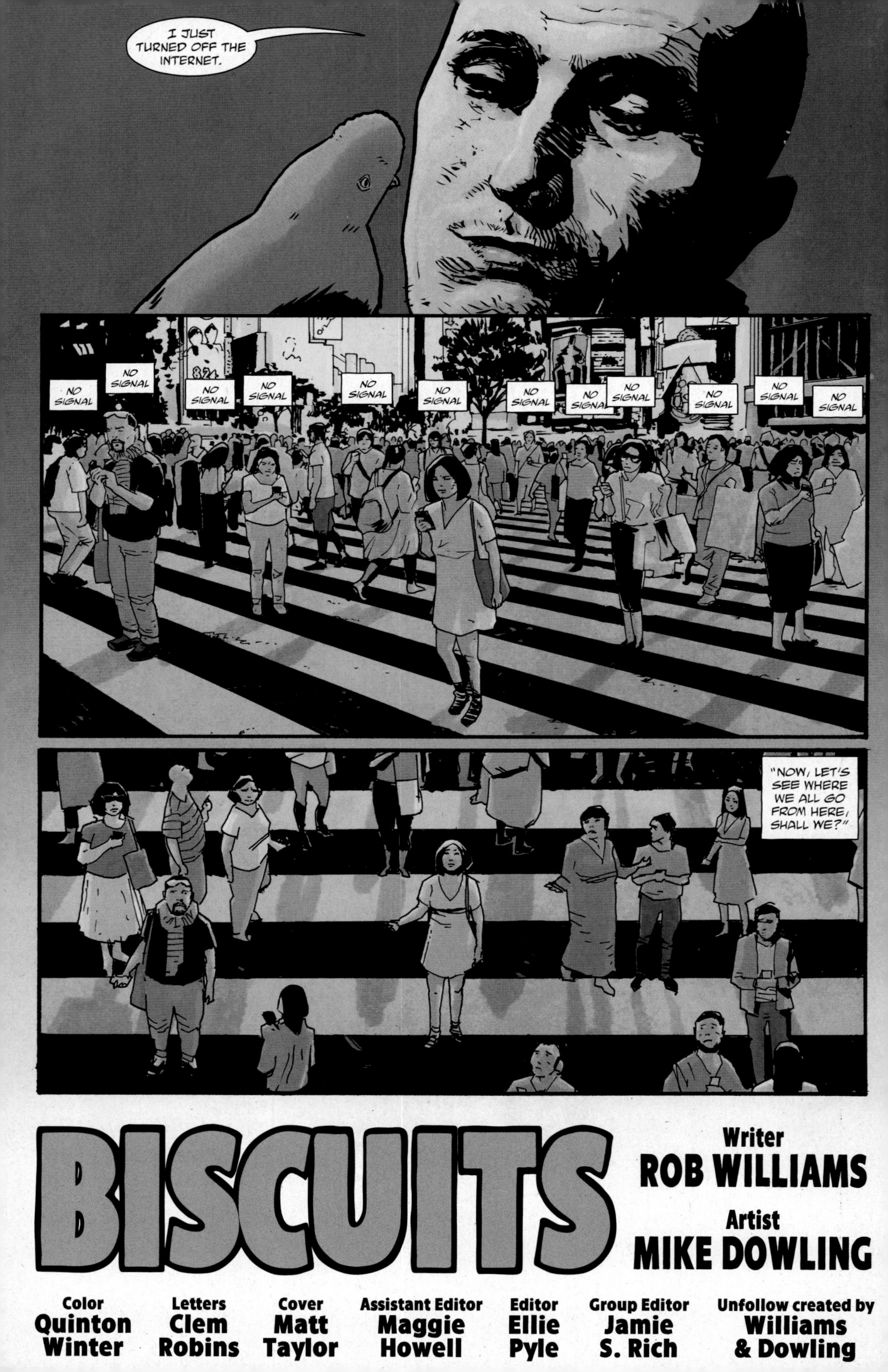
I JUST TURNED OFF THE INTERNET.
NO SIGNAL
NO SIGNAL
NO SIGNAL
NO SIGNAL
NO SIGNAL
NO SIGNAL
NO SIGNAL
NO SIGNAL
NO SIGNAL
NO SIGNAL
NO SIGNAL
NO SIGNAL
"NOW, LET'S SEE WHERE WE ALL GO FROM HERE, SHALL WE?"

BISCUITS

Writer
ROB WILLIAMS

Artist
MIKE DOWLING

Color Quinton Winter
Letters Clem Robins
Cover Matt Taylor
Assistant Editor Maggie Howell
Editor Ellie Pyle
Group Editor Jamie S. Rich
Unfollow created by Williams & Dowling

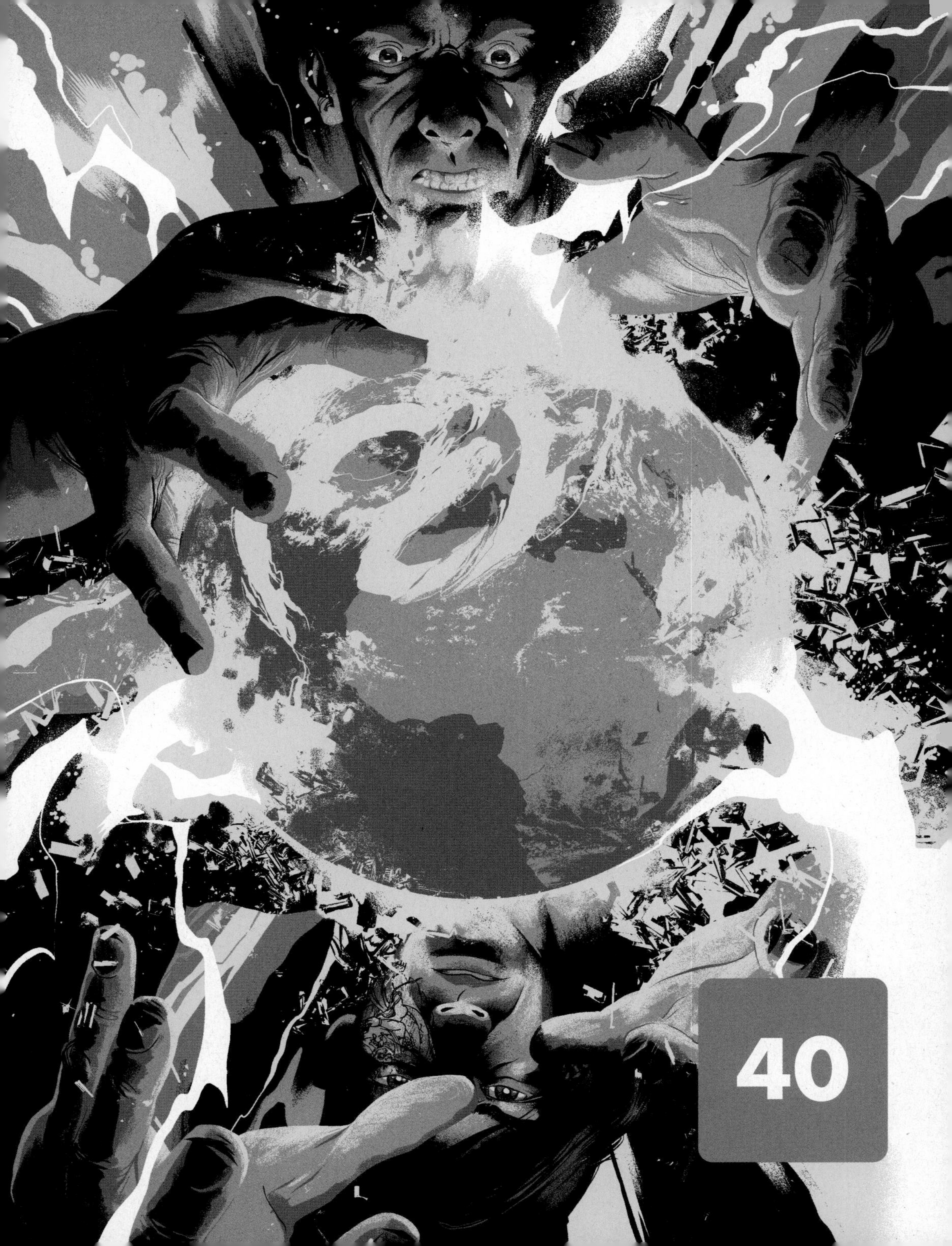
40

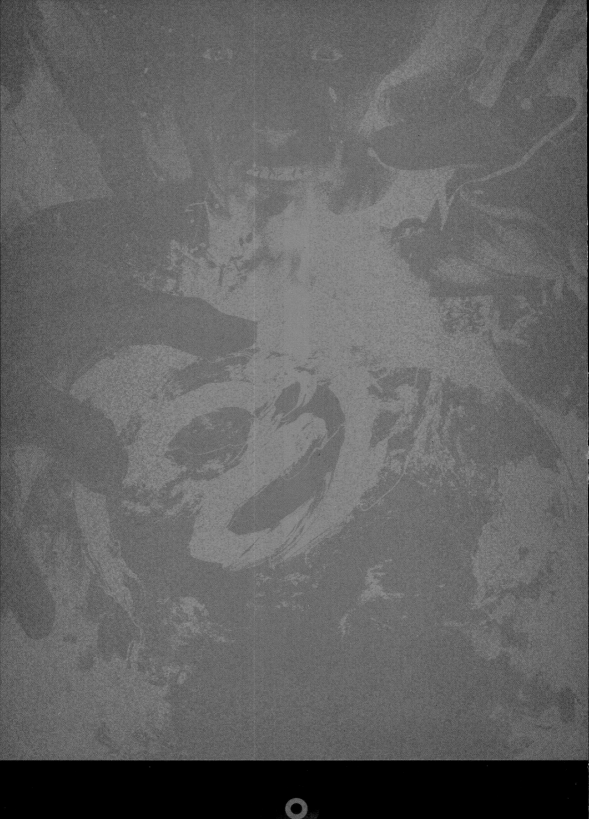

YOU CAN DEVELOP ALL THE NEW TECHNOLOGY YOU WANT, YOU KNOW.

BUT THERE ARE THREE WAYS IN WHICH YOU WILL ALWAYS BE ABLE TO CONTROL HUMAN BEINGS.

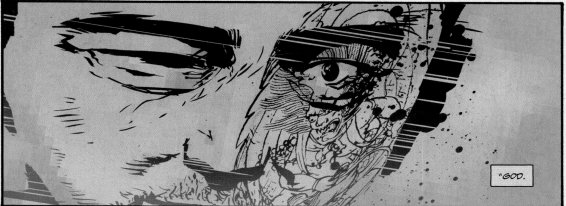

"GOD.

Larry Ferrell's net worth: $18.42 billion (divided by) 40 players remaining= $460.5 million each.

There is still $17.9 BILLION to be claimed...

"MONEY.

"AND, IF THE OTHER TWO FAIL..."

...Ah...

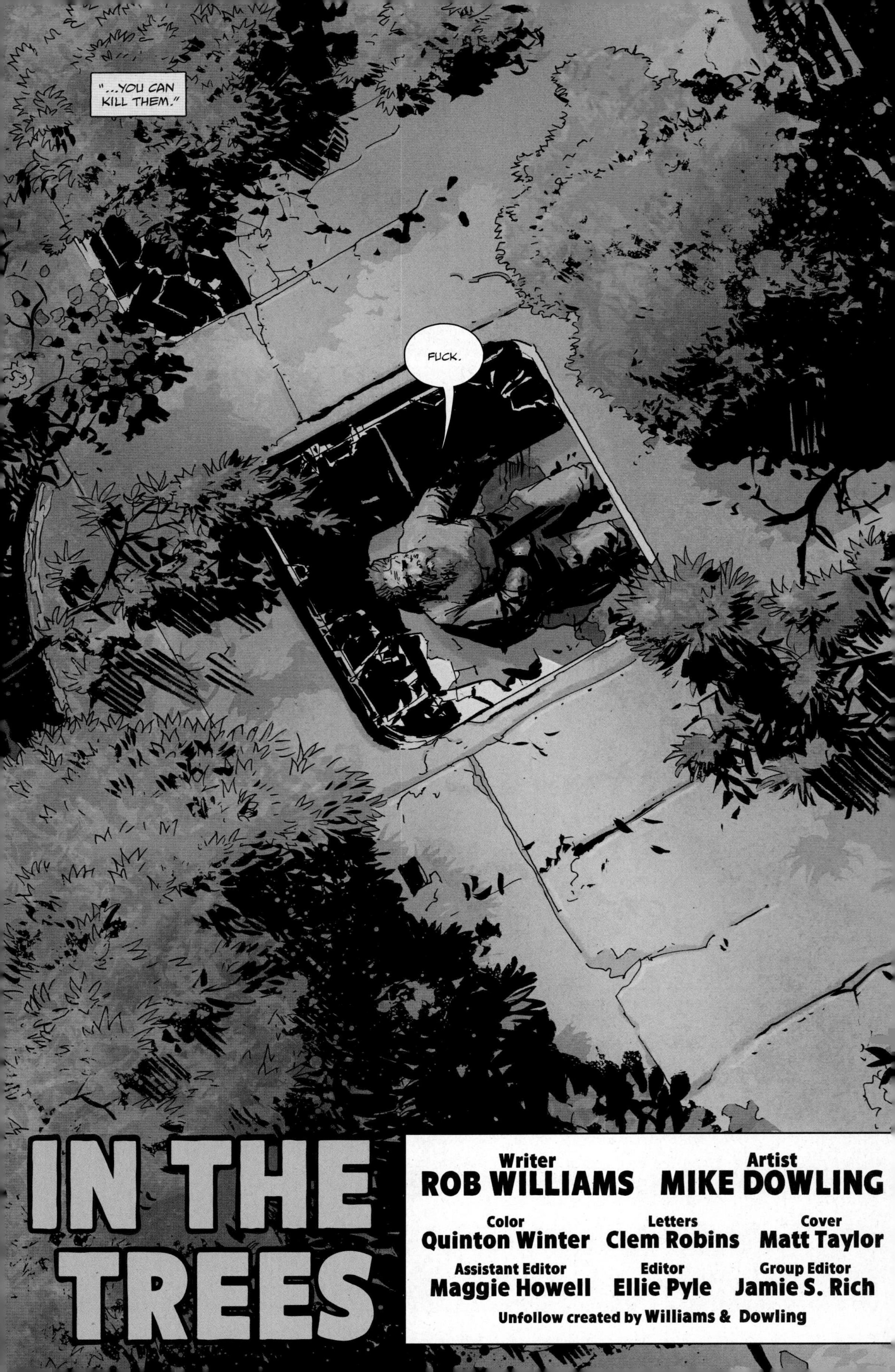
"...YOU CAN KILL THEM."
FUCK.

IN THE TREES

Writer
ROB WILLIAMS

Artist
MIKE DOWLING

Color
Quinton Winter

Letters
Clem Robins

Cover
Matt Taylor

Assistant Editor
Maggie Howell

Editor
Ellie Pyle

Group Editor
Jamie S. Rich

Unfollow created by Williams & Dowling

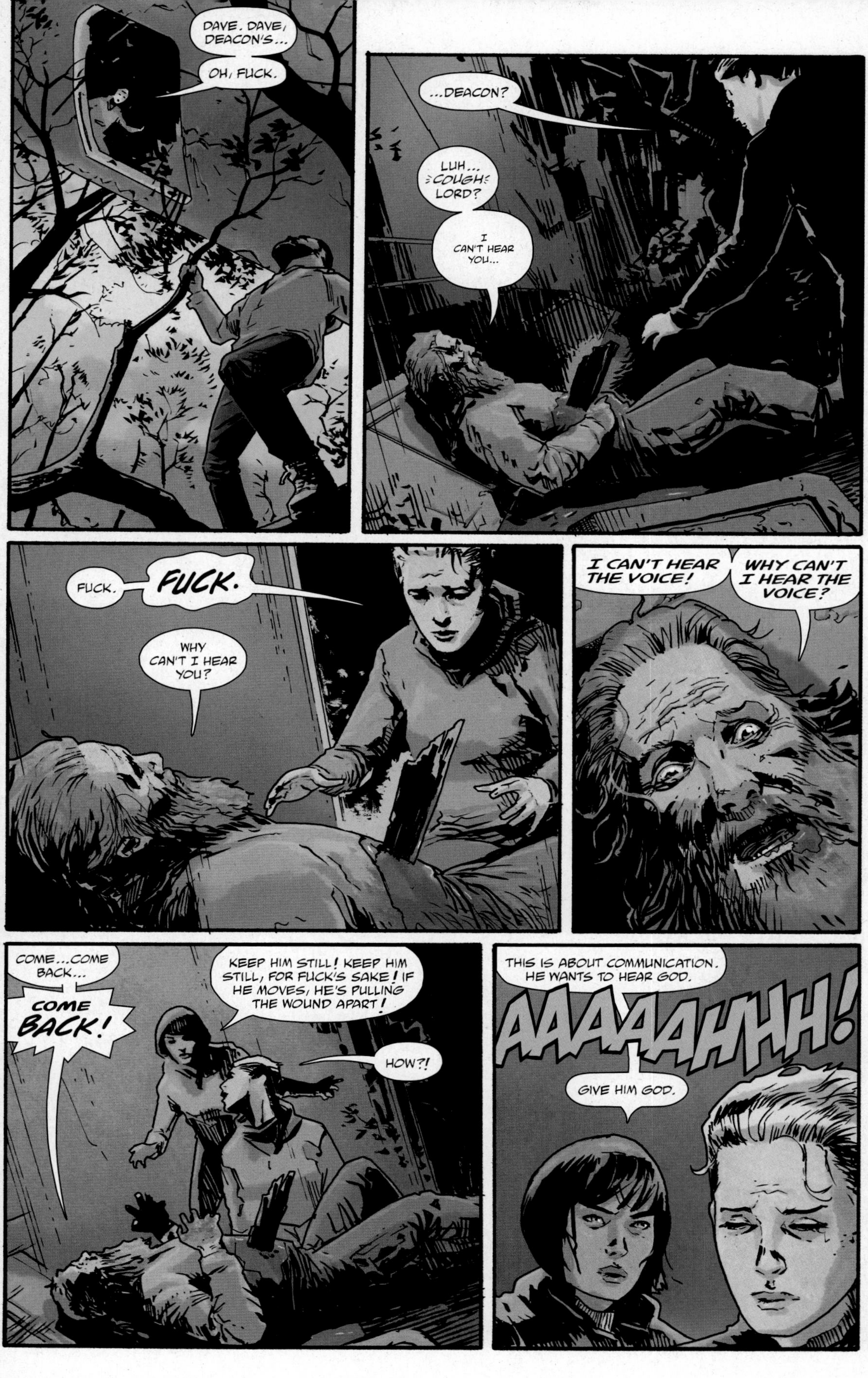
DAVE. DAVE, DEACON'S...
OH, FUCK.
...DEACON?
LUH... COUGH LORD?
I CAN'T HEAR YOU...
FUCK.
FUCK.
WHY CAN'T I HEAR YOU?
I CAN'T HEAR THE VOICE!
WHY CAN'T I HEAR THE VOICE?
COME...COME BACK...
COME BACK!
KEEP HIM STILL! KEEP HIM STILL, FOR FUCK'S SAKE! IF HE MOVES, HE'S PULLING THE WOUND APART!
HOW?!
THIS IS ABOUT COMMUNICATION. HE WANTS TO HEAR GOD.
AAAAAHHH!
GIVE HIM GOD.

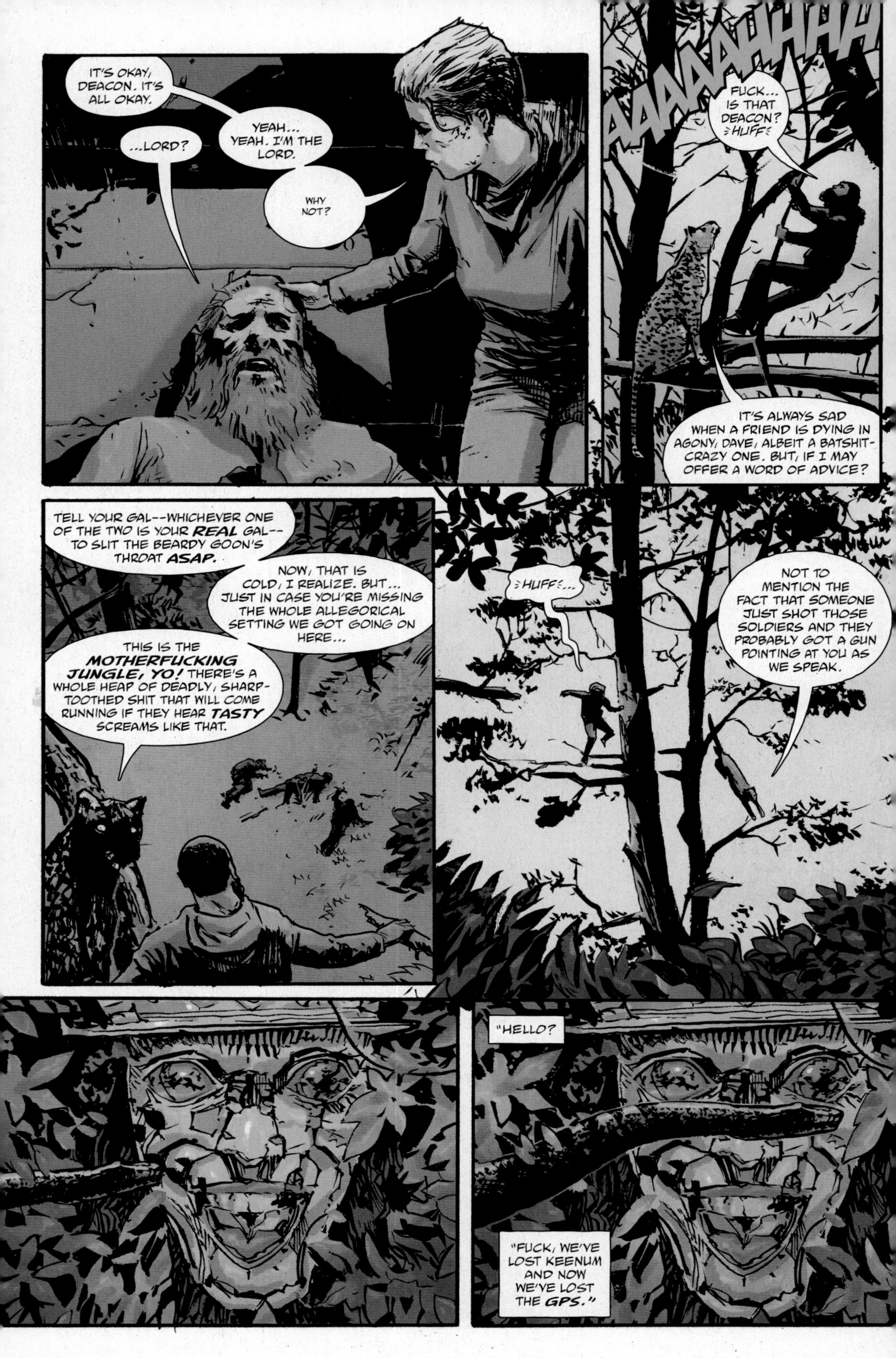
IT'S OKAY, DEACON. IT'S ALL OKAY.
...LORD?
YEAH... YEAH. I'M THE LORD.
WHY NOT?
AAAAAAHHHAH
FUCK... IS THAT DEACON? HUFF
IT'S ALWAYS SAD WHEN A FRIEND IS DYING IN AGONY, DAVE, ALBEIT A BATSHIT-CRAZY ONE. BUT, IF I MAY OFFER A WORD OF ADVICE?
TELL YOUR GAL--WHICHEVER ONE OF THE TWO IS YOUR REAL GAL--TO SLIT THE BEARDY GOON'S THROAT ASAP.
NOW, THAT IS COLD, I REALIZE. BUT... JUST IN CASE YOU'RE MISSING THE WHOLE ALLEGORICAL SETTING WE GOT GOING ON HERE...
THIS IS THE MOTHERFUCKING JUNGLE, YO! THERE'S A WHOLE HEAP OF DEADLY, SHARP-TOOTHED SHIT THAT WILL COME RUNNING IF THEY HEAR TASTY SCREAMS LIKE THAT.
HUFF...
NOT TO MENTION THE FACT THAT SOMEONE JUST SHOT THOSE SOLDIERS AND THEY PROBABLY GOT A GUN POINTING AT YOU AS WE SPEAK.
"HELLO?
"FUCK, WE'VE LOST KEENUM AND NOW WE'VE LOST THE GPS."

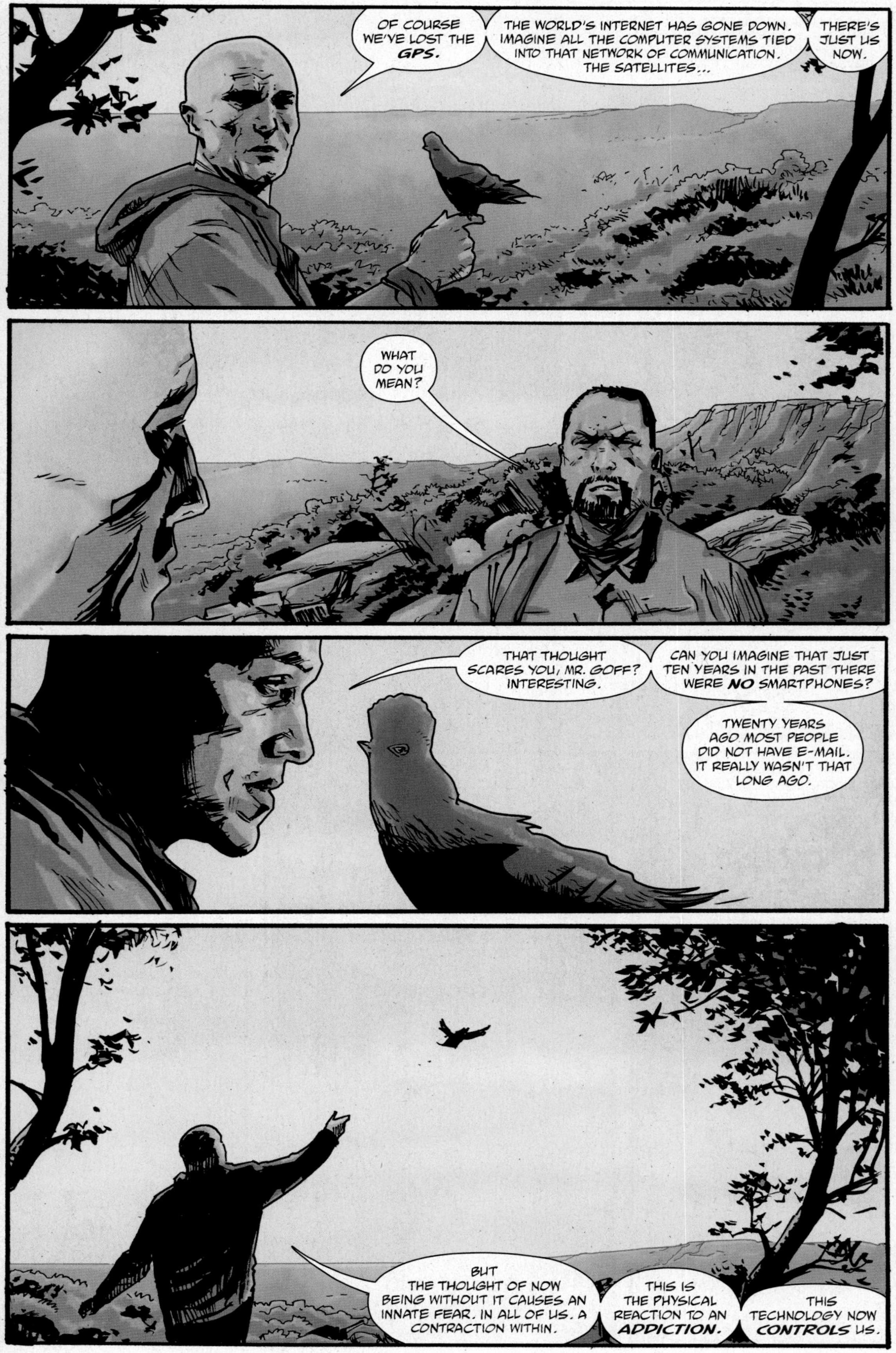
OF COURSE WE'VE LOST THE GPS.
THE WORLD'S INTERNET HAS GONE DOWN. IMAGINE ALL THE COMPUTER SYSTEMS TIED INTO THAT NETWORK OF COMMUNICATION. THE SATELLITES...
THERE'S JUST US NOW.
WHAT DO YOU MEAN?
THAT THOUGHT SCARES YOU, MR. GOFF? INTERESTING.
CAN YOU IMAGINE THAT JUST TEN YEARS IN THE PAST THERE WERE NO SMARTPHONES?
TWENTY YEARS AGO MOST PEOPLE DID NOT HAVE E-MAIL. IT REALLY WASN'T THAT LONG AGO.
BUT THE THOUGHT OF NOW BEING WITHOUT IT CAUSES AN INNATE FEAR. IN ALL OF US. A CONTRACTION WITHIN.
THIS IS THE PHYSICAL REACTION TO AN ADDICTION.
THIS TECHNOLOGY NOW CONTROLS US.

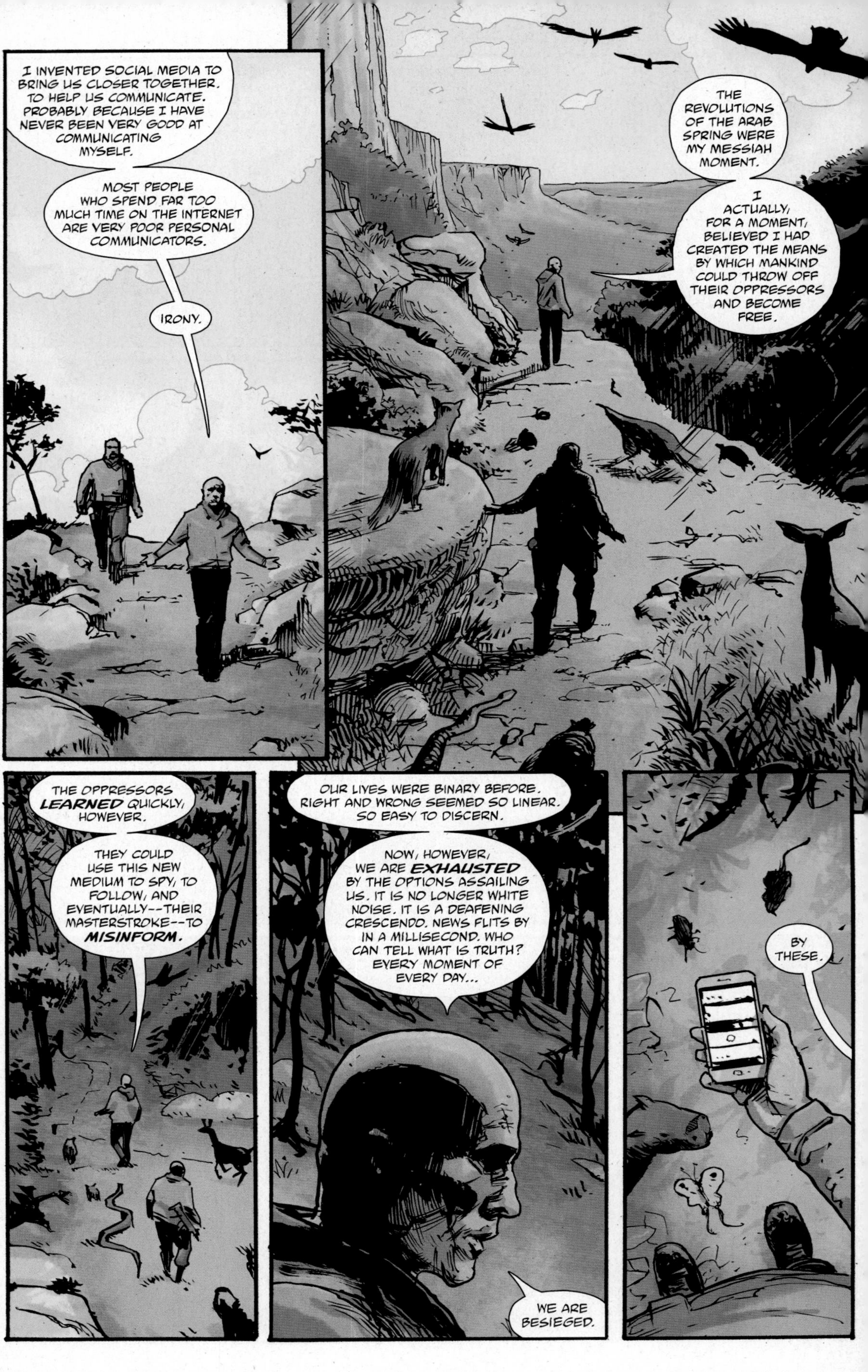
I INVENTED SOCIAL MEDIA TO BRING US CLOSER TOGETHER. TO HELP US COMMUNICATE. PROBABLY BECAUSE I HAVE NEVER BEEN VERY GOOD AT COMMUNICATING MYSELF.
MOST PEOPLE WHO SPEND FAR TOO MUCH TIME ON THE INTERNET ARE VERY POOR PERSONAL COMMUNICATORS.
IRONY.
THE REVOLUTIONS OF THE ARAB SPRING WERE MY MESSIAH MOMENT.
I ACTUALLY, FOR A MOMENT, BELIEVED I HAD CREATED THE MEANS BY WHICH MANKIND COULD THROW OFF THEIR OPPRESSORS AND BECOME FREE.
THE OPPRESSORS LEARNED QUICKLY, HOWEVER.
THEY COULD USE THIS NEW MEDIUM TO SPY, TO FOLLOW, AND EVENTUALLY--THEIR MASTERSTROKE--TO MISINFORM.
OUR LIVES WERE BINARY BEFORE. RIGHT AND WRONG SEEMED SO LINEAR. SO EASY TO DISCERN.
NOW, HOWEVER, WE ARE EXHAUSTED BY THE OPTIONS ASSAILING US. IT IS NO LONGER WHITE NOISE. IT IS A DEAFENING CRESCENDO. NEWS FLITS BY IN A MILLISECOND. WHO CAN TELL WHAT IS TRUTH? EVERY MOMENT OF EVERY DAY...
WE ARE BESIEGED.
BY THESE.

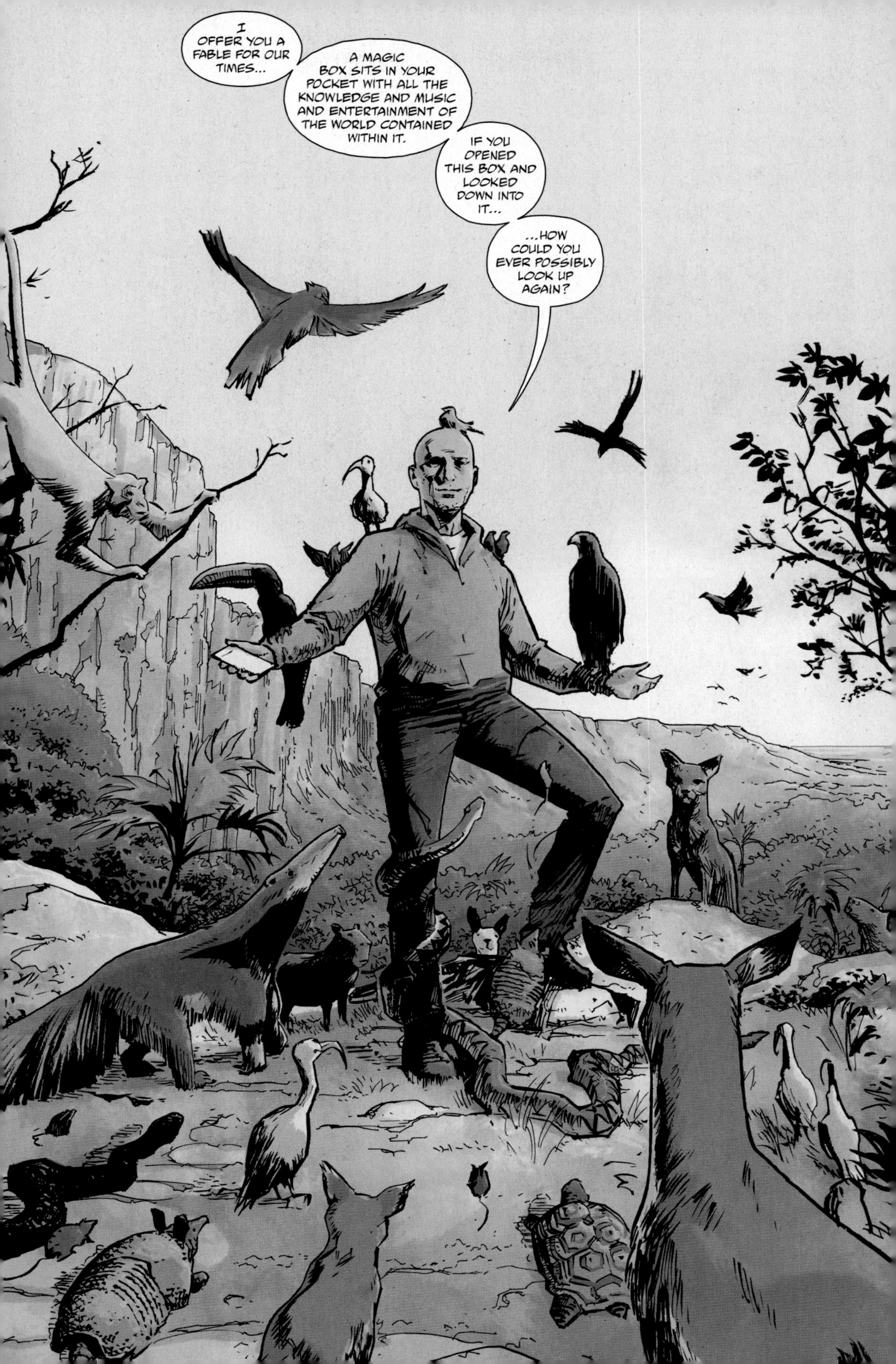
I OFFER YOU A FABLE FOR OUR TIMES...
A MAGIC BOX SITS IN YOUR POCKET WITH ALL THE KNOWLEDGE AND MUSIC AND ENTERTAINMENT OF THE WORLD CONTAINED WITHIN IT.
IF YOU OPENED THIS BOX AND LOOKED DOWN INTO IT...
...HOW COULD YOU EVER POSSIBLY LOOK UP AGAIN?

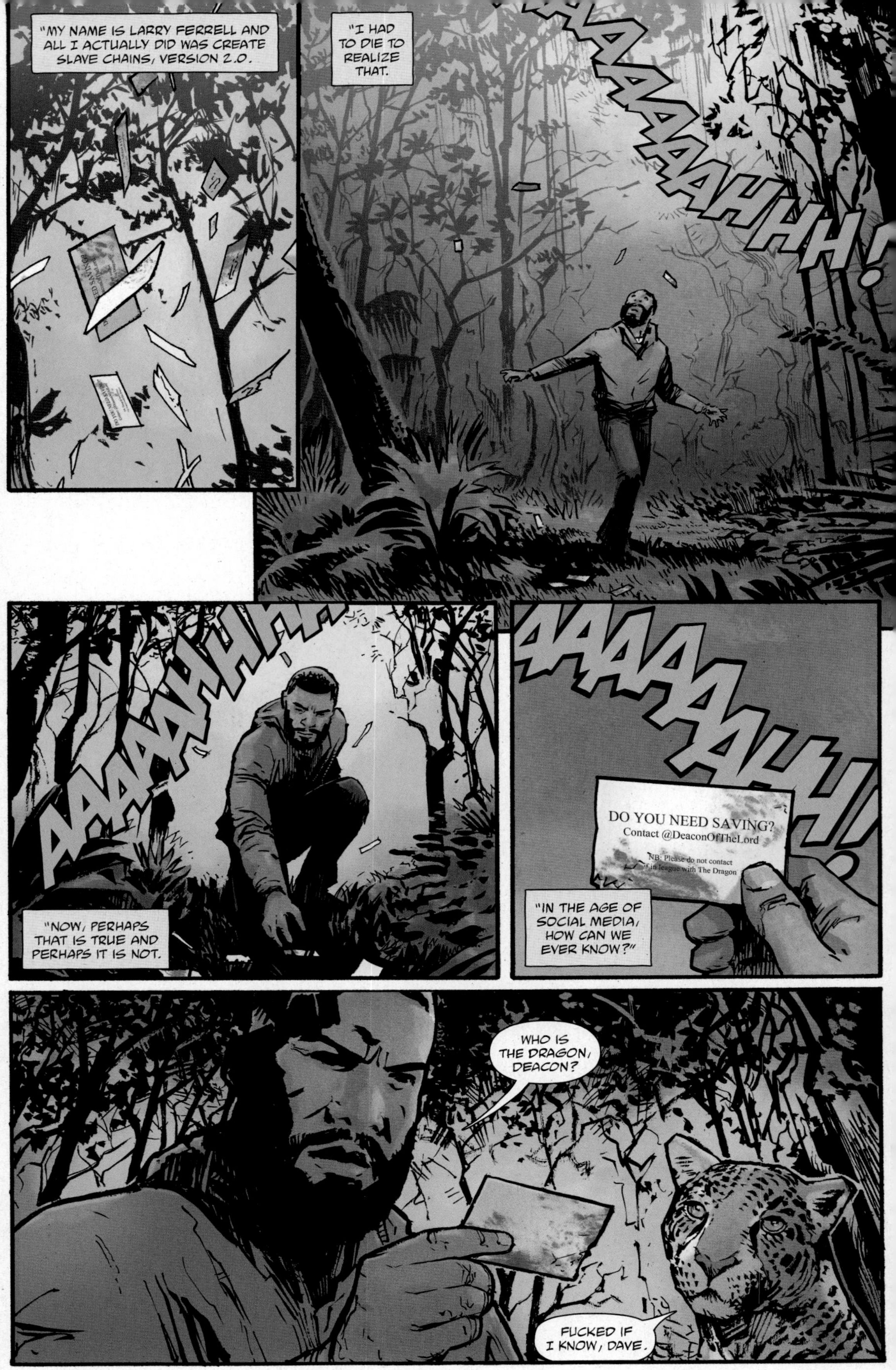
"MY NAME IS LARRY FERRELL AND ALL I ACTUALLY DID WAS CREATE SLAVE CHAINS, VERSION 2.0.
"I HAD TO DIE TO REALIZE THAT.
AAAAAAAAHHHH!
AAAAAHHH
"NOW, PERHAPS THAT IS TRUE AND PERHAPS IT IS NOT.
AAAAAAAHH!
DO YOU NEED SAVING?
Contact @DeaconOfTheLord
NB: Please do not contact
in league with The Dragon
"IN THE AGE OF SOCIAL MEDIA, HOW CAN WE EVER KNOW?"
WHO IS THE DRAGON, DEACON?
FUCKED IF I KNOW, DAVE.

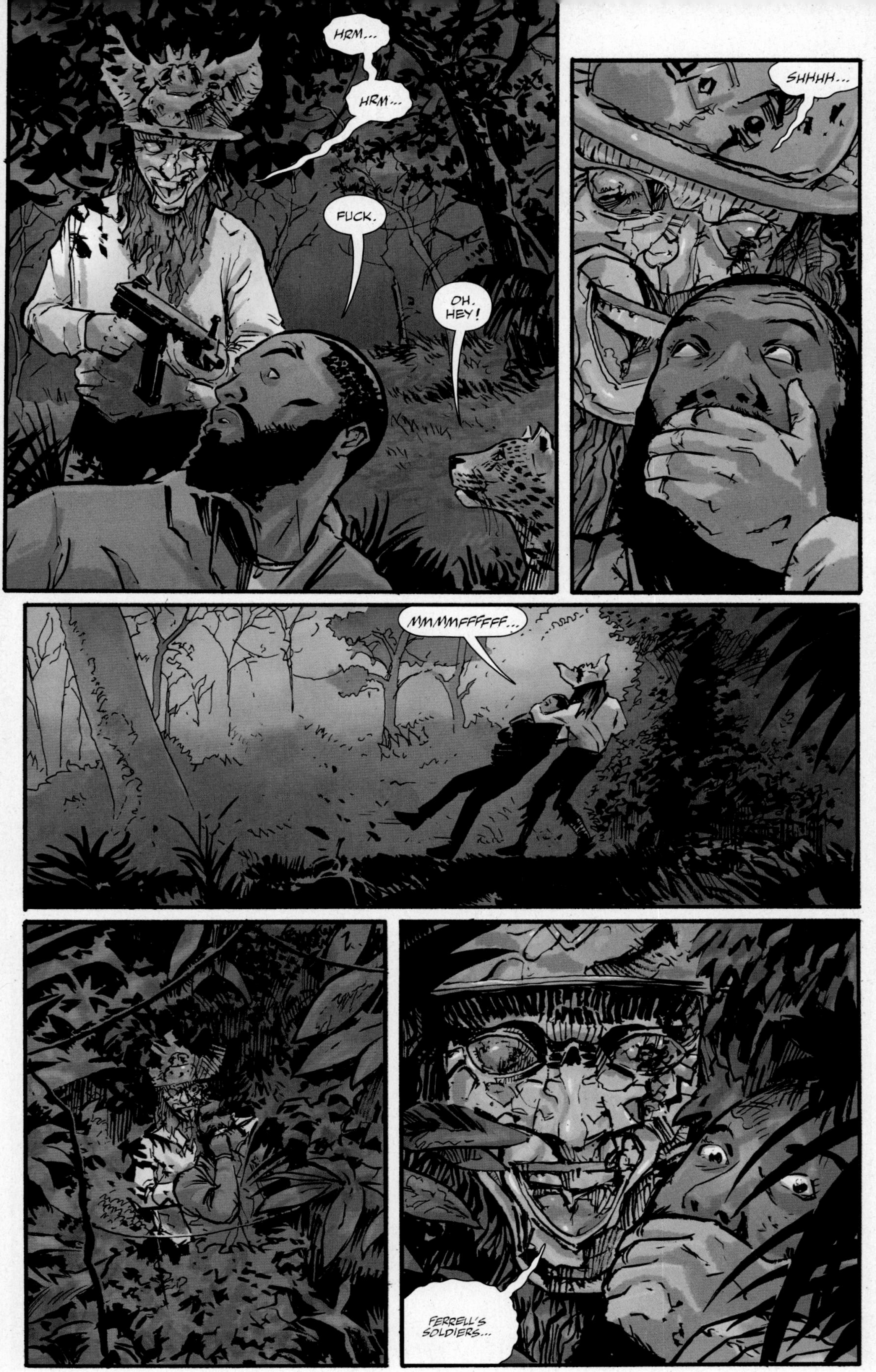
HRM...
HRM...
FUCK.
OH. HEY!
SHHHH...
MMMMFFFFFF...
FERRELL'S SOLDIERS...

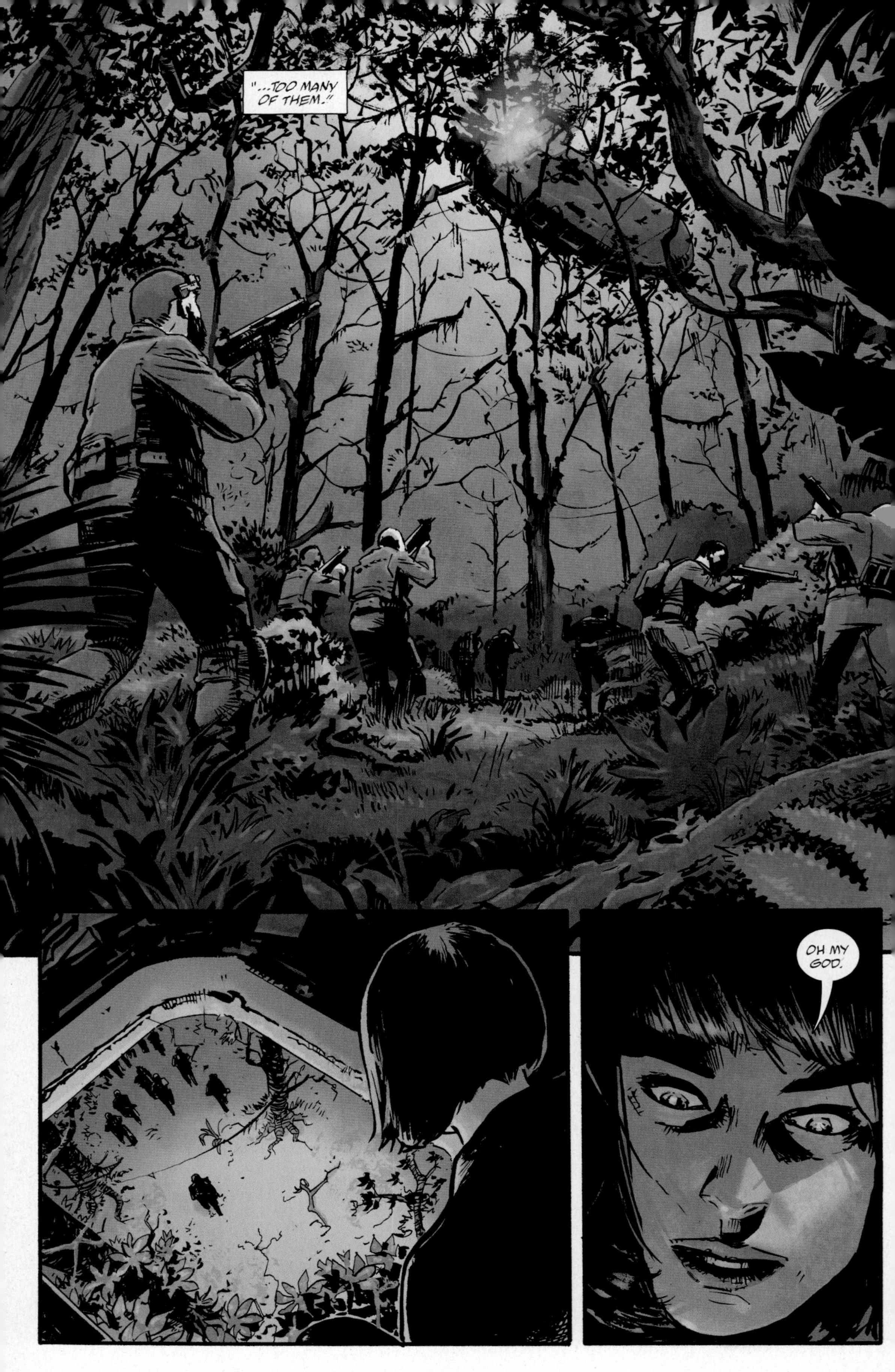
"...TOO MANY OF THEM."
OH MY GOD.

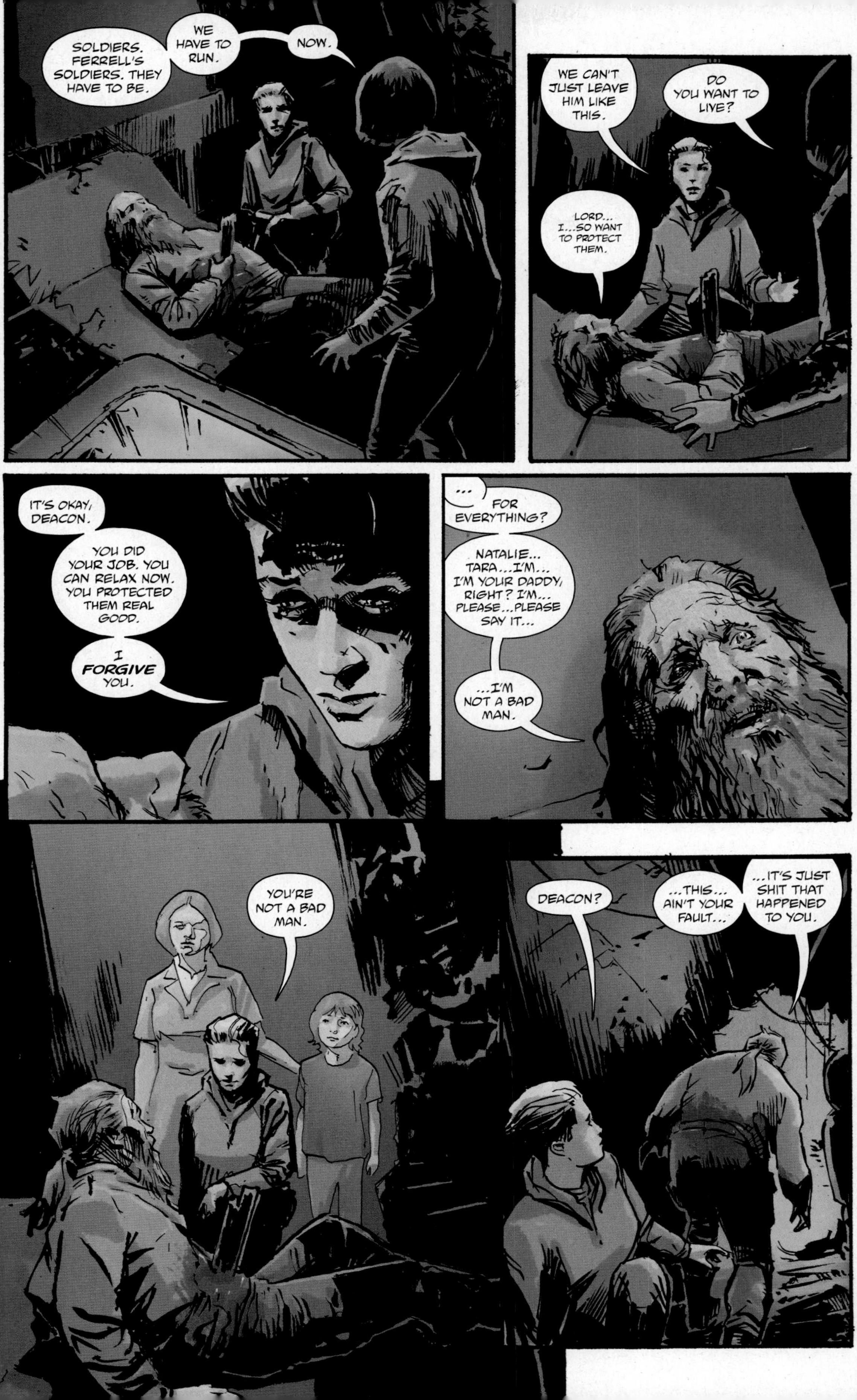

SOLDIERS. FERRELL'S SOLDIERS. THEY HAVE TO BE.
WE HAVE TO RUN.
NOW.
WE CAN'T JUST LEAVE HIM LIKE THIS.
DO YOU WANT TO LIVE?
LORD... I...SO WANT TO PROTECT THEM.
IT'S OKAY, DEACON.
YOU DID YOUR JOB. YOU CAN RELAX NOW. YOU PROTECTED THEM REAL GOOD.
I **FORGIVE** YOU.
...
FOR EVERYTHING?
NATALIE... TARA...I'M... I'M YOUR DADDY, RIGHT? I'M... PLEASE...PLEASE SAY IT...
...I'M NOT A BAD MAN.
YOU'RE NOT A BAD MAN.
DEACON?
...THIS... AIN'T YOUR FAULT...
...IT'S JUST SHIT THAT HAPPENED TO YOU.

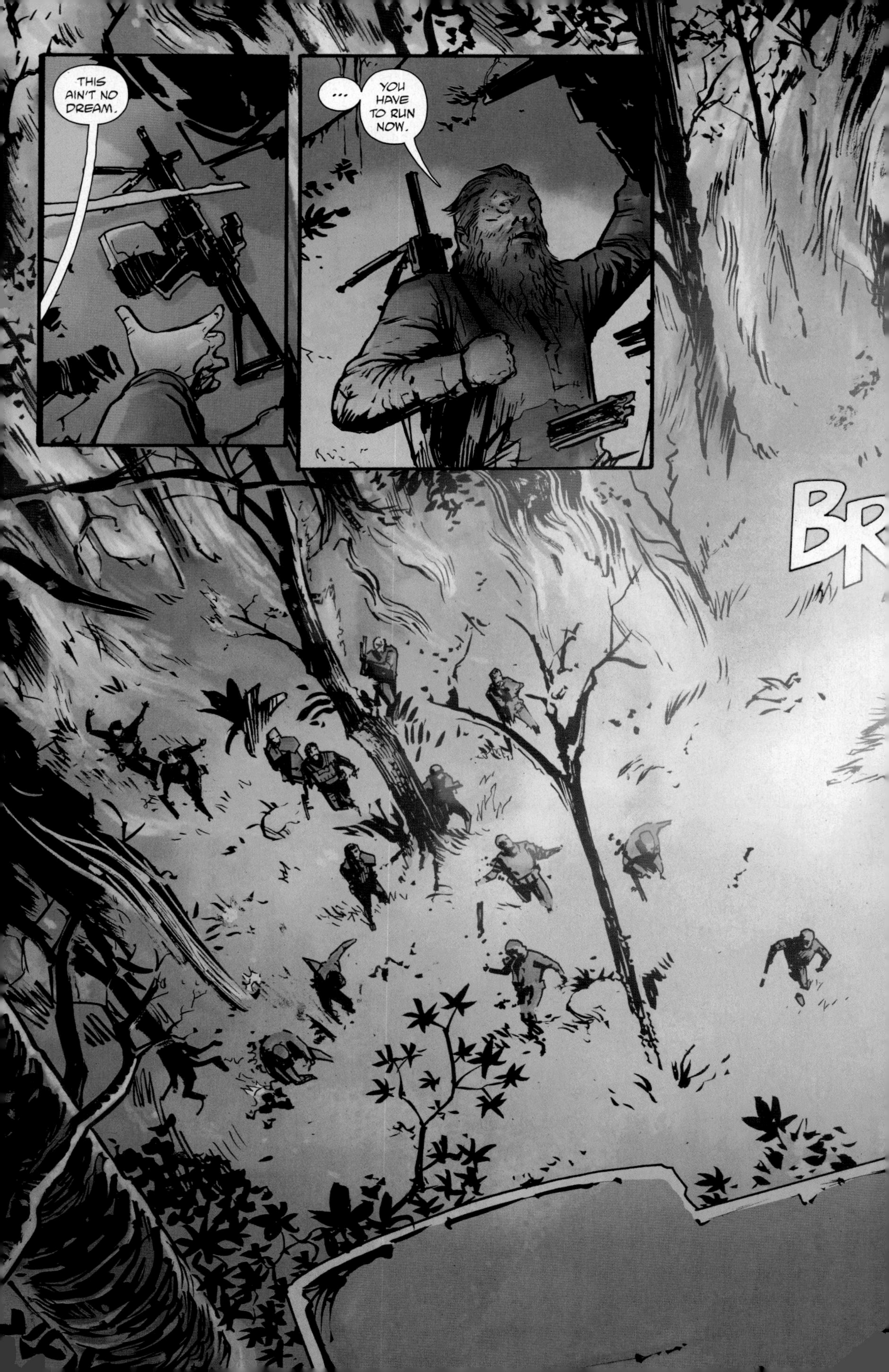
THIS AIN'T NO DREAM.
...
YOU HAVE TO RUN NOW.
BR

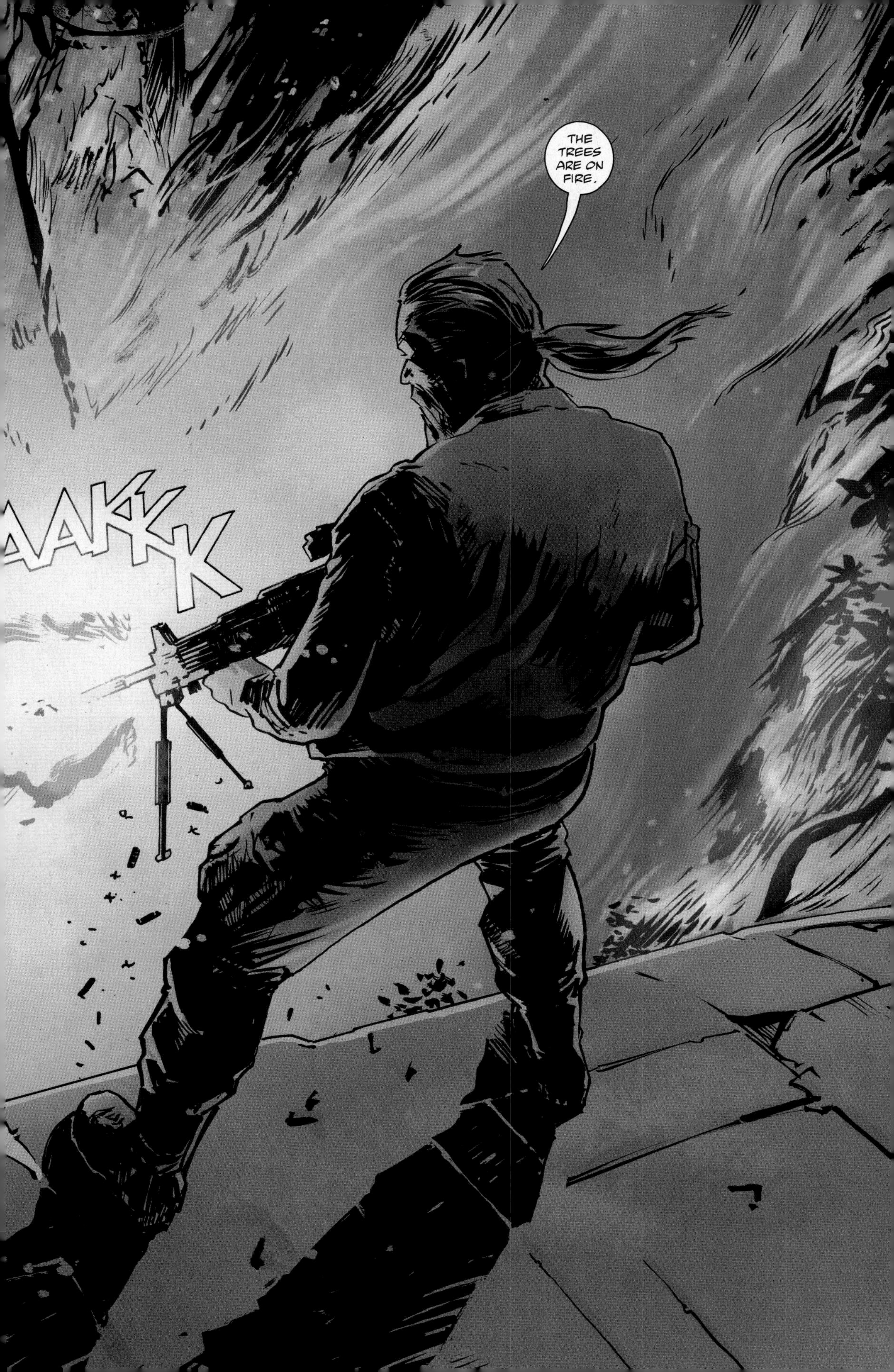
THE TREES ARE ON FIRE.
AAKKK

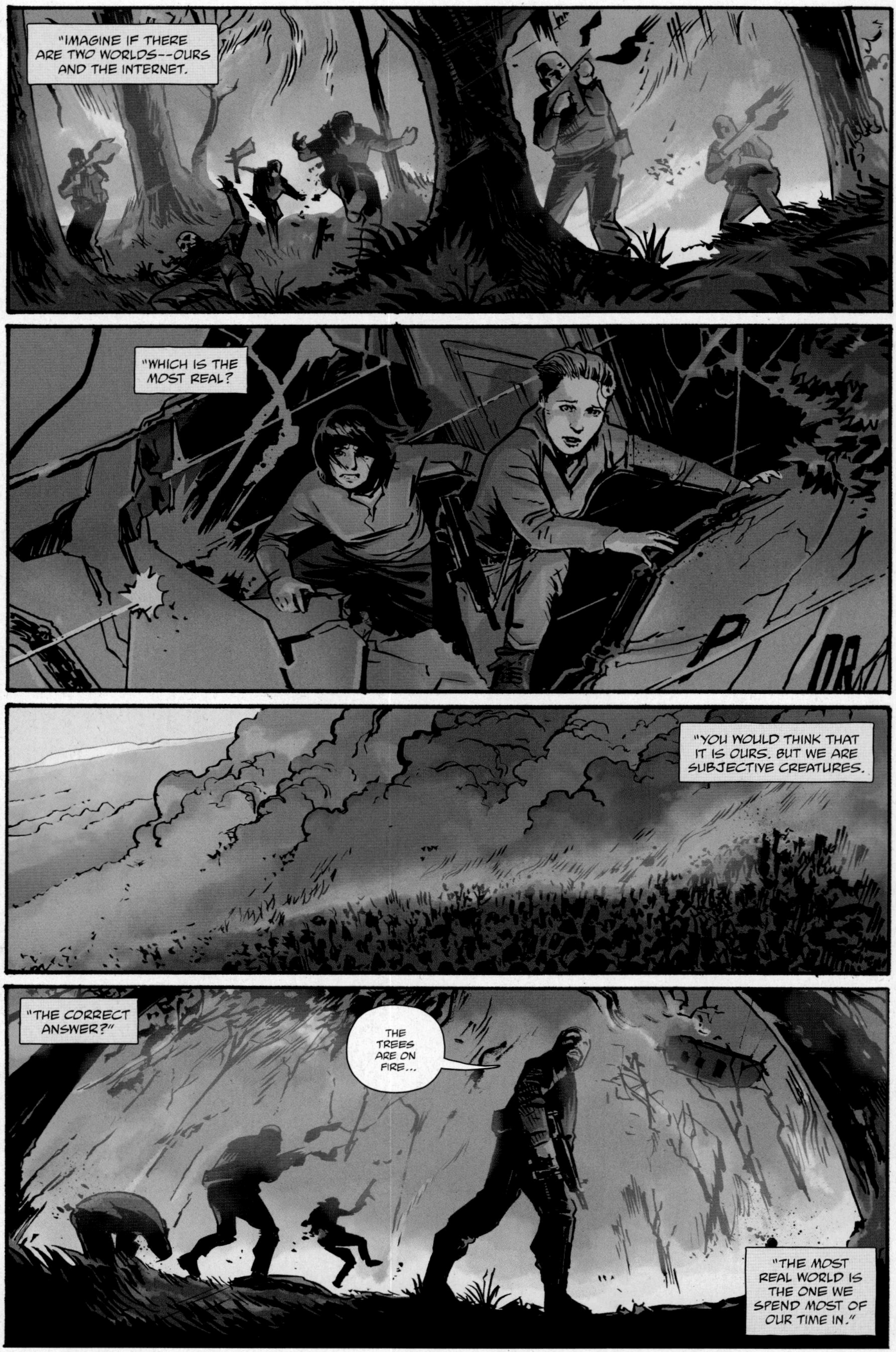
"IMAGINE IF THERE ARE TWO WORLDS--OURS AND THE INTERNET.
"WHICH IS THE MOST REAL?
"YOU WOULD THINK THAT IT IS OURS. BUT WE ARE SUBJECTIVE CREATURES.
"THE CORRECT ANSWER?"
THE TREES ARE ON FIRE...
"THE MOST REAL WORLD IS THE ONE WE SPEND MOST OF OUR TIME IN."

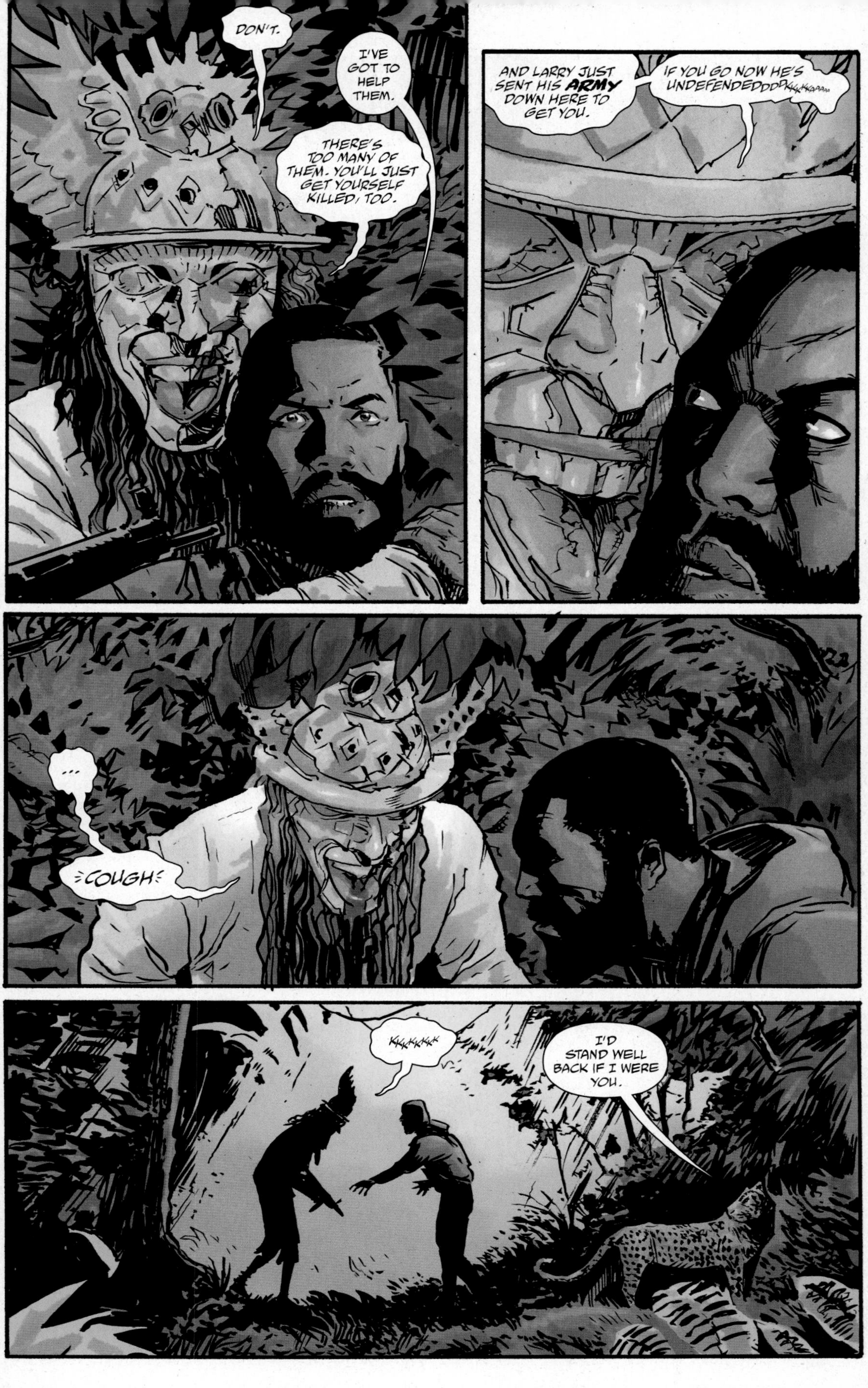
DON'T.
I'VE GOT TO HELP THEM.
THERE'S TOO MANY OF THEM. YOU'LL JUST GET YOURSELF KILLED, TOO.
AND LARRY JUST SENT HIS **ARMY** DOWN HERE TO GET YOU.
IF YOU GO NOW HE'S UNDEFENDEDDDDKKKKKaaaa
...
COUGH
KKKKKKKKK
I'D STAND WELL BACK IF I WERE YOU.

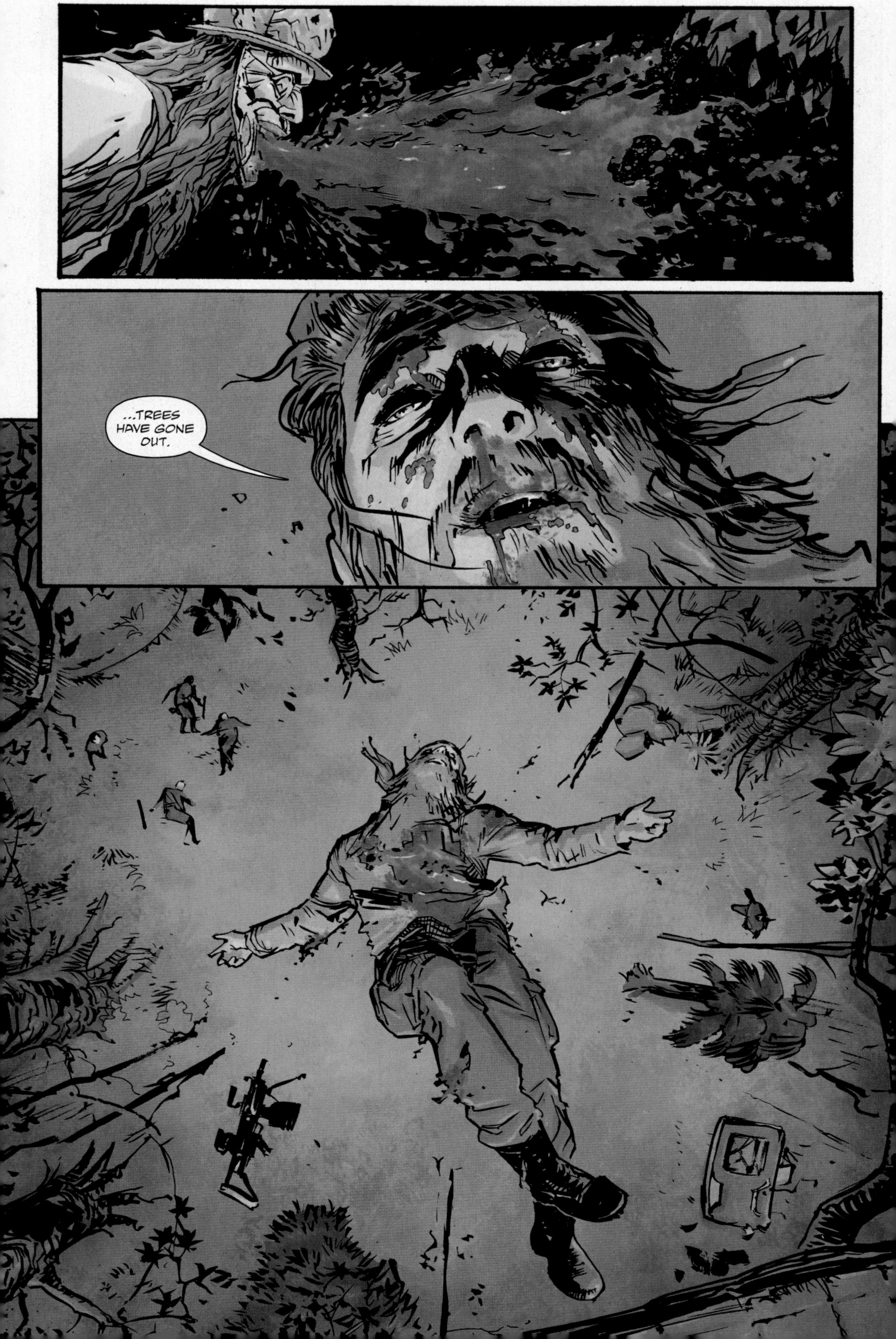
...TREES HAVE GONE OUT.

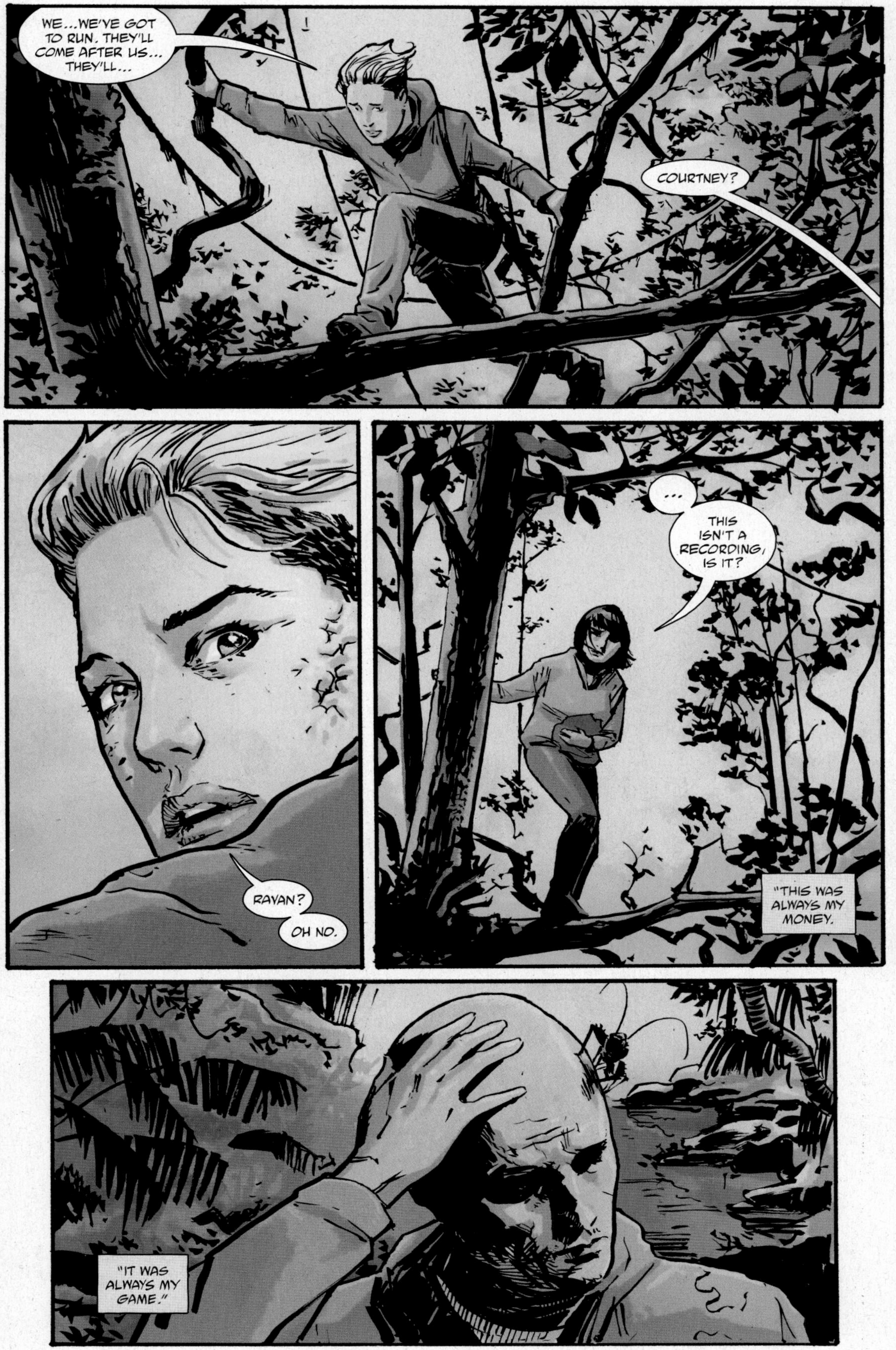
WE...WE'VE GOT TO RUN. THEY'LL COME AFTER US... THEY'LL...
!
COURTNEY?
RAVAN?
OH NO.
...
THIS ISN'T A RECORDING, IS IT?
"THIS WAS ALWAYS MY MONEY.
"IT WAS ALWAYS MY GAME."

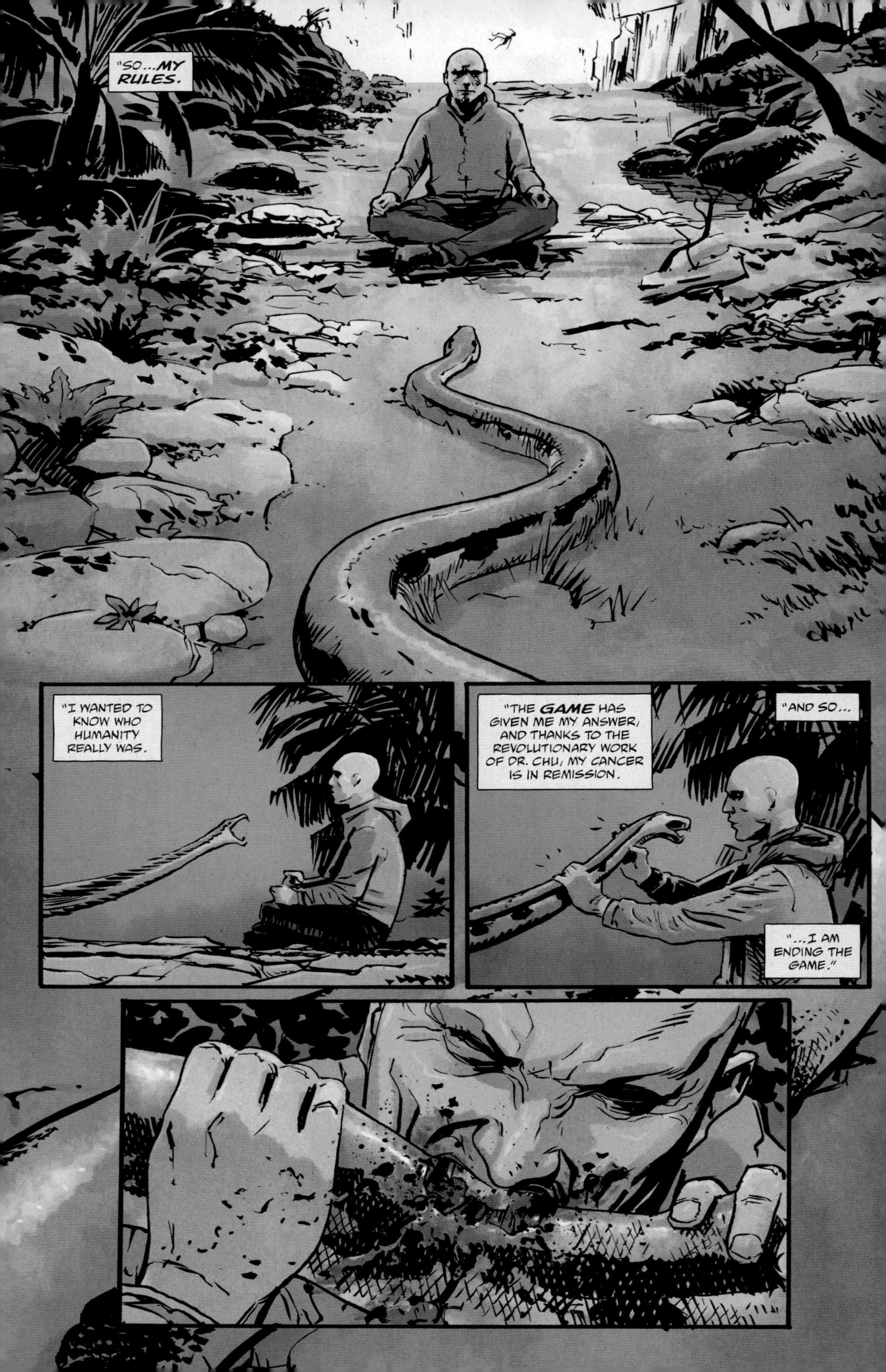
"SO... MY RULES.
"I WANTED TO KNOW WHO HUMANITY REALLY WAS.
"THE GAME HAS GIVEN ME MY ANSWER, AND THANKS TO THE REVOLUTIONARY WORK OF DR. CHU, MY CANCER IS IN REMISSION.
"AND SO...
"...I AM ENDING THE GAME."

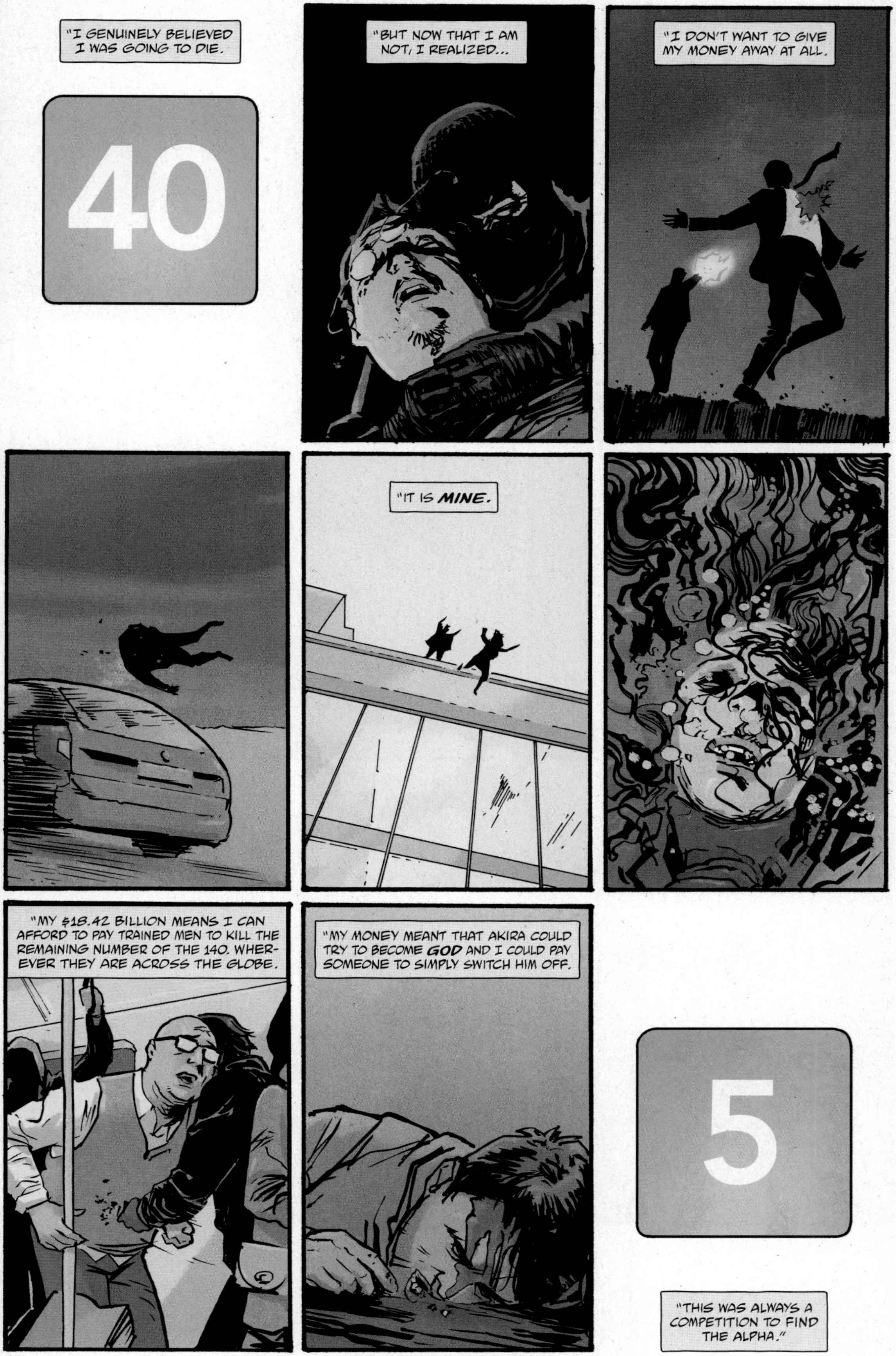
"I GENUINELY BELIEVED I WAS GOING TO DIE.
40
"BUT NOW THAT I AM NOT, I REALIZED...
"I DON'T WANT TO GIVE MY MONEY AWAY AT ALL.
"IT IS **MINE**.
"MY $18.42 BILLION MEANS I CAN AFFORD TO PAY TRAINED MEN TO KILL THE REMAINING NUMBER OF THE 140. WHEREVER THEY ARE ACROSS THE GLOBE.
"MY MONEY MEANT THAT AKIRA COULD TRY TO BECOME **GOD** AND I COULD PAY SOMEONE TO SIMPLY SWITCH HIM OFF.
5
"THIS WAS ALWAYS A COMPETITION TO FIND THE ALPHA."

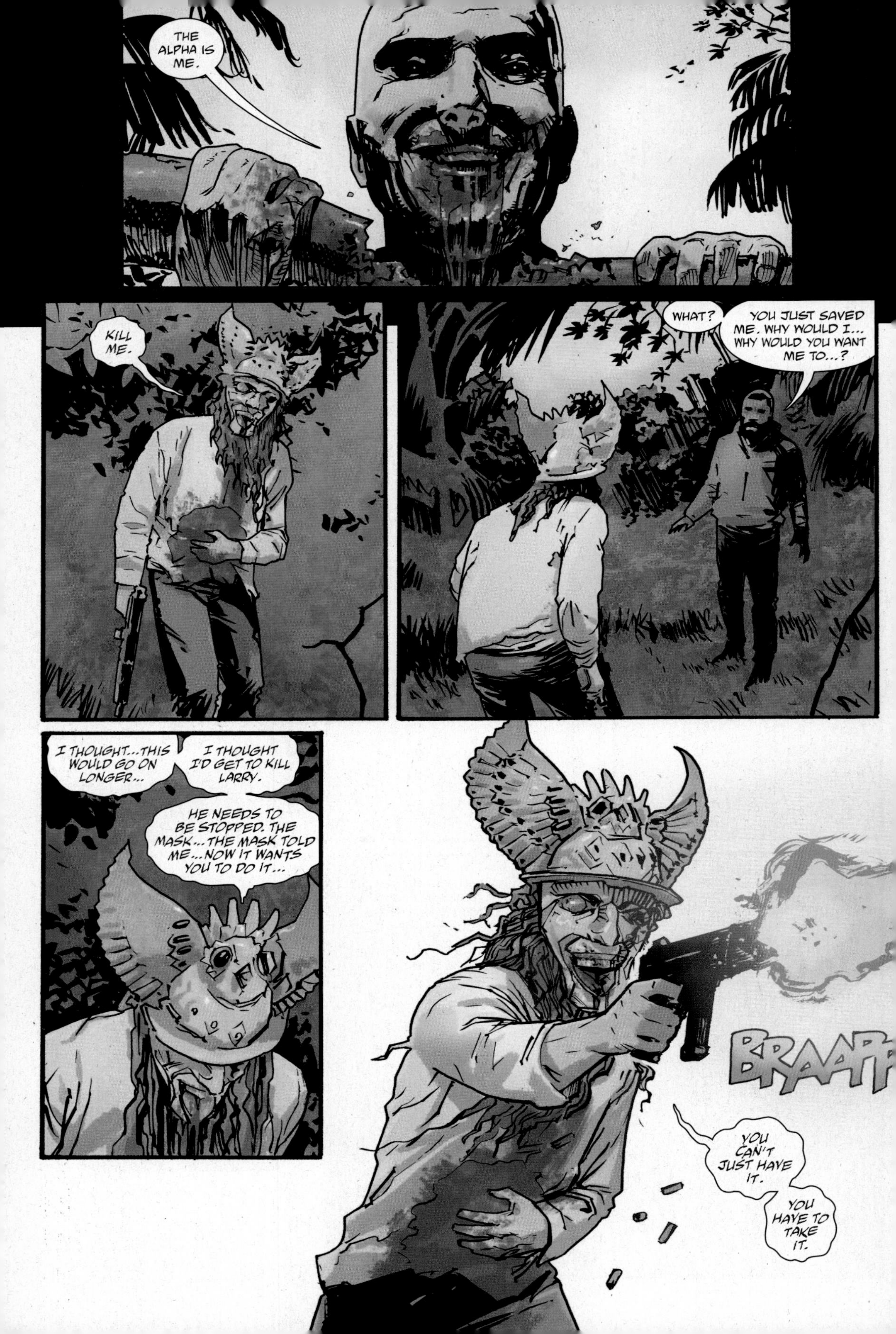
THE ALPHA IS ME.
KILL ME.
WHAT?
YOU JUST SAVED ME. WHY WOULD I... WHY WOULD YOU WANT ME TO...?
I THOUGHT...THIS WOULD GO ON LONGER...
I THOUGHT I'D GET TO KILL LARRY.
HE NEEDS TO BE STOPPED. THE MASK...THE MASK TOLD ME...NOW IT WANTS YOU TO DO IT...
BRAAPP
YOU CAN'T JUST HAVE IT.
YOU HAVE TO TAKE IT.

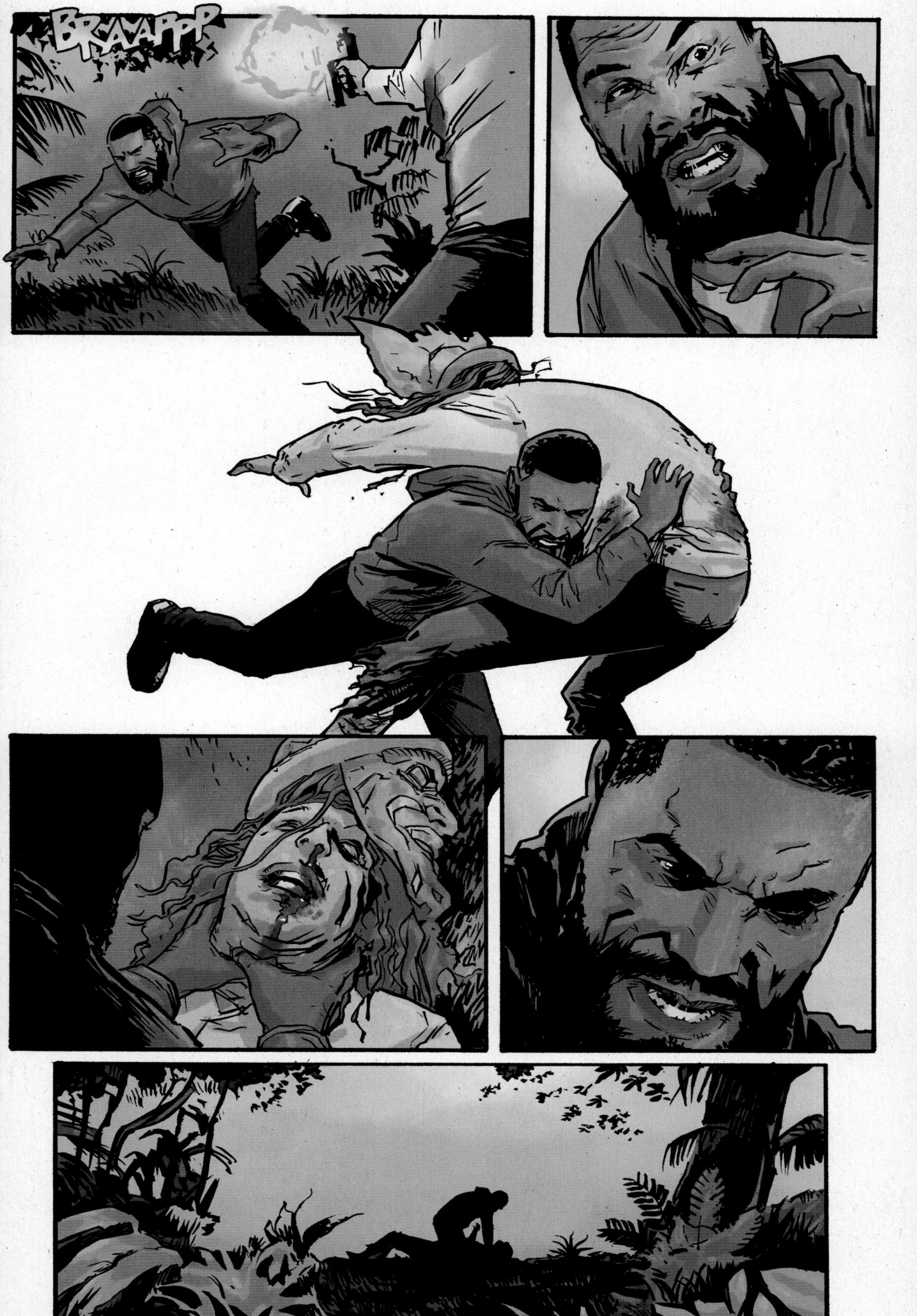
BRAAPPP

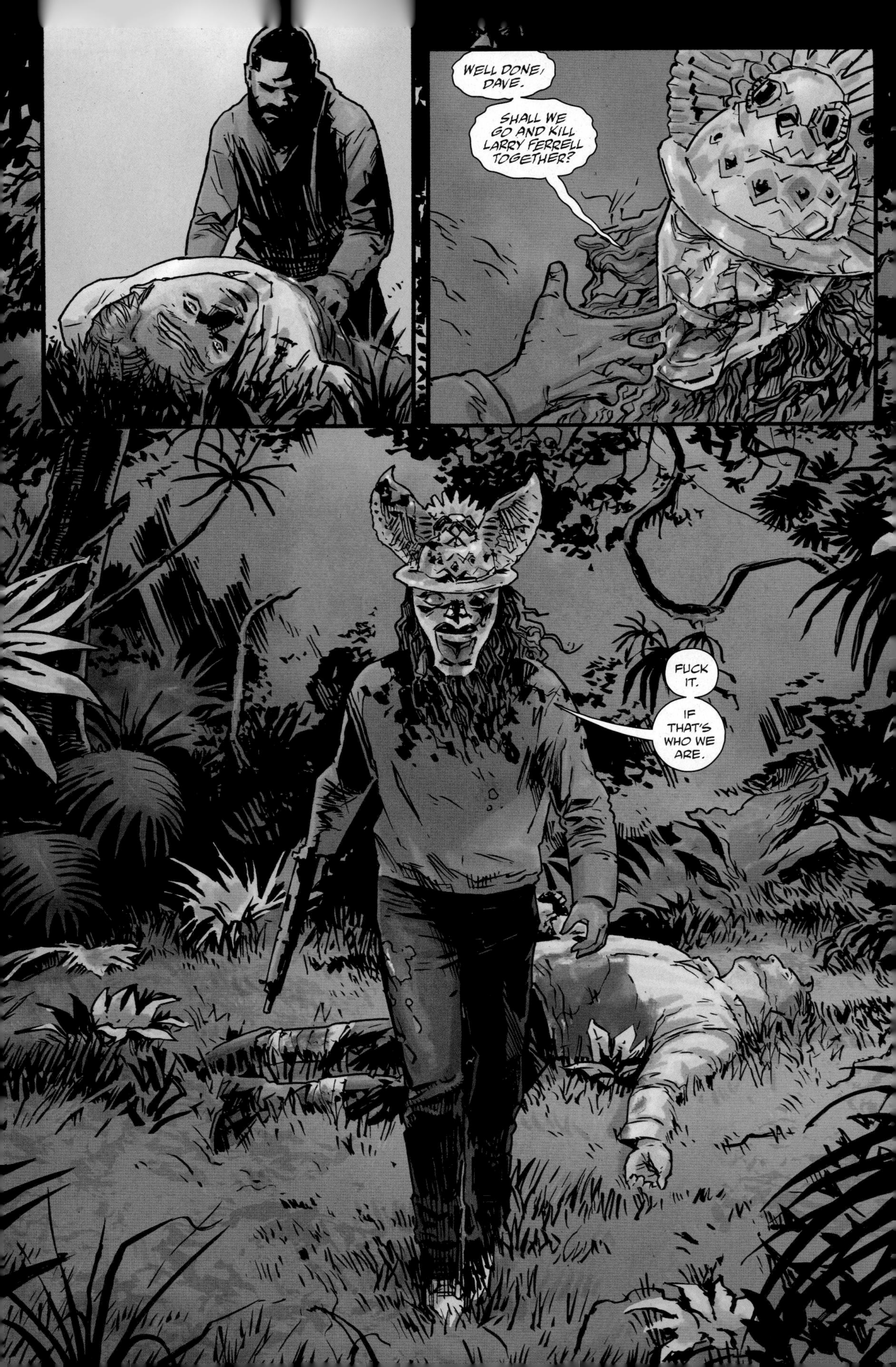
WELL DONE, DAVE.
SHALL WE GO AND KILL LARRY FERRELL TOGETHER?
FUCK IT.
IF THAT'S WHO WE ARE.

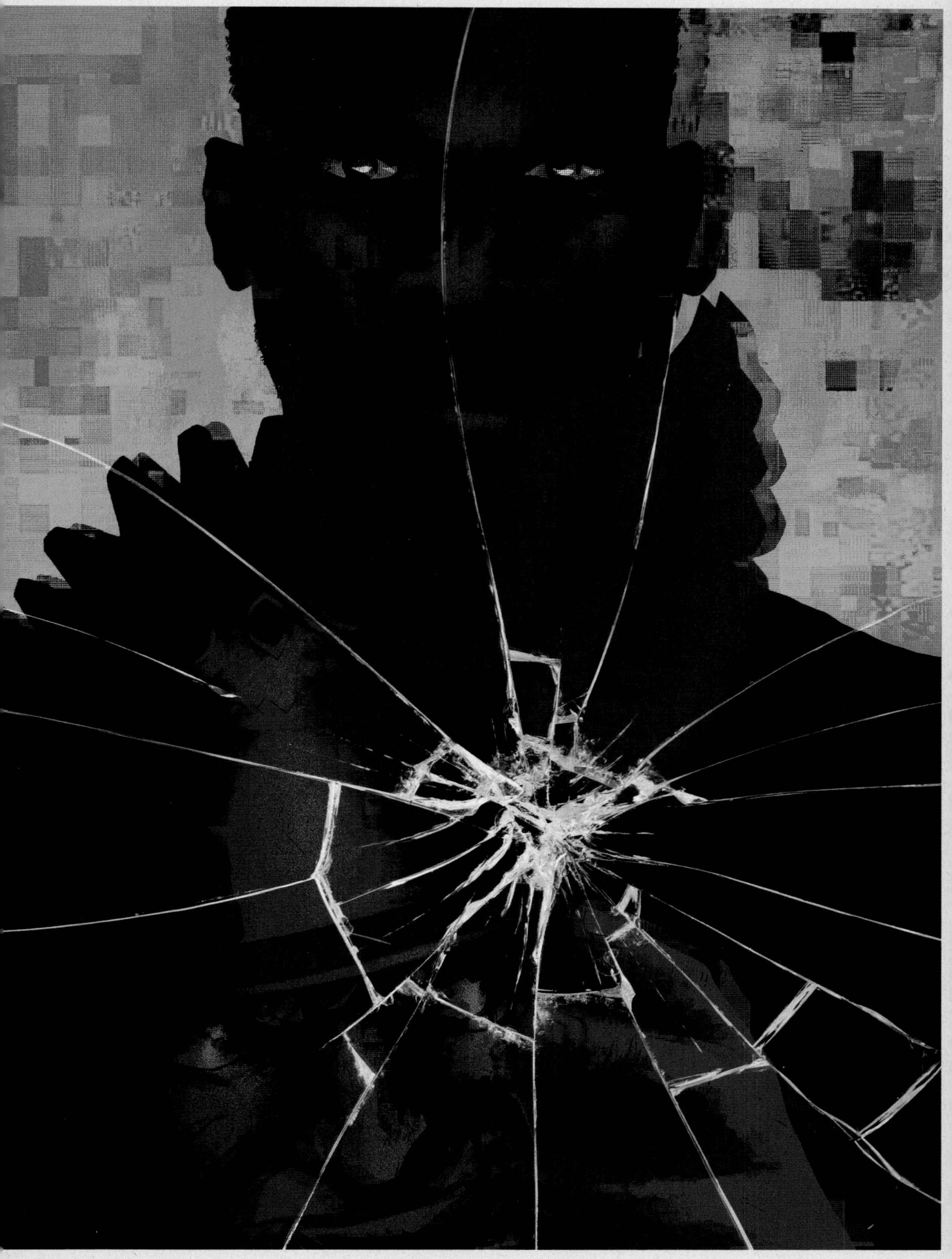

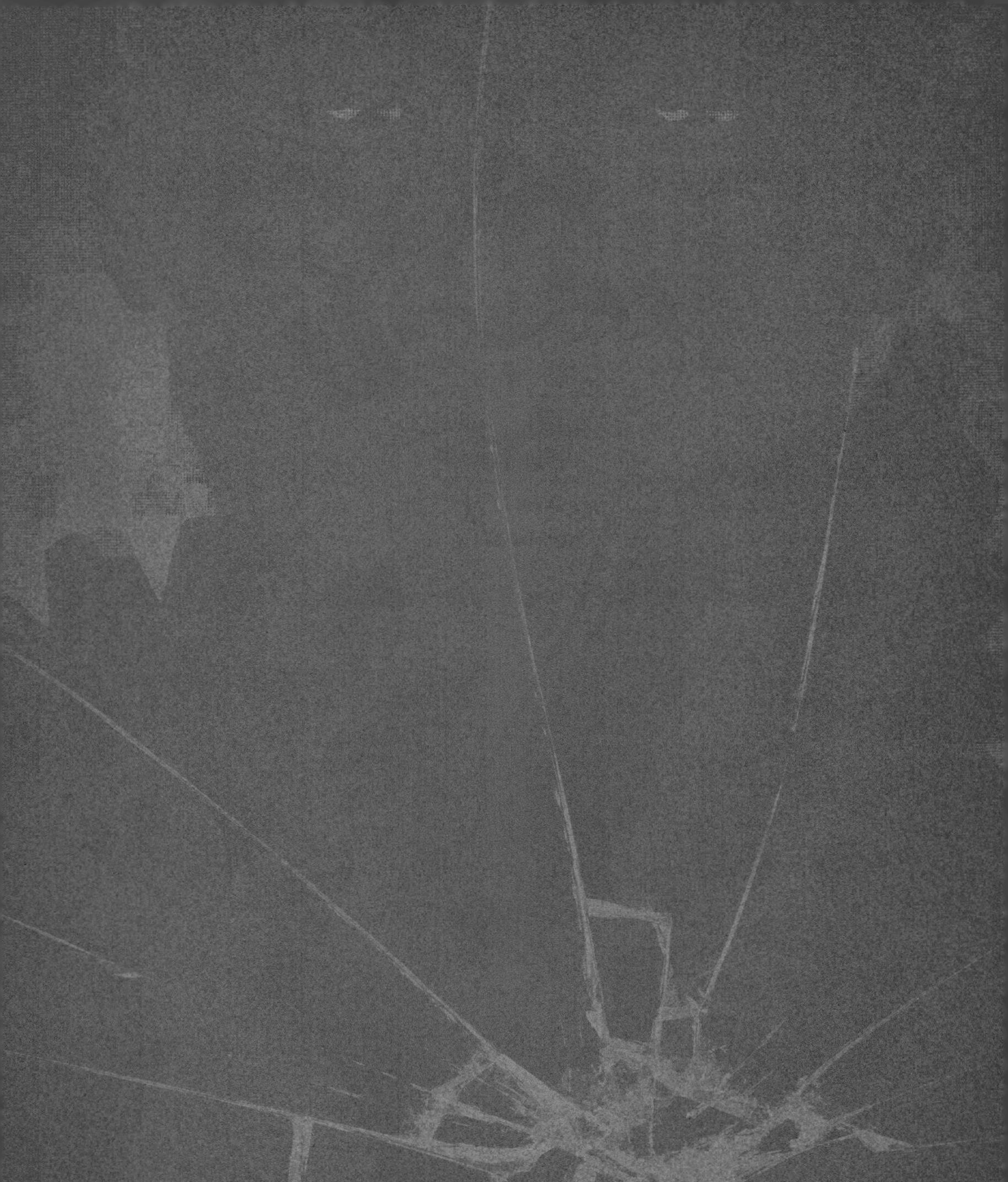

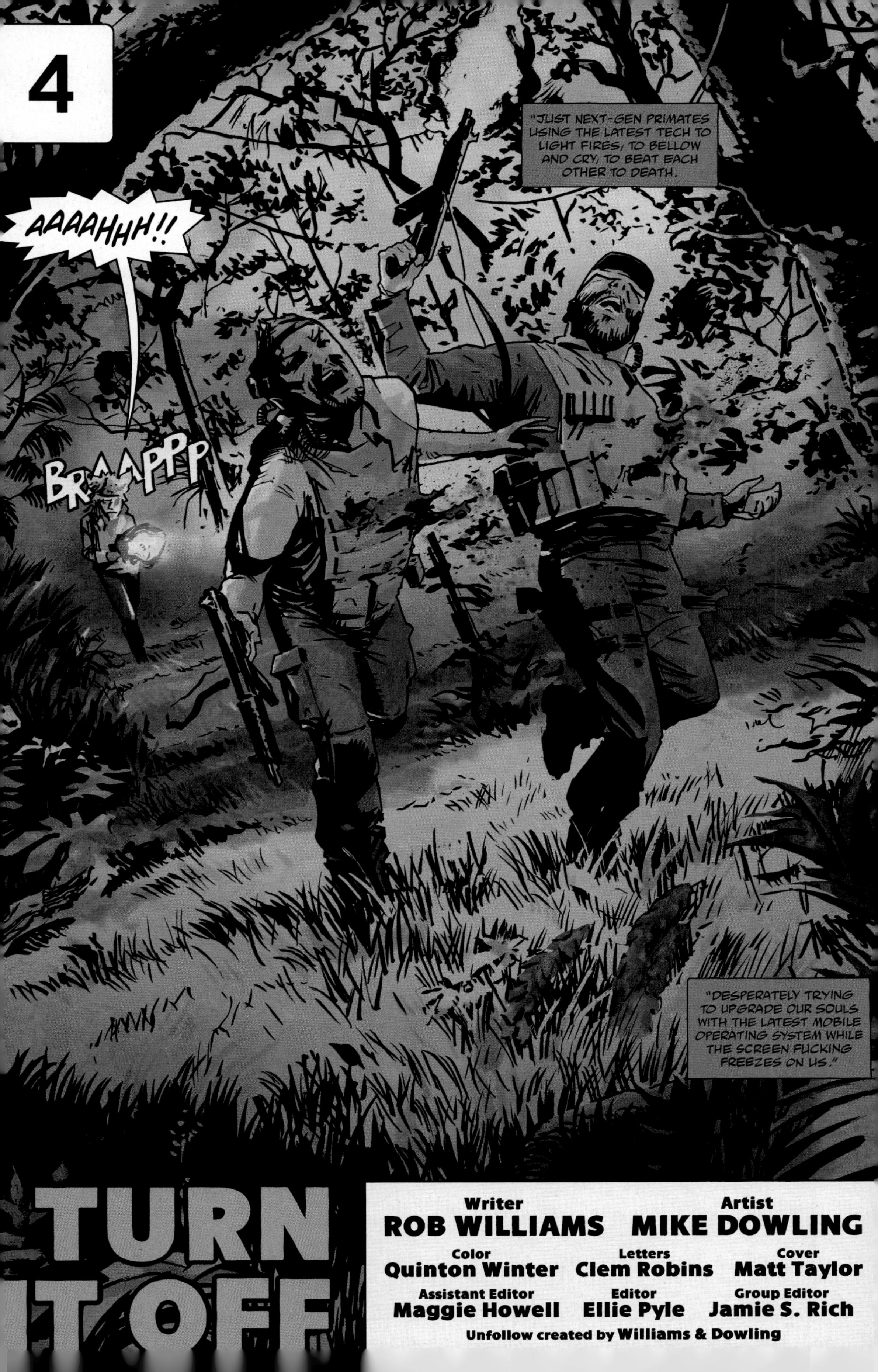
4
"JUST NEXT-GEN PRIMATES USING THE LATEST TECH TO LIGHT FIRES, TO BELLOW AND CRY, TO BEAT EACH OTHER TO DEATH.
AAAAHHH!!
BRAAAPPP
"DESPERATELY TRYING TO UPGRADE OUR SOULS WITH THE LATEST MOBILE OPERATING SYSTEM WHILE THE SCREEN FUCKING FREEZES ON US."
TURN IT OFF

Writer
ROB WILLIAMS

Artist
MIKE DOWLING

Color
Quinton Winter

Letters
Clem Robins

Cover
Matt Taylor

Assistant Editor
Maggie Howell

Editor
Ellie Pyle

Group Editor
Jamie S. Rich

Unfollow created by Williams & Dowling

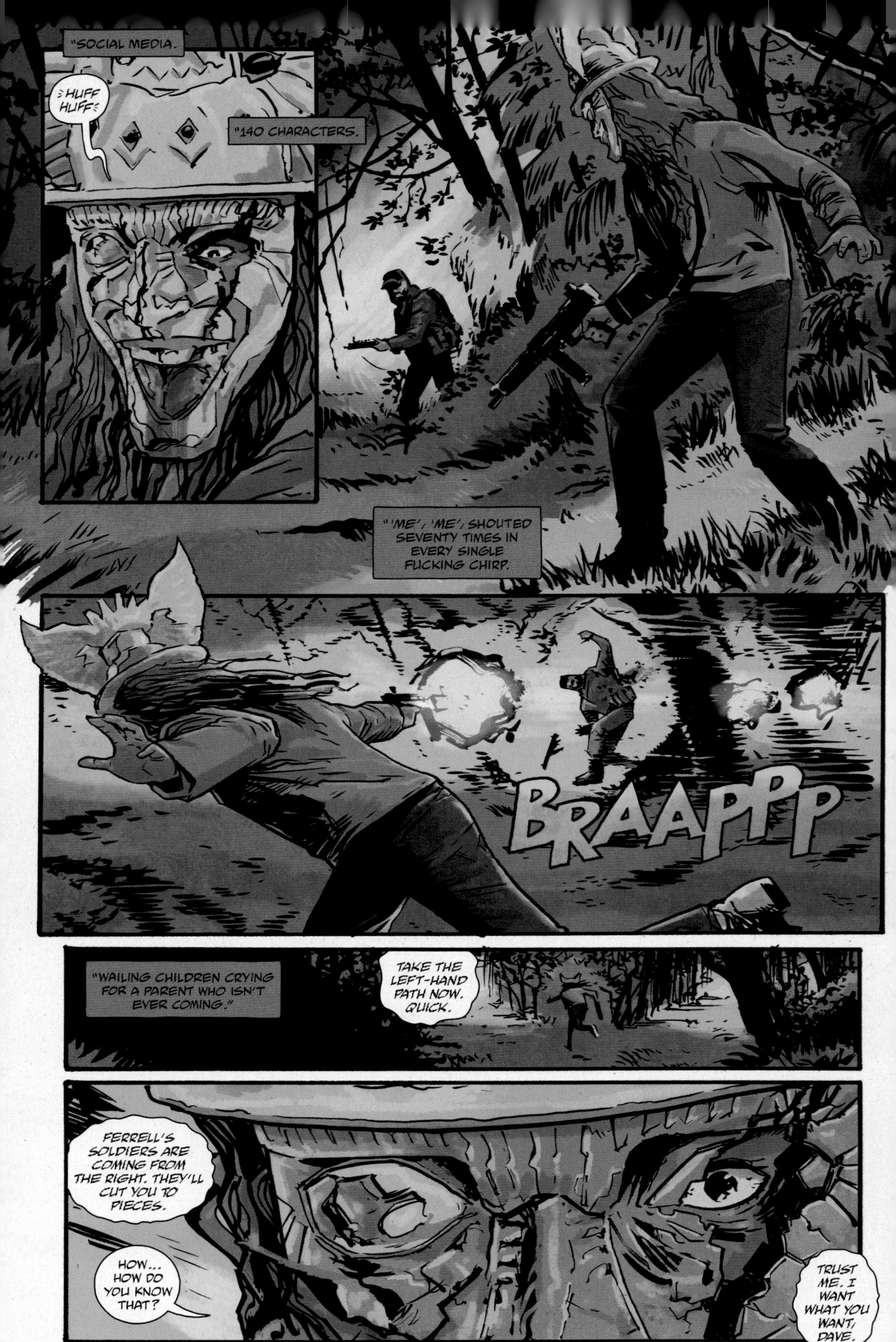
"SOCIAL MEDIA.
HUFF HUFF
"140 CHARACTERS.
"'ME', 'ME', SHOUTED SEVENTY TIMES IN EVERY SINGLE FUCKING CHIRP.
BRAAPPP
"WAILING CHILDREN CRYING FOR A PARENT WHO ISN'T EVER COMING."
TAKE THE LEFT-HAND PATH NOW. QUICK.
FERRELL'S SOLDIERS ARE COMING FROM THE RIGHT. THEY'LL CUT YOU TO PIECES.
HOW... HOW DO YOU KNOW THAT?
TRUST ME. I WANT WHAT YOU WANT, DAVE.

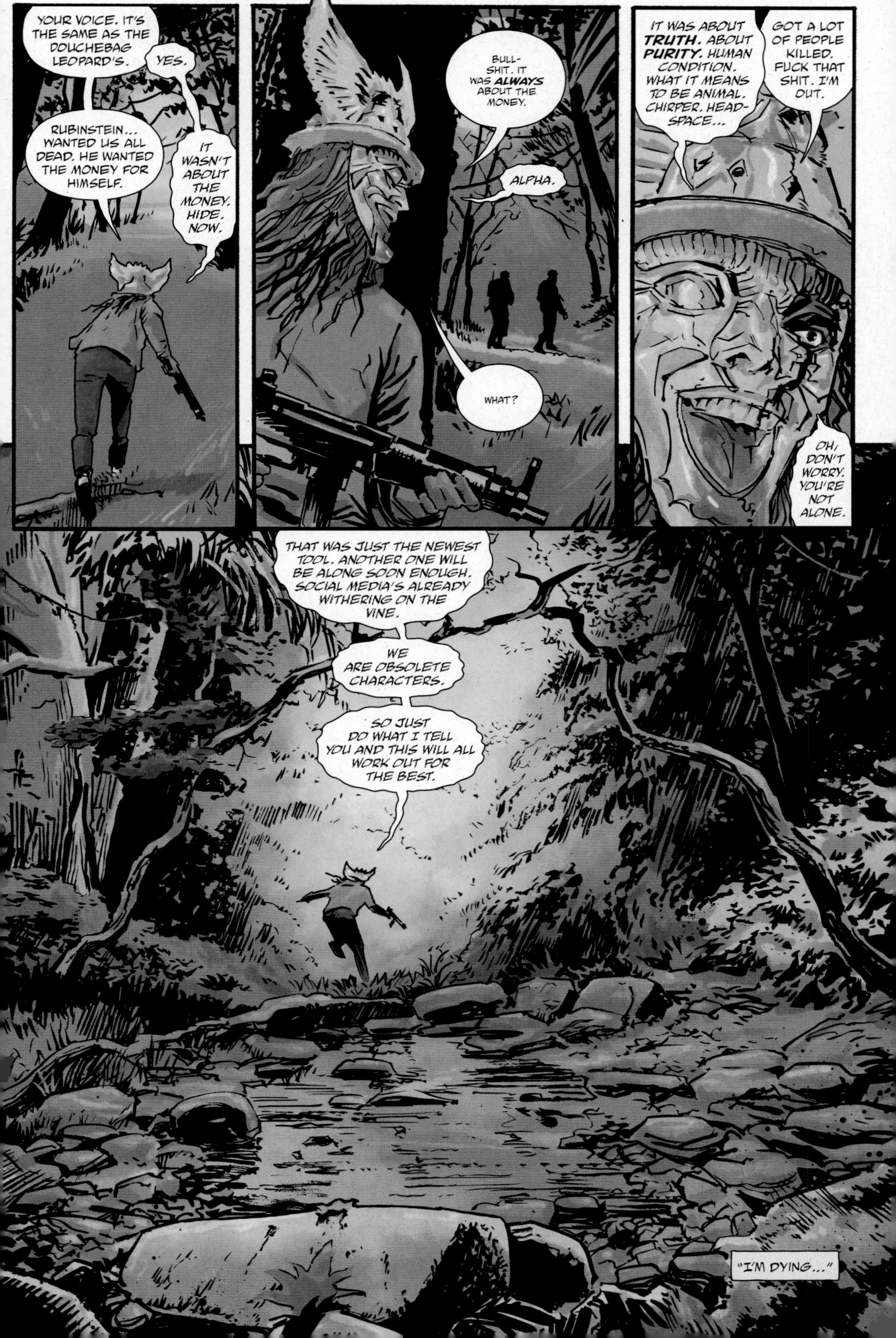

YOUR VOICE. IT'S THE SAME AS THE DOUCHEBAG LEOPARD'S.
YES.
RUBINSTEIN... WANTED US ALL DEAD. HE WANTED THE MONEY FOR HIMSELF.
IT WASN'T ABOUT THE MONEY. HIDE. NOW.
BULL-SHIT. IT WAS **ALWAYS** ABOUT THE MONEY.
ALPHA.
WHAT?
IT WAS ABOUT **TRUTH**. ABOUT **PURITY**. HUMAN CONDITION. WHAT IT MEANS TO BE ANIMAL. CHIRPER. HEAD-SPACE...
GOT A LOT OF PEOPLE KILLED. FUCK THAT SHIT. I'M OUT.
OH, DON'T WORRY. YOU'RE NOT ALONE.
THAT WAS JUST THE NEWEST TOOL. ANOTHER ONE WILL BE ALONG SOON ENOUGH. SOCIAL MEDIA'S ALREADY WITHERING ON THE VINE.
WE ARE OBSOLETE CHARACTERS.
SO JUST DO WHAT I TELL YOU AND THIS WILL ALL WORK OUT FOR THE BEST.
"I'M DYING..."

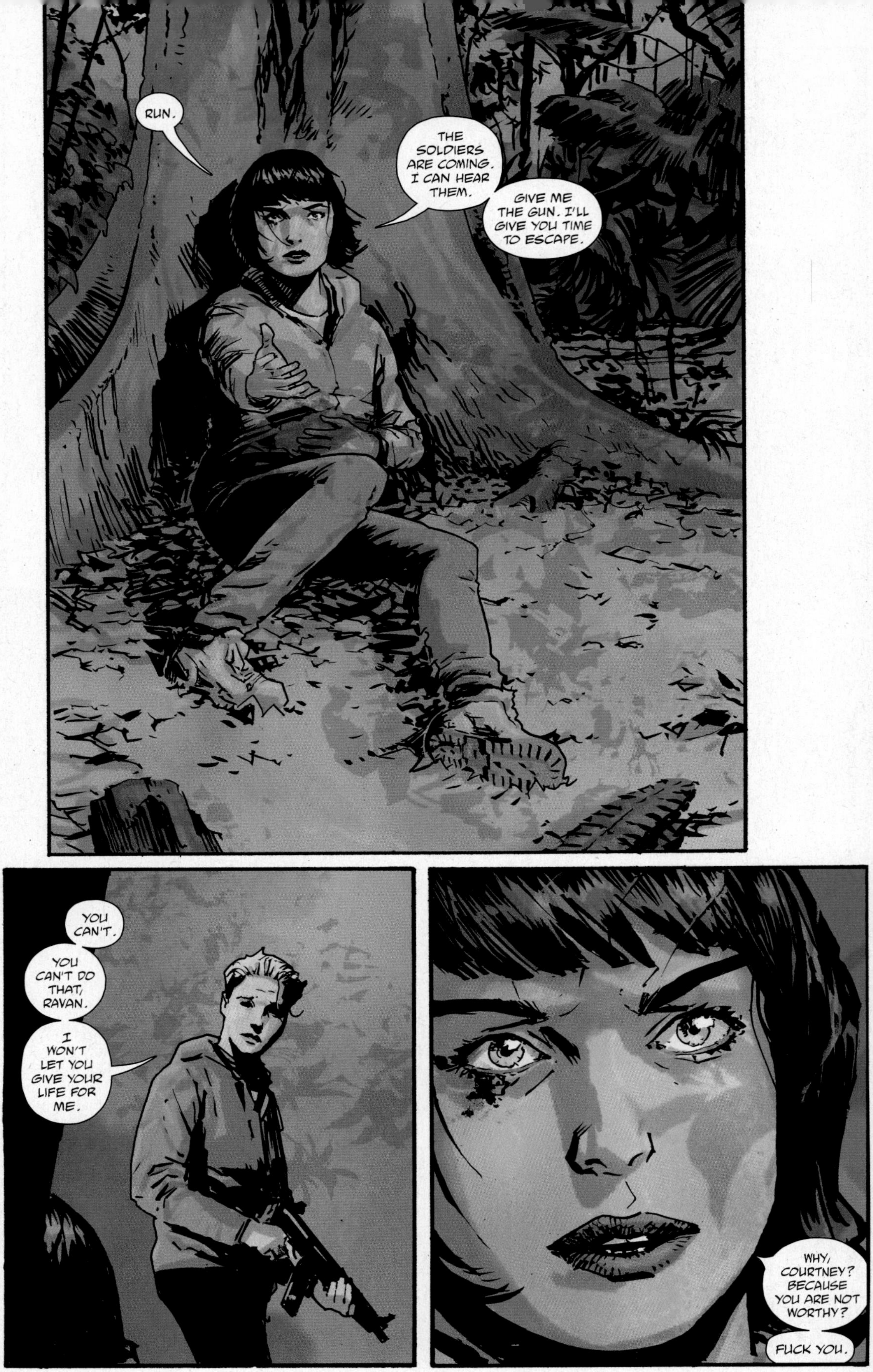
RUN.
THE SOLDIERS ARE COMING. I CAN HEAR THEM.
GIVE ME THE GUN. I'LL GIVE YOU TIME TO ESCAPE.
YOU CAN'T.
YOU CAN'T DO THAT, RAVAN.
I WON'T LET YOU GIVE YOUR LIFE FOR ME.
WHY, COURTNEY? BECAUSE YOU ARE NOT WORTHY?
FUCK YOU.

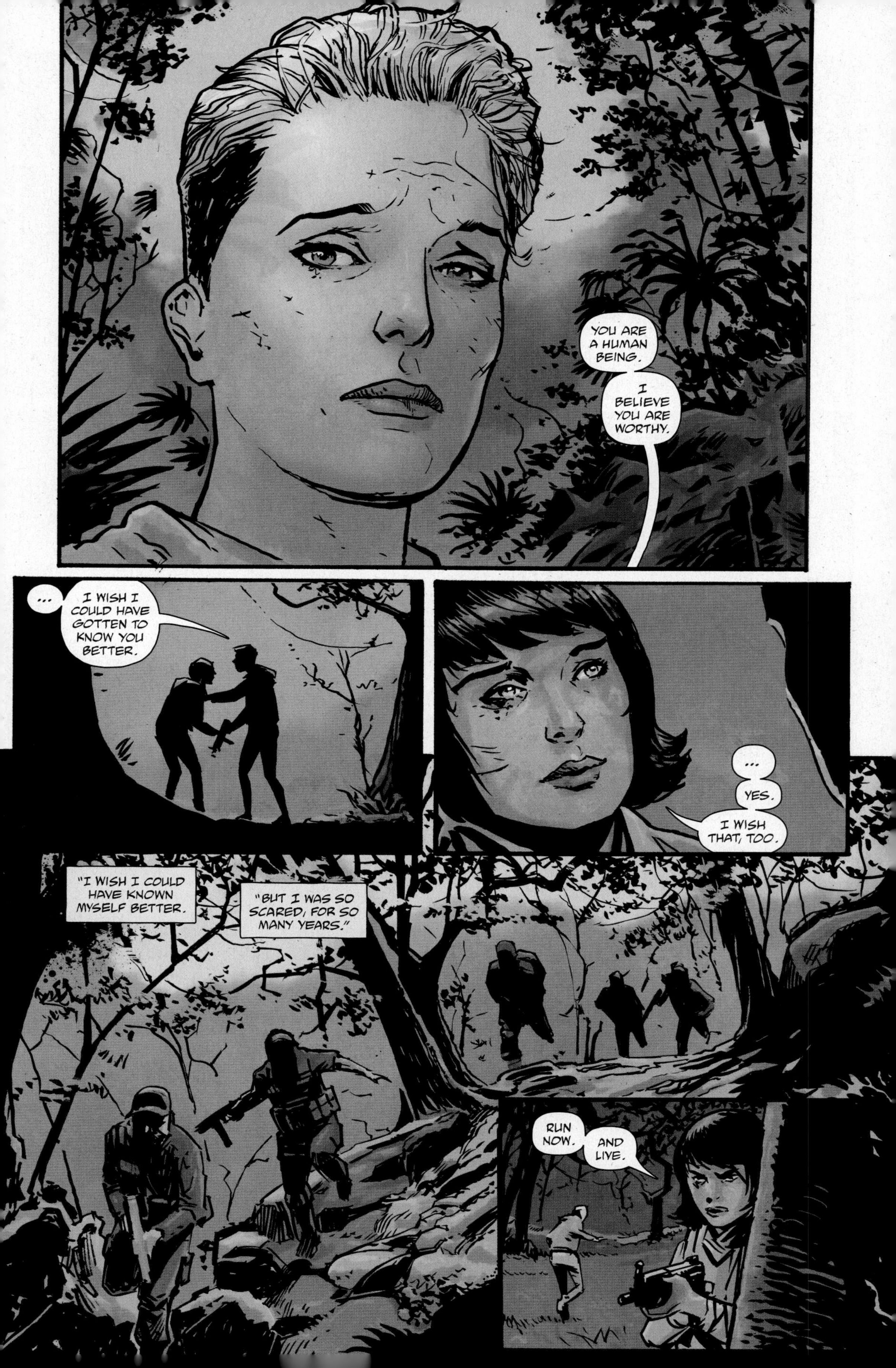
YOU ARE A HUMAN BEING.
I BELIEVE YOU ARE WORTHY.
...
I WISH I COULD HAVE GOTTEN TO KNOW YOU BETTER.
...
YES.
I WISH THAT, TOO.
"I WISH I COULD HAVE KNOWN MYSELF BETTER.
"BUT I WAS SO SCARED, FOR SO MANY YEARS."
RUN NOW.
AND LIVE.

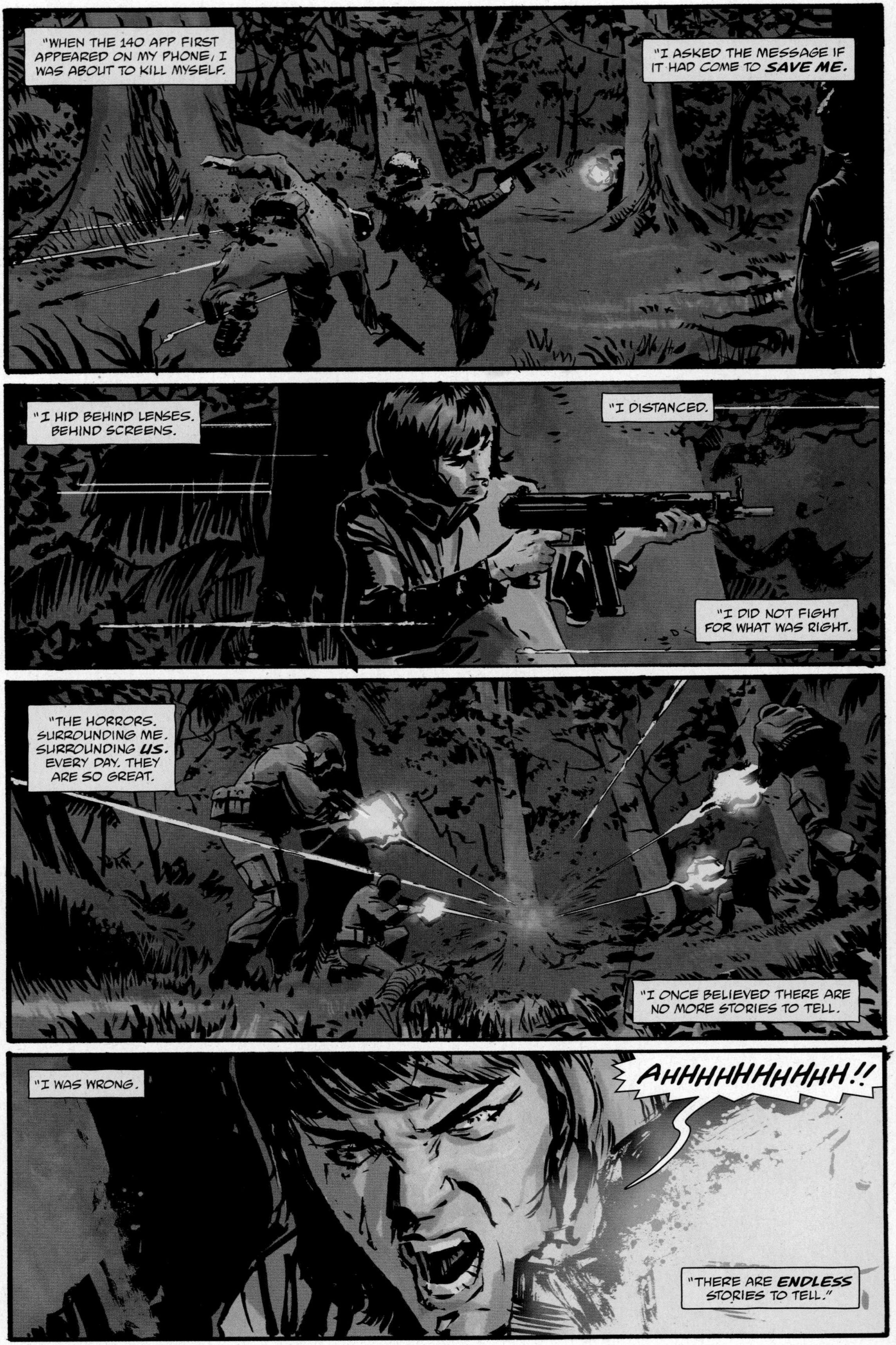
"WHEN THE 140 APP FIRST APPEARED ON MY PHONE, I WAS ABOUT TO KILL MYSELF.
"I ASKED THE MESSAGE IF IT HAD COME TO SAVE ME.
"I HID BEHIND LENSES. BEHIND SCREENS.
"I DISTANCED.
"I DID NOT FIGHT FOR WHAT WAS RIGHT.
"THE HORRORS. SURROUNDING ME. SURROUNDING US. EVERY DAY. THEY ARE SO GREAT.
"I ONCE BELIEVED THERE ARE NO MORE STORIES TO TELL.
"I WAS WRONG.
AHHHHHHHHH!!
"THERE ARE ENDLESS STORIES TO TELL."

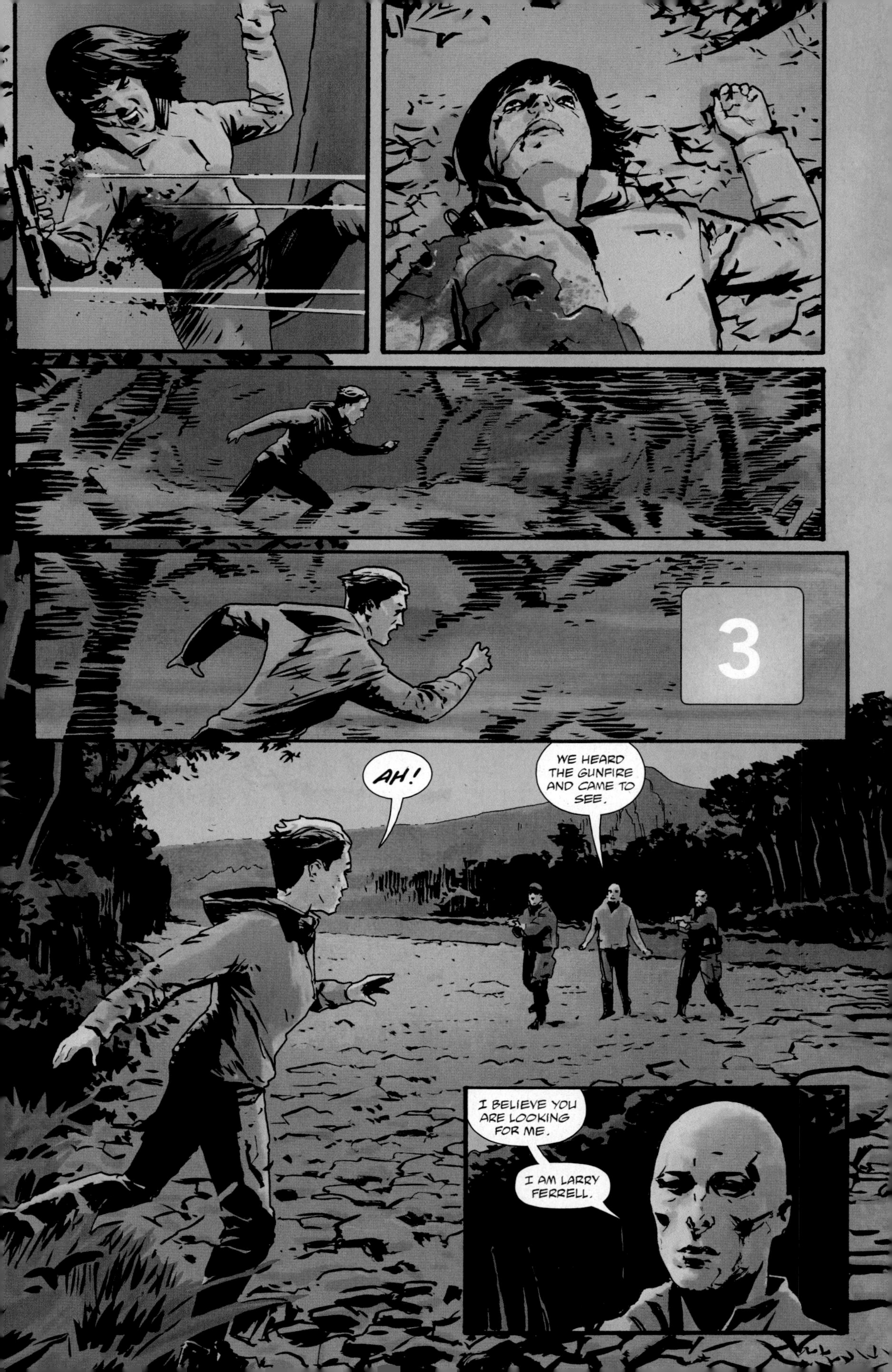
3
AH!
WE HEARD THE GUNFIRE AND CAME TO SEE.
I BELIEVE YOU ARE LOOKING FOR ME.
I AM LARRY FERRELL.

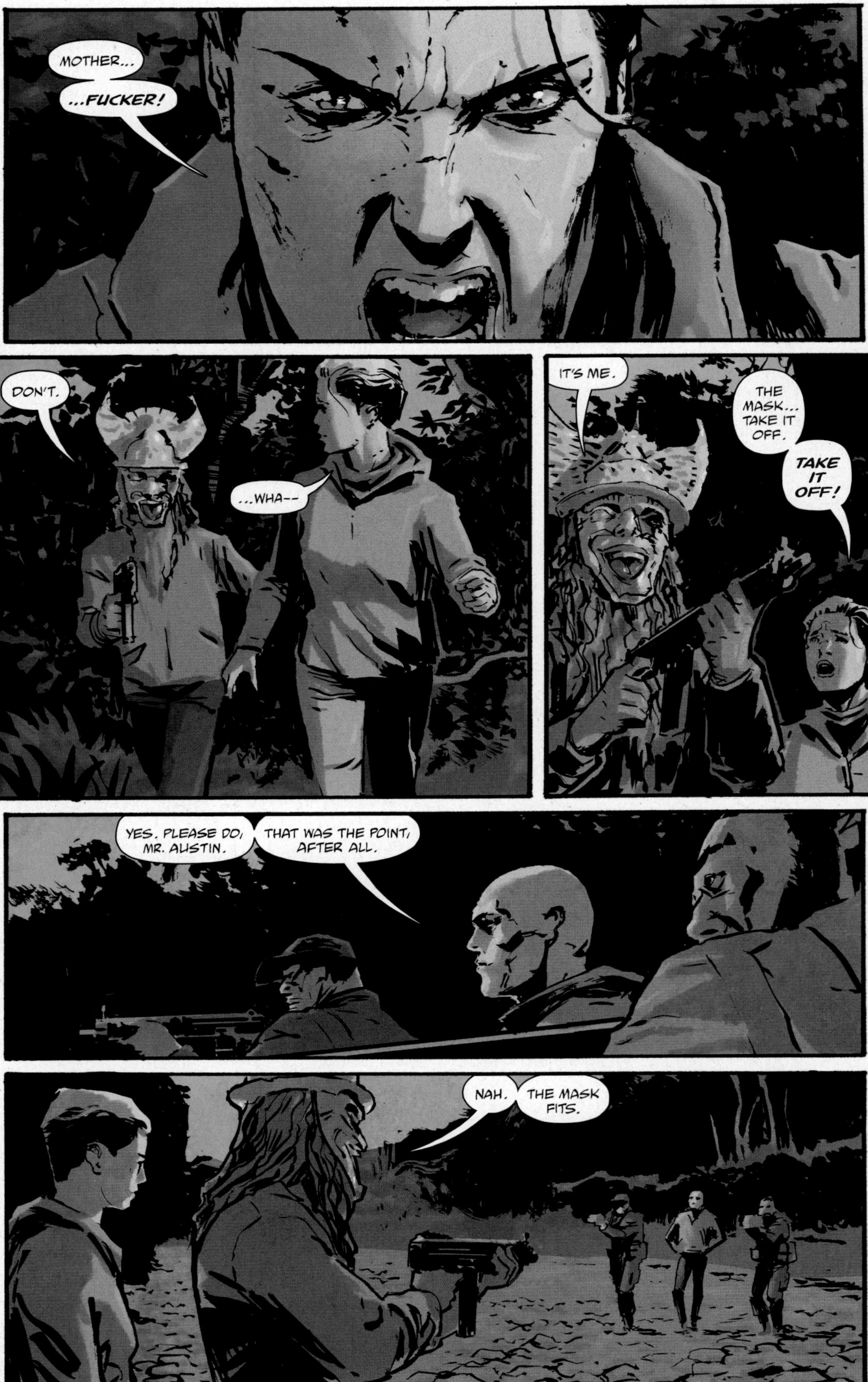
MOTHER...
...FUCKER!
DON'T.
...WHA--
IT'S ME.
THE MASK... TAKE IT OFF.
TAKE IT OFF!
YES. PLEASE DO, MR. AUSTIN.
THAT WAS THE POINT, AFTER ALL.
NAH.
THE MASK FITS.

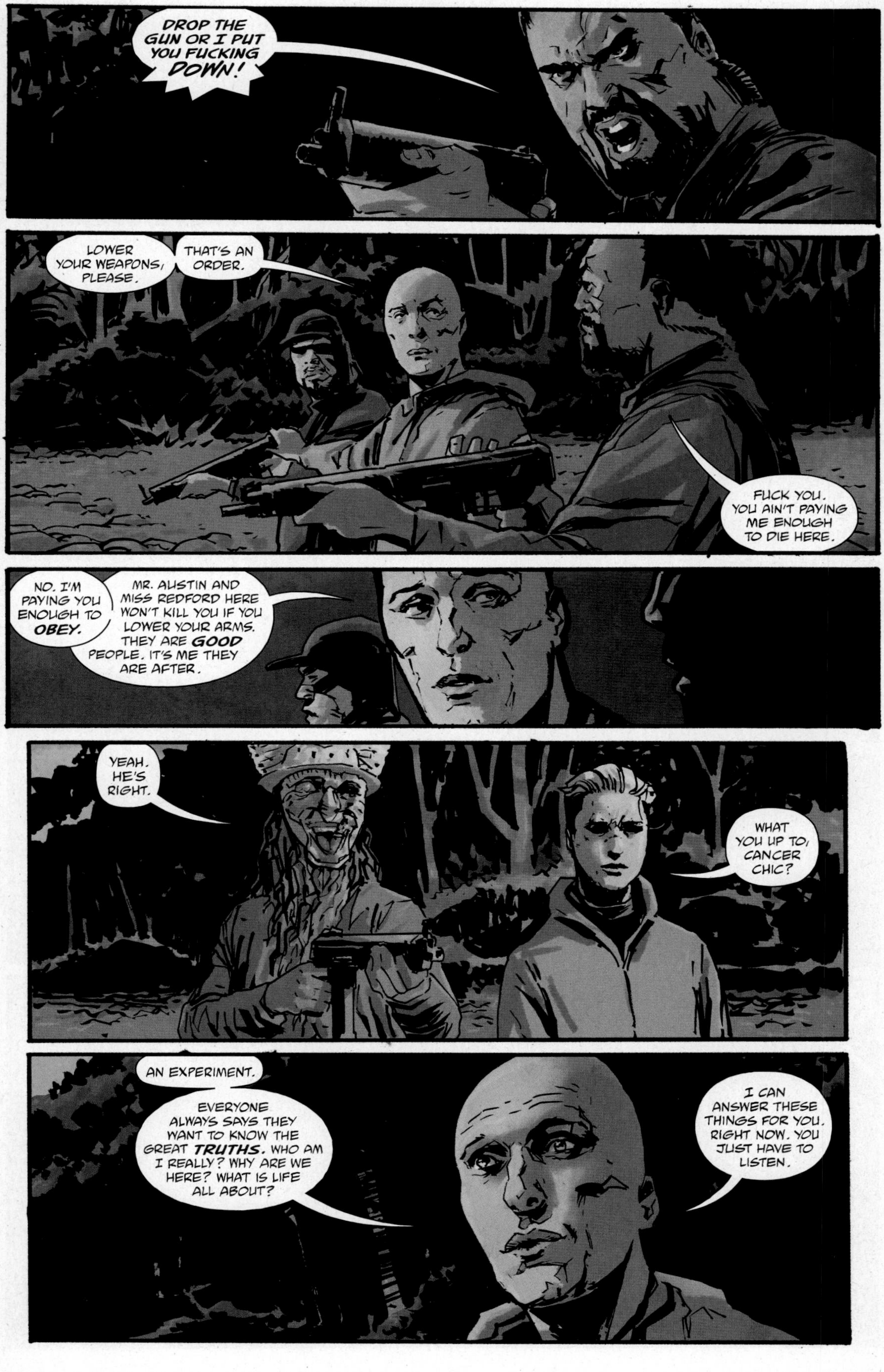
DROP THE GUN OR I PUT YOU FUCKING DOWN!
LOWER YOUR WEAPONS, PLEASE.
THAT'S AN ORDER.
FUCK YOU. YOU AIN'T PAYING ME ENOUGH TO DIE HERE.
NO. I'M PAYING YOU ENOUGH TO OBEY.
MR. AUSTIN AND MISS REDFORD HERE WON'T KILL YOU IF YOU LOWER YOUR ARMS. THEY ARE GOOD PEOPLE. IT'S ME THEY ARE AFTER.
YEAH. HE'S RIGHT.
WHAT YOU UP TO, CANCER CHIC?
AN EXPERIMENT.
EVERYONE ALWAYS SAYS THEY WANT TO KNOW THE GREAT TRUTHS. WHO AM I REALLY? WHY ARE WE HERE? WHAT IS LIFE ALL ABOUT?
I CAN ANSWER THESE THINGS FOR YOU. RIGHT NOW. YOU JUST HAVE TO LISTEN.

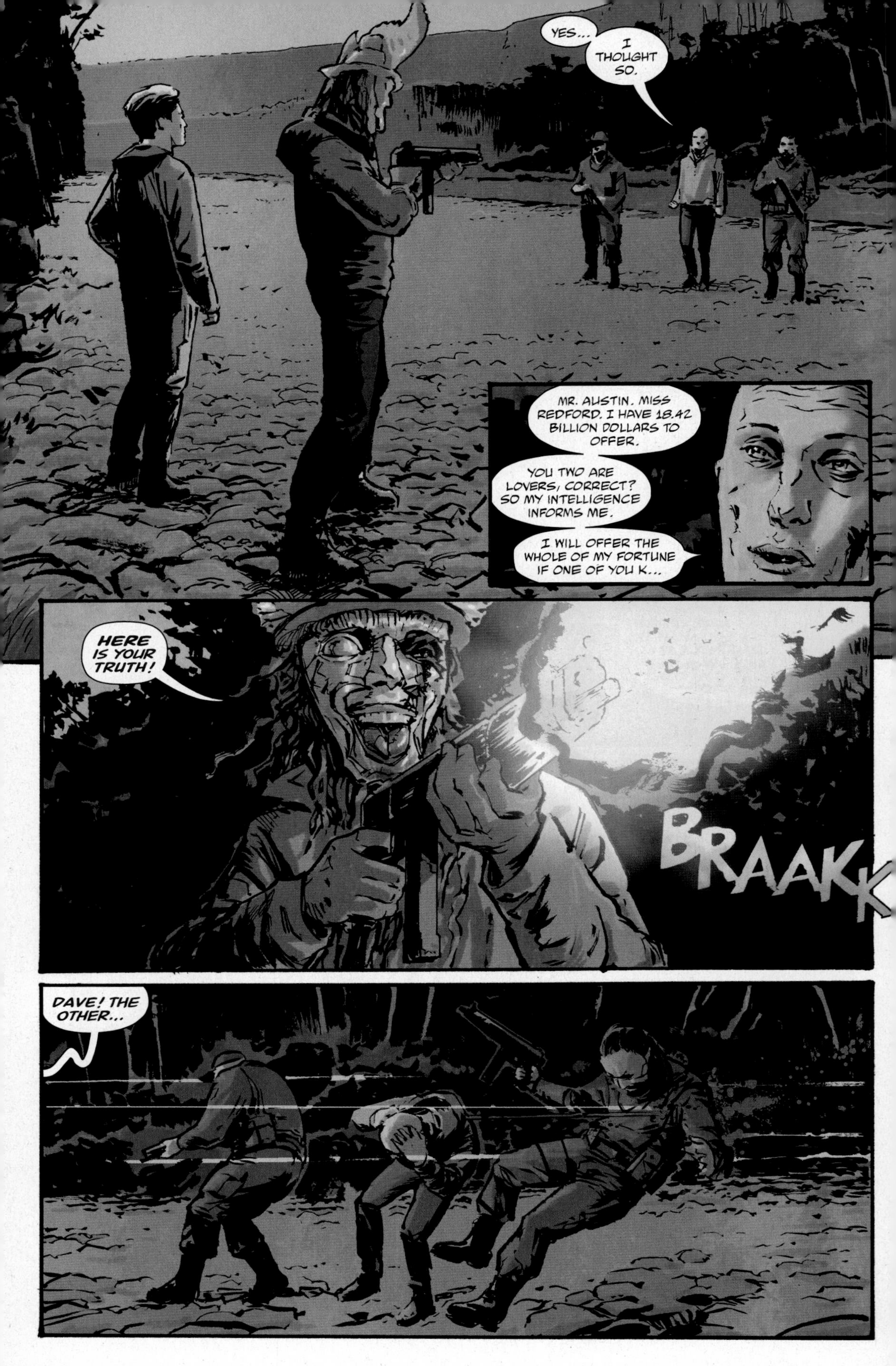
YES... I THOUGHT SO.
MR. AUSTIN. MISS REDFORD. I HAVE 18.42 BILLION DOLLARS TO OFFER.
YOU TWO ARE LOVERS, CORRECT? SO MY INTELLIGENCE INFORMS ME.
I WILL OFFER THE WHOLE OF MY FORTUNE IF ONE OF YOU K...
HERE IS YOUR TRUTH!
BRAAKK
DAVE! THE OTHER...

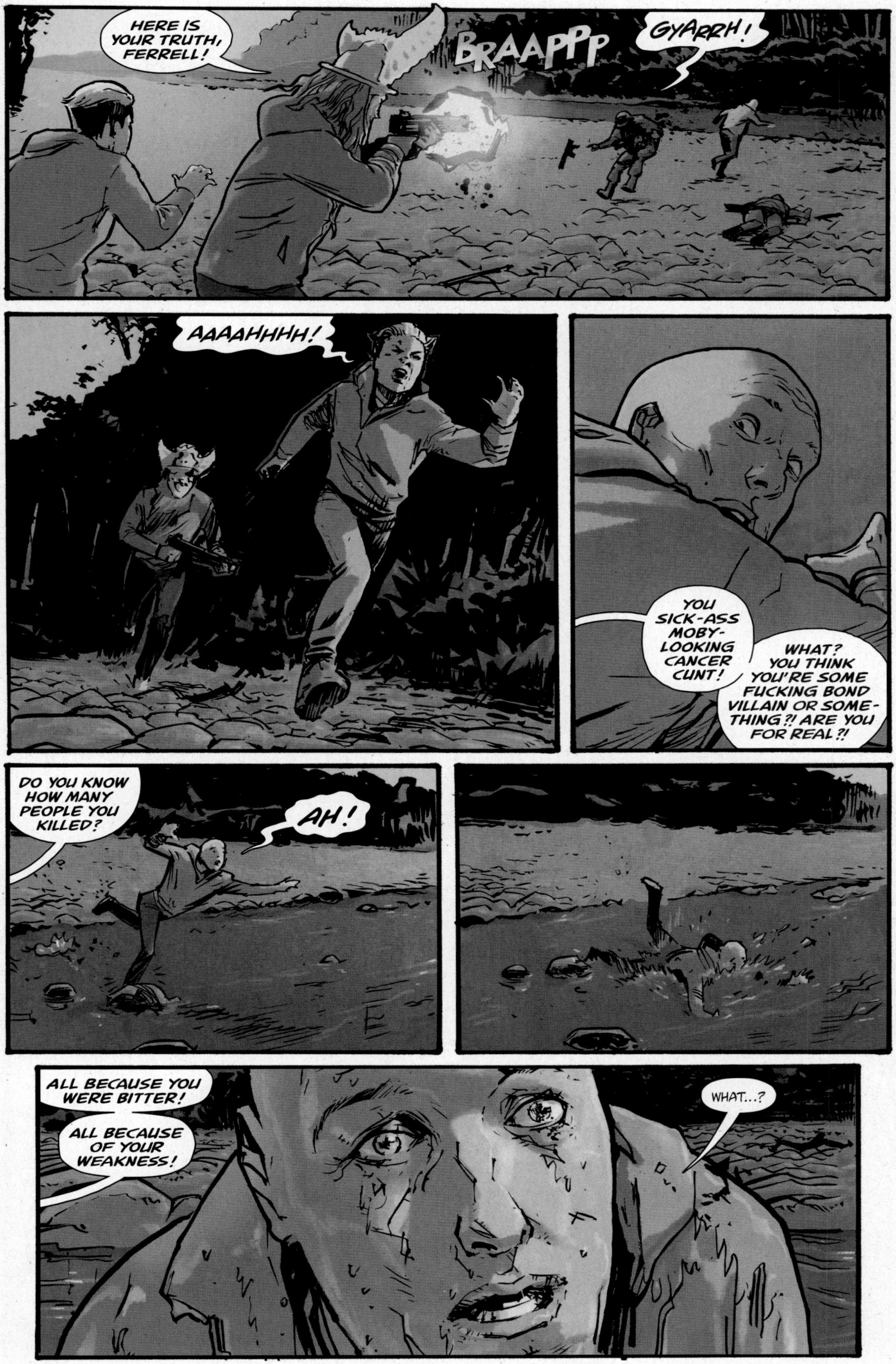
HERE IS YOUR TRUTH, FERRELL!
BRAAPPP
GYARRH!
AAAAHHHH!
YOU SICK-ASS MOBY-LOOKING CANCER CUNT!
WHAT? YOU THINK YOU'RE SOME FUCKING BOND VILLAIN OR SOME-THING?! ARE YOU FOR REAL?!
DO YOU KNOW HOW MANY PEOPLE YOU KILLED?
AH!
ALL BECAUSE YOU WERE BITTER!
ALL BECAUSE OF YOUR WEAKNESS!
WHAT...?

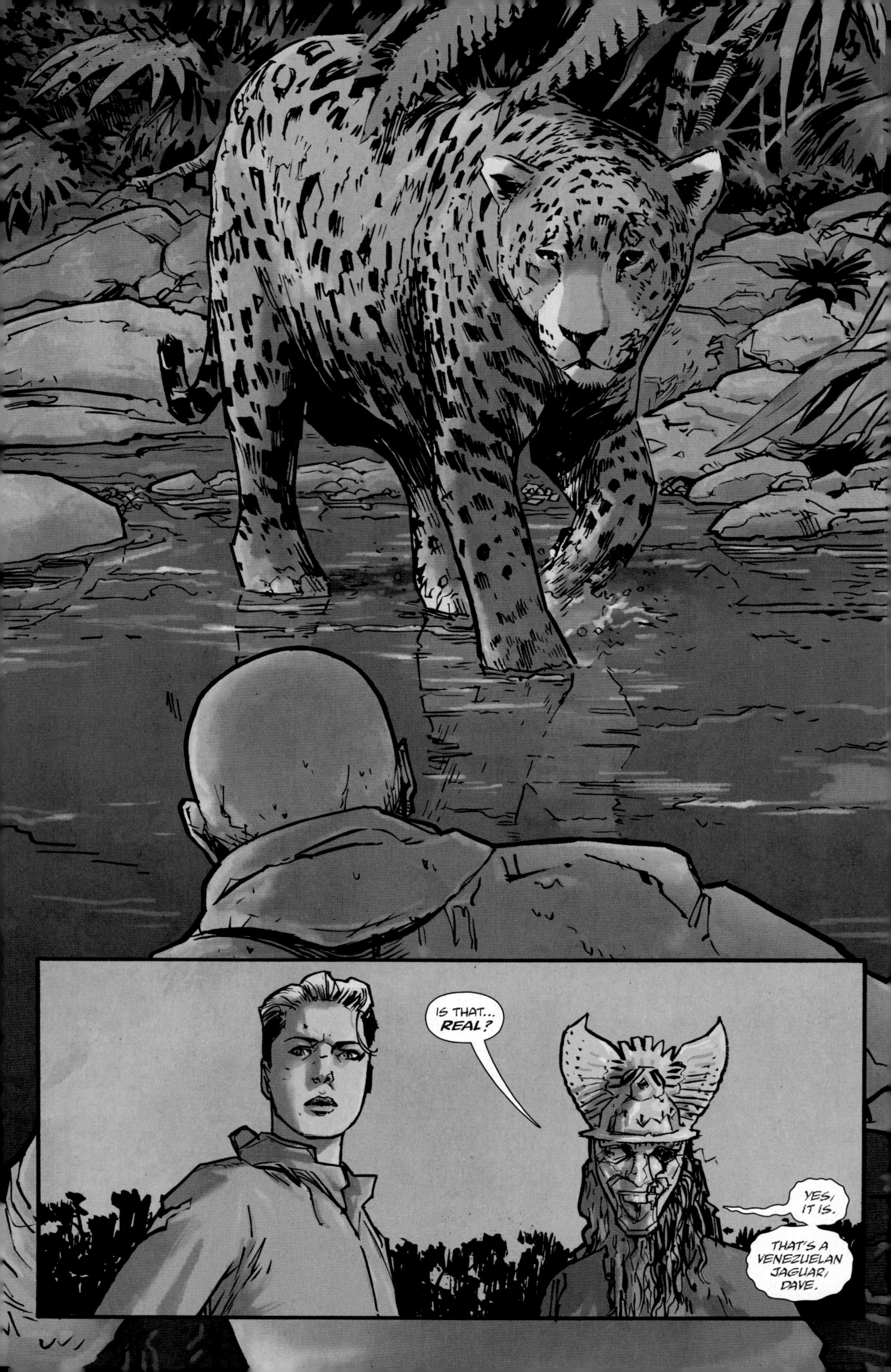
IS THAT... REAL?
YES, IT IS.
THAT'S A VENEZUELAN JAGUAR, DAVE.

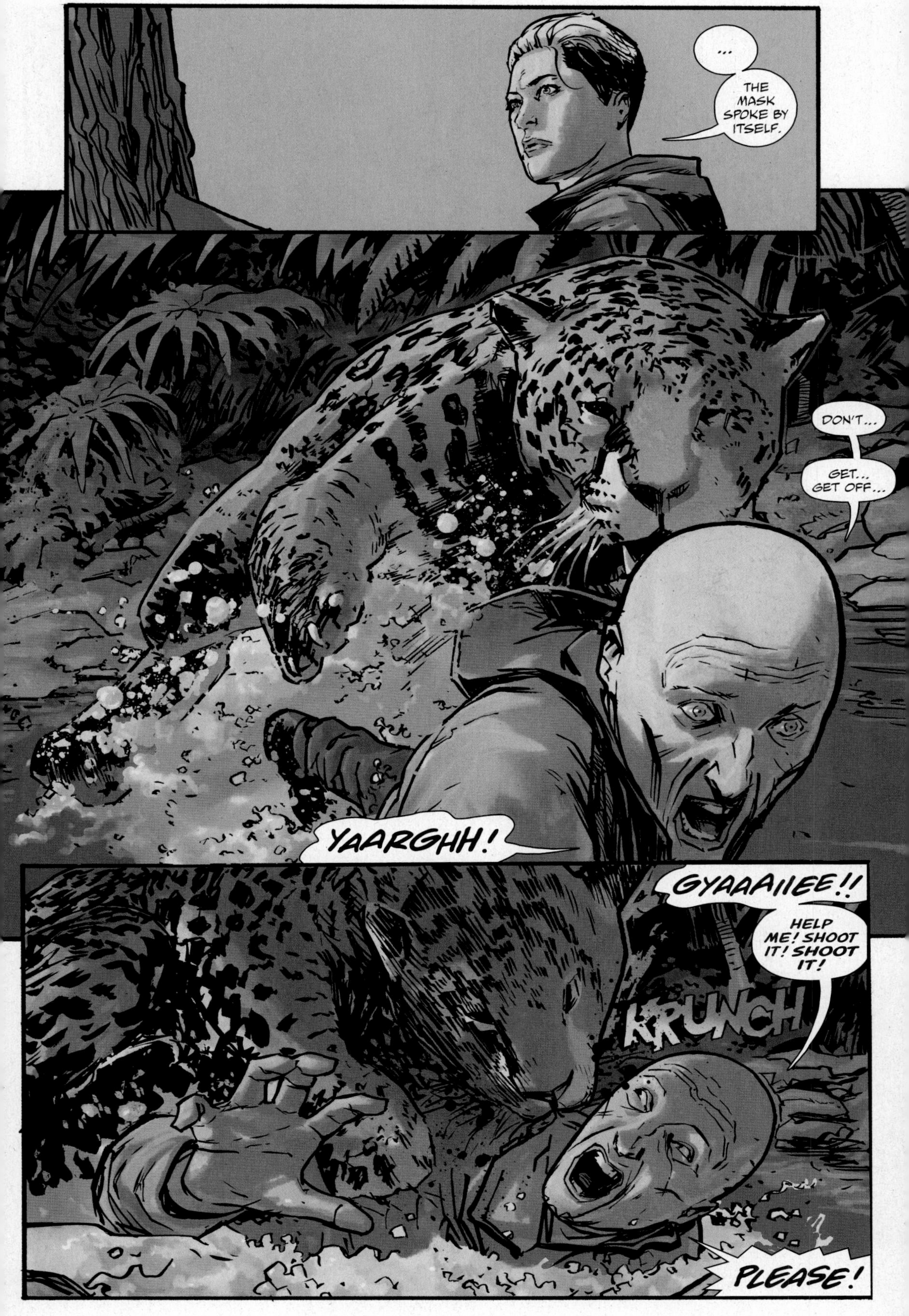
...
THE MASK SPOKE BY ITSELF.
DON'T...
GET... GET OFF...
YAARGHH!
GYAAAIIEE!!
HELP ME! SHOOT IT! SHOOT IT!
KRUNCH
PLEASE!

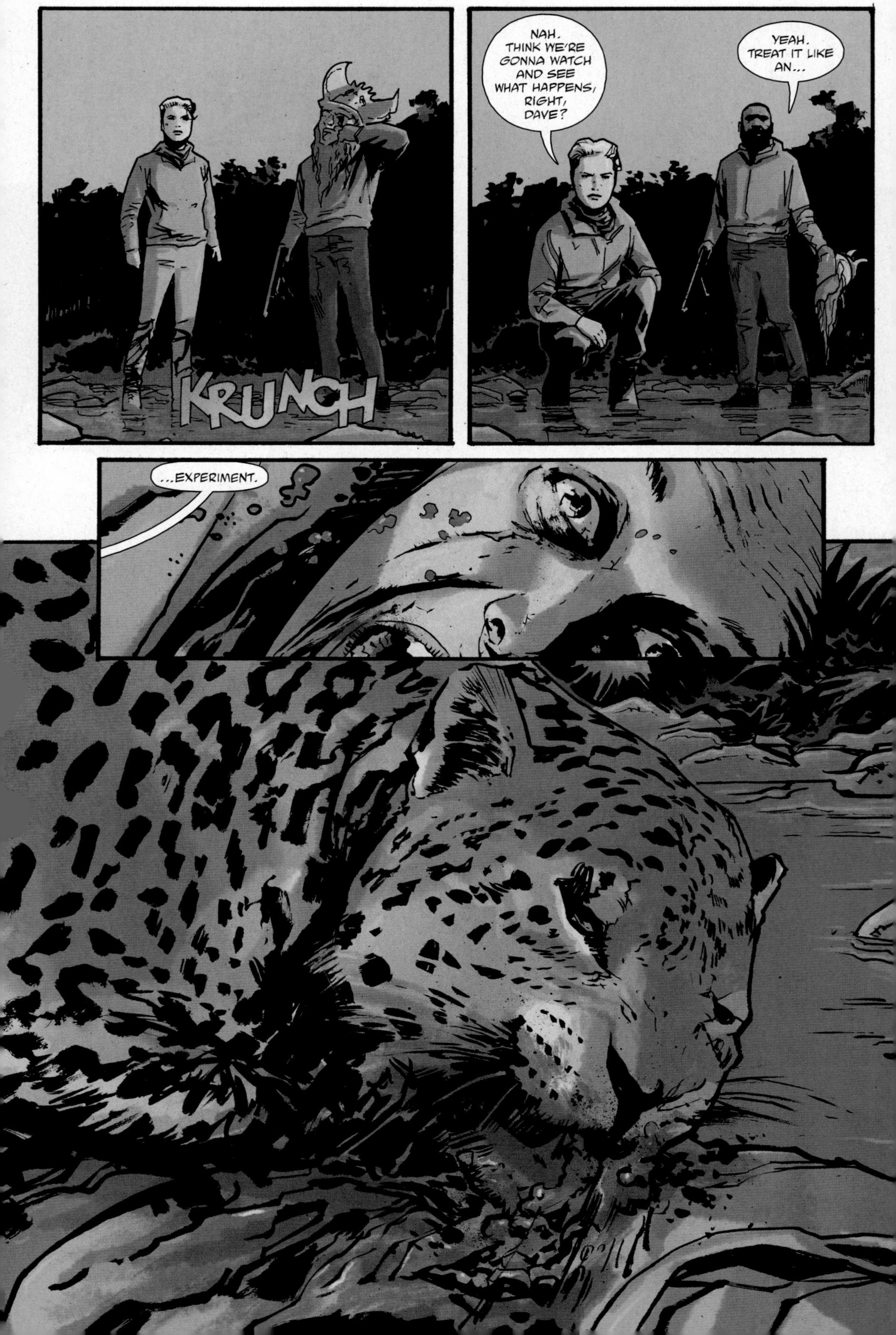
KRUNCH
NAH. THINK WE'RE GONNA WATCH AND SEE WHAT HAPPENS, RIGHT, DAVE?
YEAH. TREAT IT LIKE AN...
...EXPERIMENT.

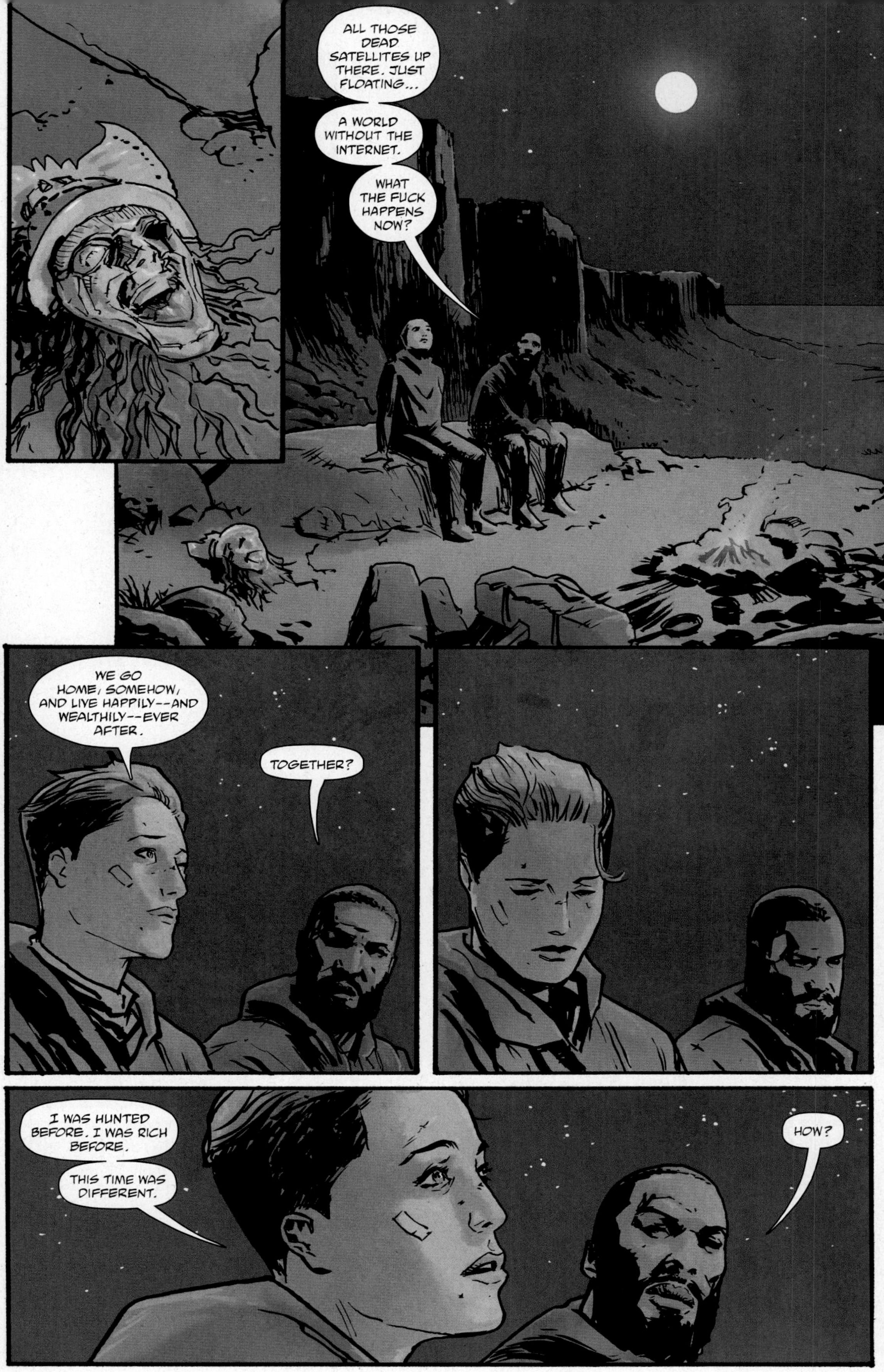
ALL THOSE DEAD SATELLITES UP THERE. JUST FLOATING...
A WORLD WITHOUT THE INTERNET.
WHAT THE FUCK HAPPENS NOW?
WE GO HOME, SOMEHOW, AND LIVE HAPPILY--AND WEALTHILY--EVER AFTER.
TOGETHER?
I WAS HUNTED BEFORE. I WAS RICH BEFORE.
THIS TIME WAS DIFFERENT.
HOW?

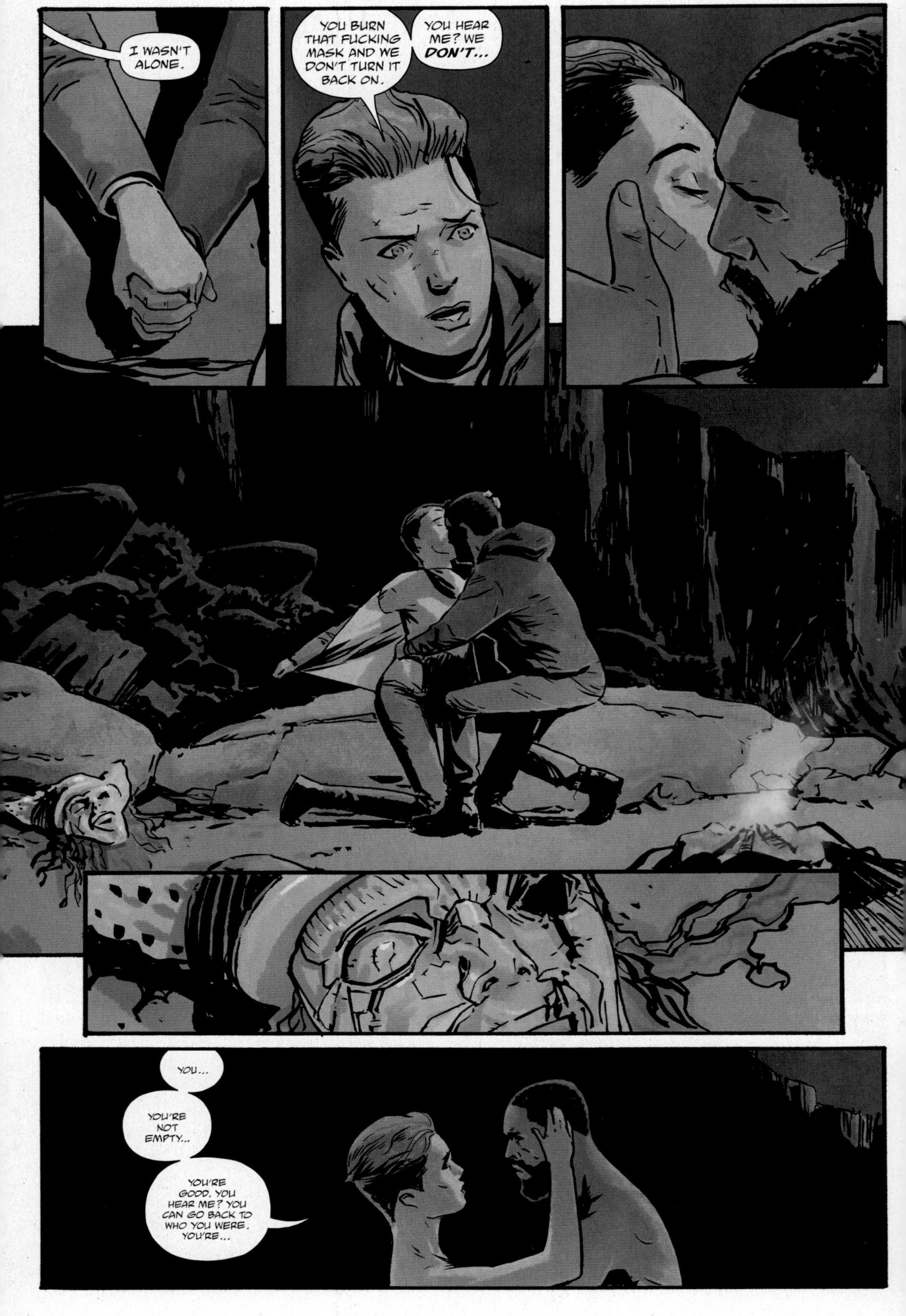
I WASN'T ALONE.
YOU BURN THAT FUCKING MASK AND WE DON'T TURN IT BACK ON.
YOU HEAR ME? WE **DON'T...**
YOU...
YOU'RE NOT EMPTY...
YOU'RE GOOD. YOU HEAR ME? YOU CAN GO BACK TO WHO YOU WERE. YOU'RE...

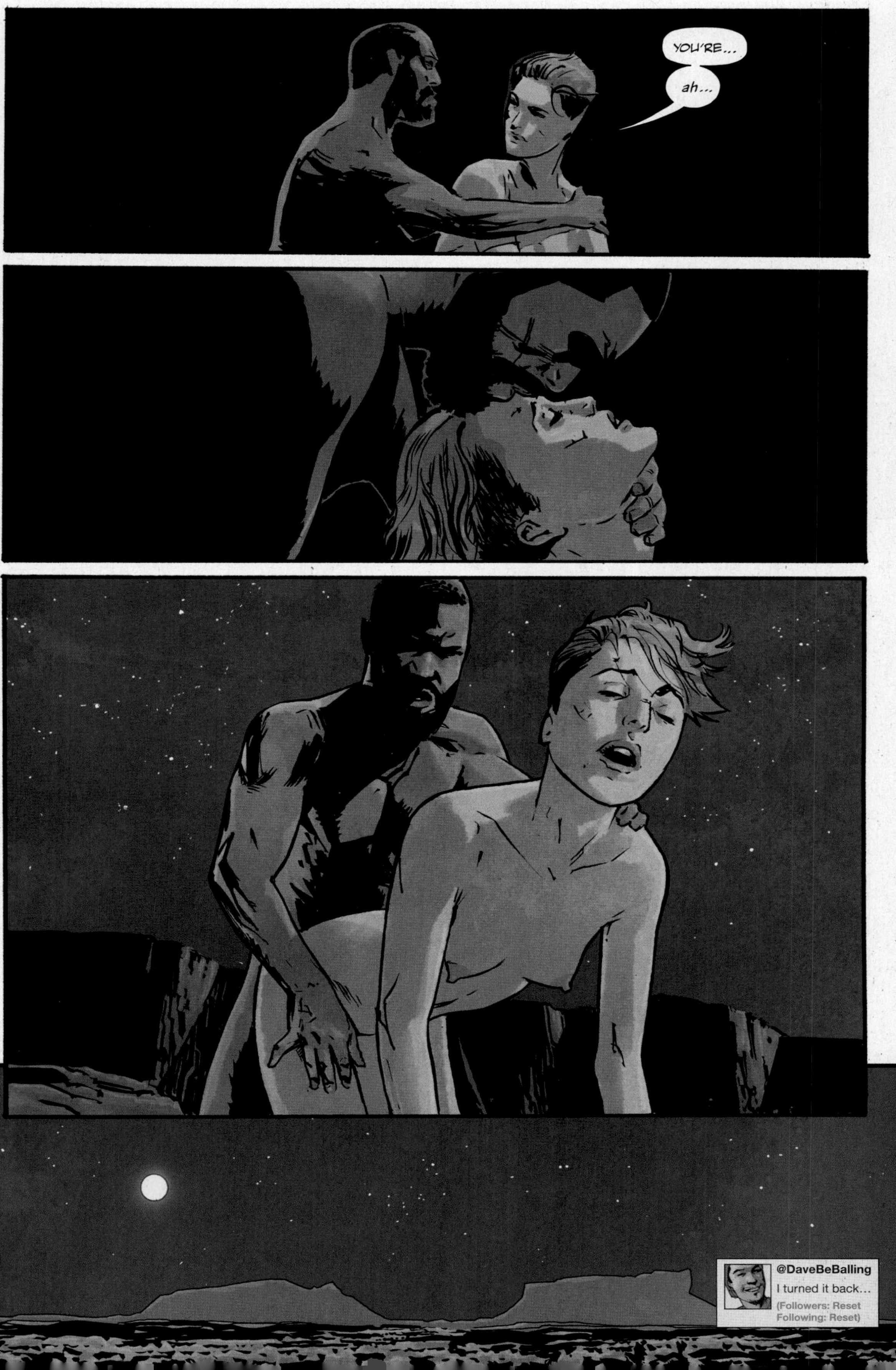
YOU'RE...
ah...
@DaveBeBalling
I turned it back...
(Followers: Reset
Following: Reset)

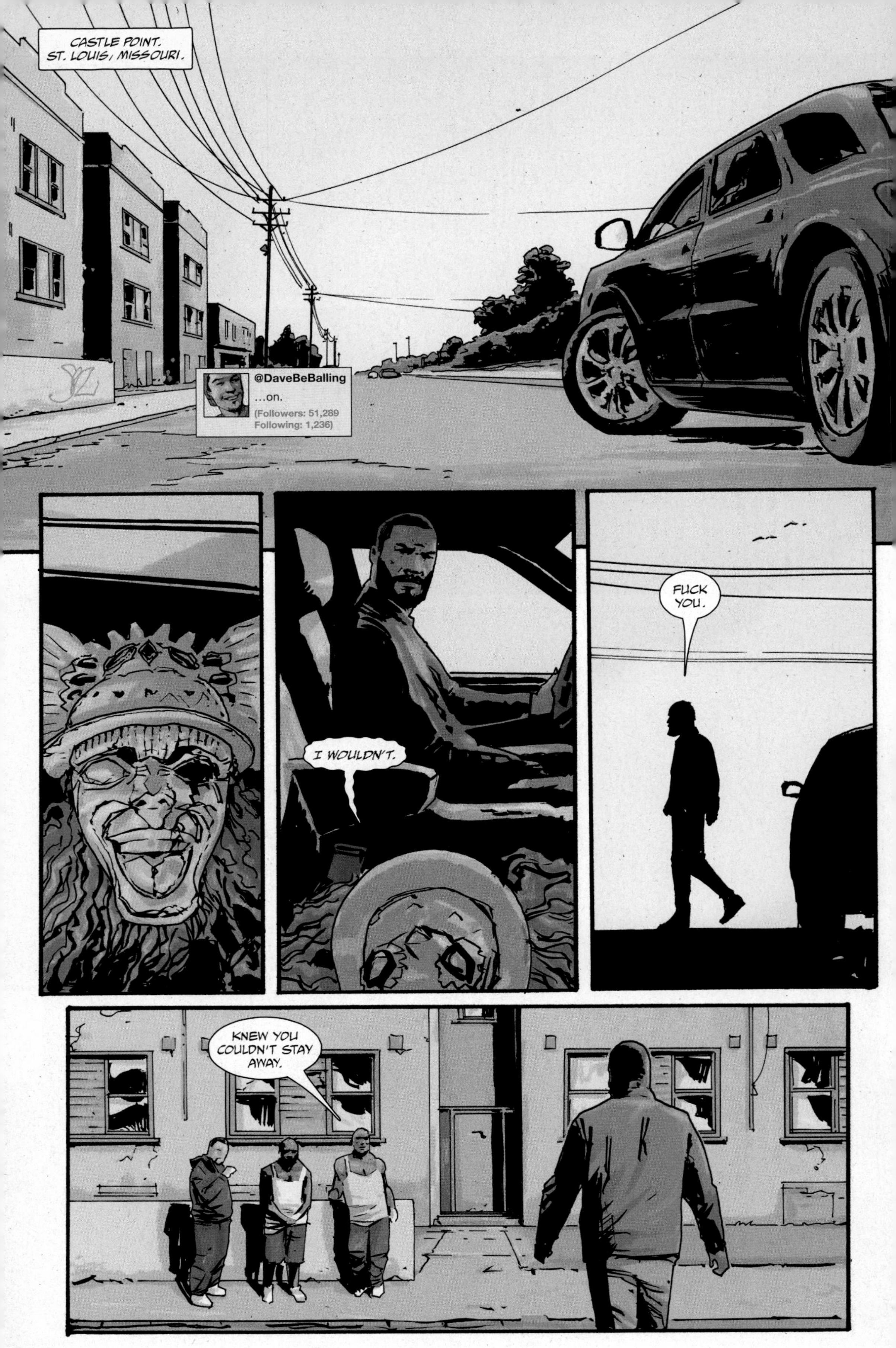
CASTLE POINT.
ST. LOUIS, MISSOURI.
@DaveBeBalling
...on.
(Followers: 51,289
Following: 1,236)
I WOULDN'T.
FUCK YOU.
KNEW YOU COULDN'T STAY AWAY.

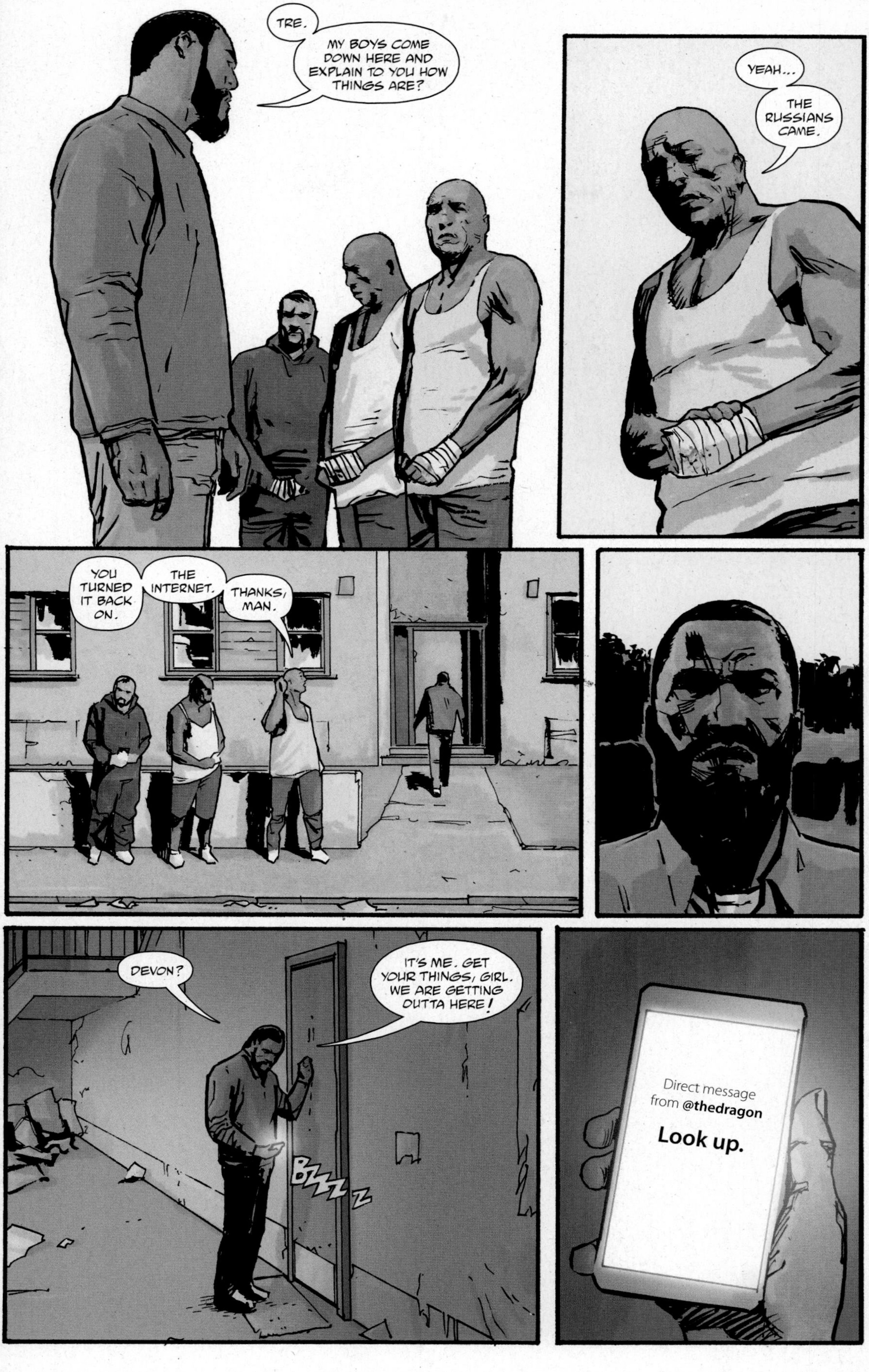
TRE.
MY BOYS COME DOWN HERE AND EXPLAIN TO YOU HOW THINGS ARE?
YEAH...
THE RUSSIANS CAME.
YOU TURNED IT BACK ON.
THE INTERNET.
THANKS, MAN.
DEVON?
IT'S ME. GET YOUR THINGS, GIRL. WE ARE GETTING OUTTA HERE!
BZZZZ
Direct message from @thedragon
Look up.

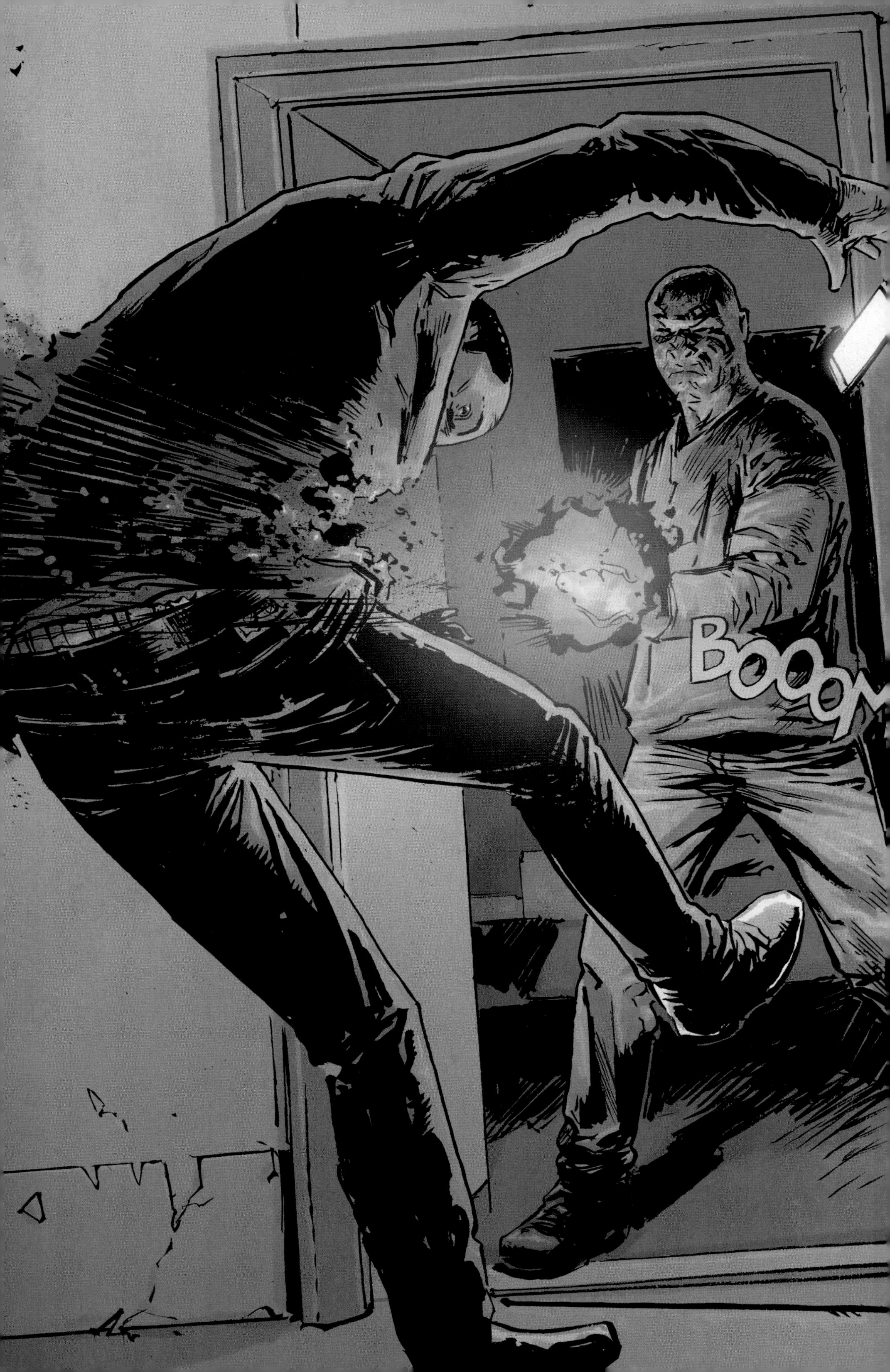
BOOOM

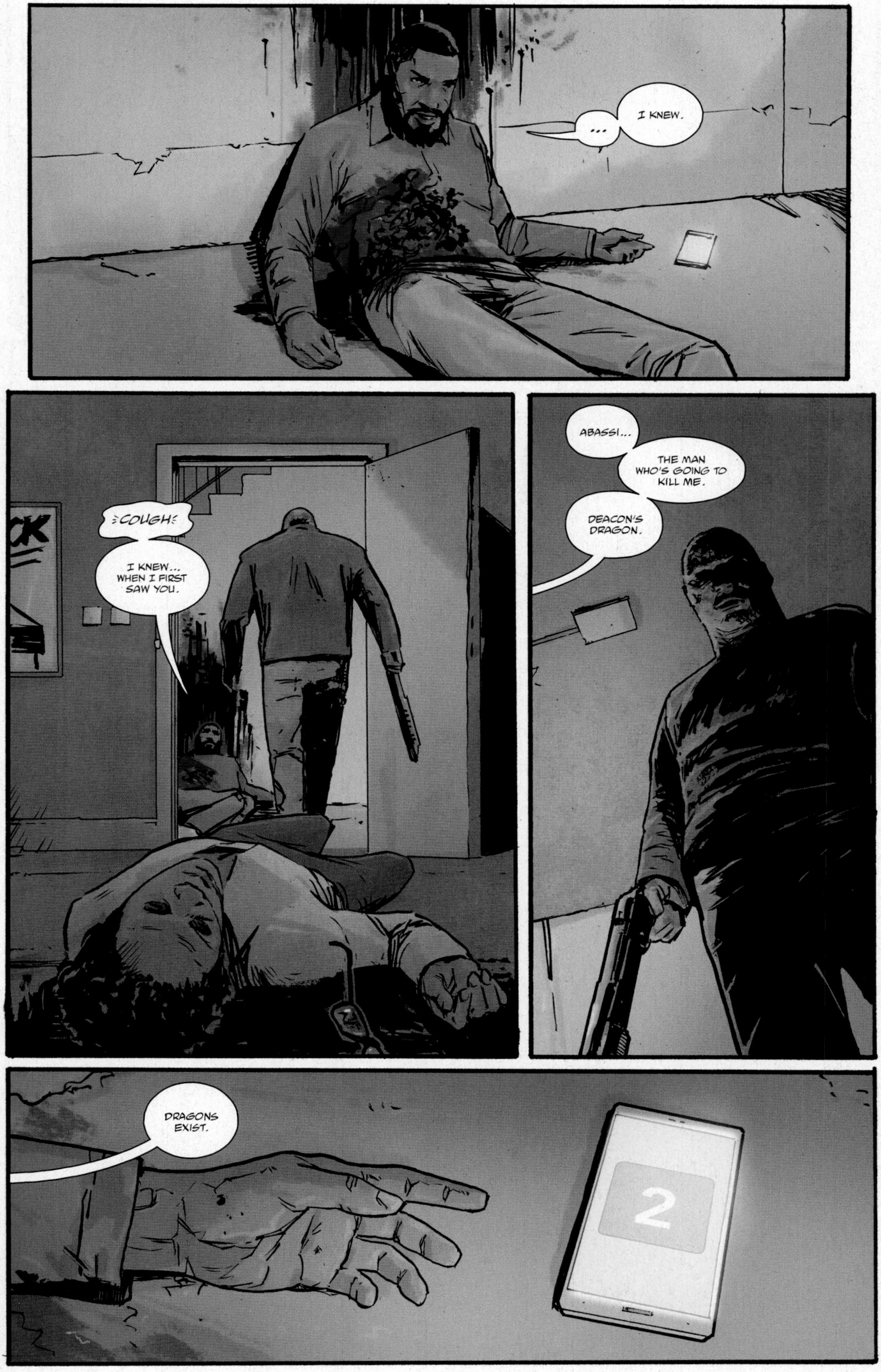
...
I KNEW.
COUGH
I KNEW... WHEN I FIRST SAW YOU.
ABASSI...
THE MAN WHO'S GOING TO KILL ME.
DEACON'S DRAGON.
DRAGONS EXIST.
2

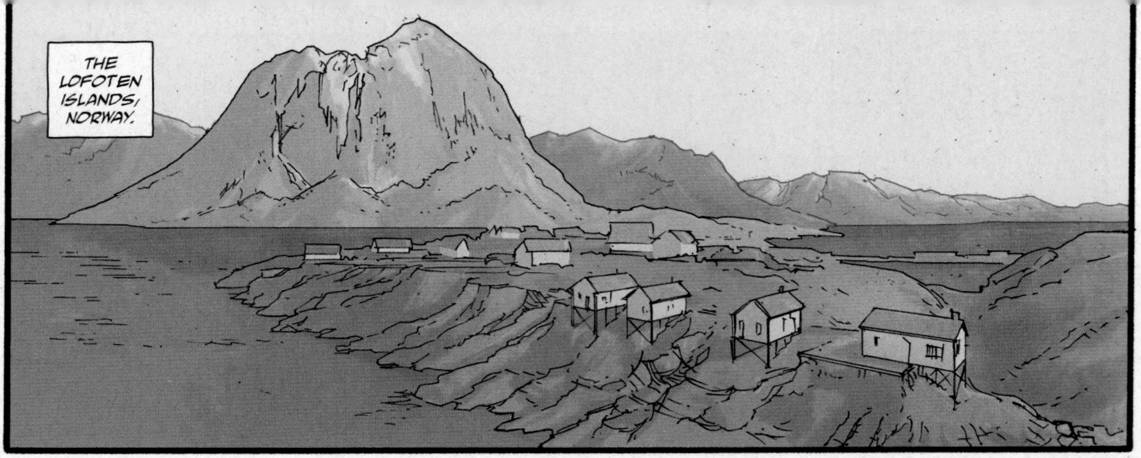
THE LOFOTEN ISLANDS, NORWAY.

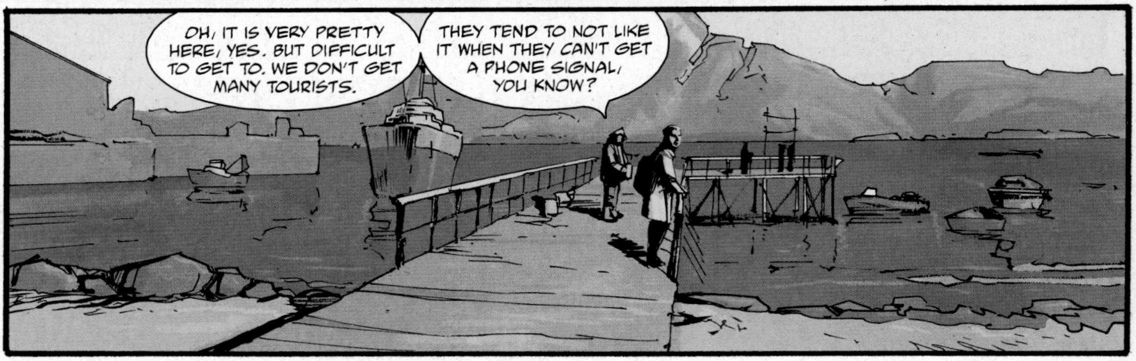
OH, IT IS VERY PRETTY HERE, YES. BUT DIFFICULT TO GET TO. WE DON'T GET MANY TOURISTS.
THEY TEND TO NOT LIKE IT WHEN THEY CAN'T GET A PHONE SIGNAL, YOU KNOW?

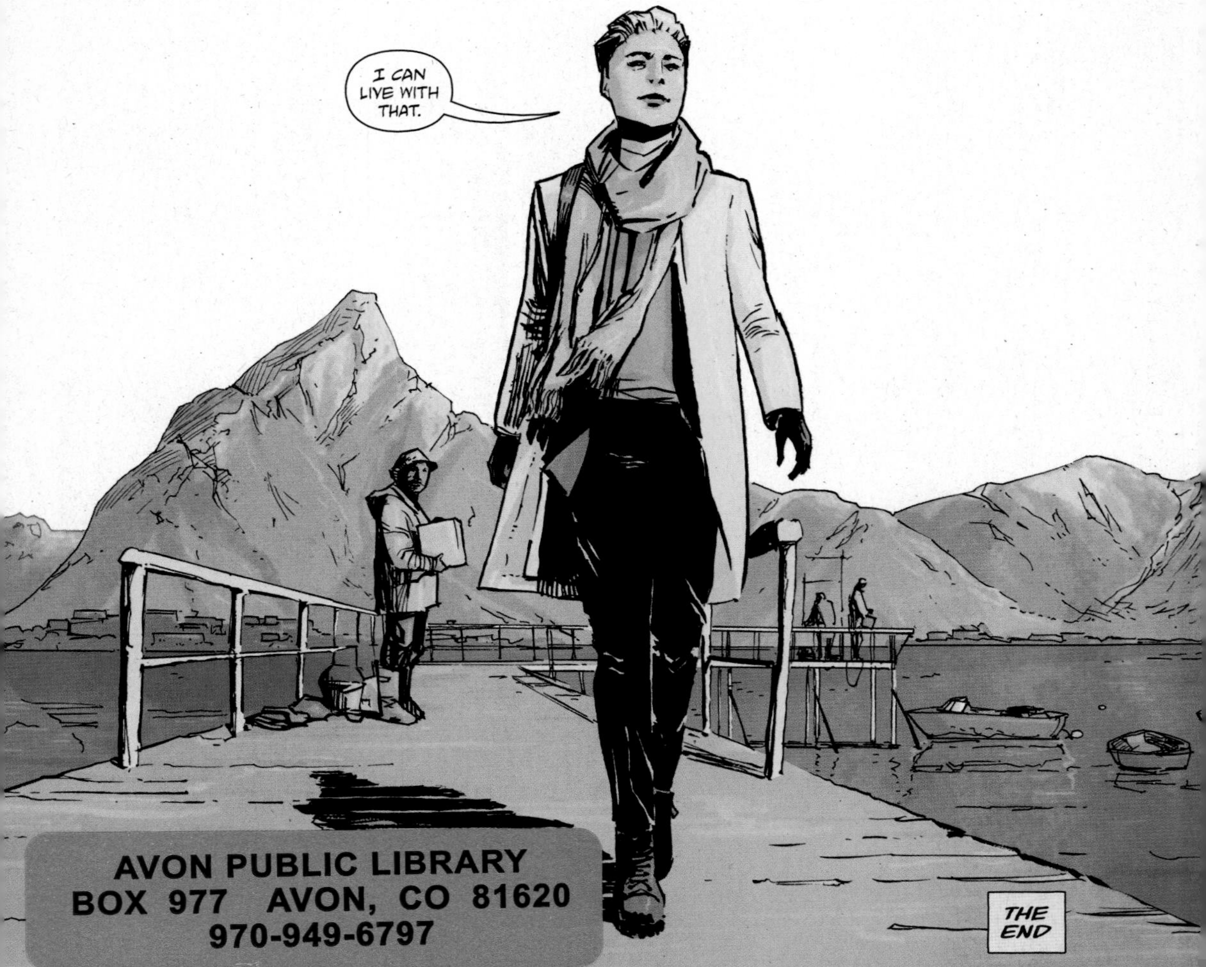
I CAN LIVE WITH THAT.
THE END